How to Do Everything with Your Tablet PC

D0924071

Bill Mann

McGraw-Hill/Osborne

New York   Chicago   San Francisco
Lisbon   London   Madrid   Mexico City
Milan   New Delhi   San Juan
Seoul   Singapore   Sydney   Toronto

The *McGraw·Hill* Companies

McGraw-Hill/Osborne
2100 Powell Street, Floor 10
Emeryville, California 94608
U.S.A.

To arrange bulk purchase discounts for sales promotions, premiums, or fund-raisers, please contact **McGraw-Hill**/Osborne at the above address. For information on translations or book distributors outside the U.S.A., please see the International Contact Information page immediately following the index of this book.

How to Do Everything with Your Tablet PC

234567890 FGR FGR 019876543

ISBN 0-07-222771-0

Publisher	Brandon A. Nordin
Vice President & Associate Publisher	Scott Rogers
Acquisitions Editor	Megg Morin
Project Editors	Jenn Tust, Carolyn Welch
Acquisitions Coordinator	Tana Allen
Technical Editor	Chris De Herrera
Copy Editors	Chrisa Hotchkiss, Marcia Baker, Bob Campbell
Proofreader	Marian Selig
Indexer	Claire Splan
Computer Designers	Lucie Ericksen, Apollo Printing Services
Illustrators	Michael Mueller, Lyssa Wald
Series Design	Mickey Galicia
Cover Series Design	Dodie Shoemaker

This book was composed with Corel VENTURA™ Publisher.

This book is for Patti and Jenn, who once again put up with the crazy hours and endless evenings at the keyboard I put in to get this project done. You two are great. In addition, this book is dedicated to the newest member of our household, Lightning the kitten, for her clear love for my Tablet PC and the many "paragraphs" she typed into the manuscript when I wasn't looking.

About the Author

Bill Mann (Bedford, NH) is the author of more than a dozen books, plus numerous technology articles for publications including Internet World, TECH Edge, Palm Power, and Computer Bits. Bill's past projects for McGraw-Hill/Osborne include *I Want My MP3! How to Download, Rip, & Play Digital Music* and *Genealogy Online Special America Online Edition*. He specializes in mobile and wireless gadgets, and has written about most of the major handheld and wireless devices available in the U.S. When not writing, Bill spends his time with his family and plays far too many computer games.

About the Technical Editor

Chris De Herrera is webmaster of Tablet PC Talk (http://www.tabletpctalk.com), a leading resource on Tablet PC news. His website, CEWindows.NET (http://www.cewindows.net), assists users of Pocket PCs and Windows CE devices. He has been recognized for the past five years as a Microsoft Most Valuable Professional for Mobile Devices, which include the Pocket PC and SmartPhone. You can contact Chris at chrisd@tabletpctalk.com.

Contents

Acknowledgments

I want to thank everyone at McGraw-Hill/Osborne who was involved in this project, in particular Megg, Jenn, Carolyn, and Tana. It was a pleasure to work with you, and I hope to do so again. In owe Tina a big thank you for getting me the hardware I needed to do the project, and Chris the same for this tech editing. Margot, thanks for handling this and all my other book projects. Last, but certainly not least, my sincere thanks to all the folks who provided me with the information (and the cool toys!) I needed to do the job.

Introduction

The Tablet PCs are finally here. We've been hearing about them for years—small, light, capable machines that you can write on as if they were a pad of paper or a personal digital assistant. These three-pound powerhouses run a version of Windows XP, so you can use them like high-end notebook computers and run all your favorite applications. But you can also use them like virtually endless digital notebooks or sketchbooks, entering information with a digital pen in environments where a desktop or notebook computer just won't cut it. You can even talk to them.

People have built tablet computers before. Some were ill-conceived, some were underpowered, most were just ahead of their time. Even so, tablet computers have found some niches where their unique characteristics have made them the computer of choice. Now Microsoft and its partners have built the first Tablet PCs that provide real benefits for general users like you and me.

Tablet PCs stake out a unique place in the market. They give you much of the convenience of a personal digital assistant (PDA) like the Palm or Pocket PC devices, but have the power to do real work. And with pen and voice for input, you don't have to do that work by sitting down and typing somewhere. If you need to be able to take serious processing power with you wherever you go, or if you spend a lot of time taking notes in meetings (where regular notebook computers and the tappety-tap of their keyboards have become unwelcome), the Tablet PC may be exactly what you need.

This book is meant to be your guide to the new breed of Tablet PC. This isn't some encyclopedic reference guide that covers every possible aspect of using a Tablet PC. Instead, it is designed to be your guide to the things that you'll need to know to set up, use, and maintain your new machine. Beyond that, this book introduces many of the new applications designed to take advantage of the capabilities of the Tablet PC. I think you'll find that this book tells you how to do everything you're likely to do with your machine.

I've divided the book into four parts. In Part I, "Get Acquainted with Your Tablet PC," you'll do exactly that. We start at the very beginning, by examining your Tablet PC and figuring out how to start it up, using the pen in lieu of a mouse, and navigating around the user interface. Once you have the bare basics down, we get down to work with a whirlwind tour of some of the unique benefits of the Tablet PC. But this is no lecture—we fire up applications like Windows Journal, the Tablet PC Input Panel, even a game. You get to experience for yourself some of what makes the Tablet PC special.

In Part II, "Set Up Your Tablet PC," we'll get into the nitty-gritty aspects of owning and using a Tablet PC. By the end of this section, you'll be able to configure your software and manage your hardware, and generally set up your shiny new Tablet PC to work the way you want it to. You'll also be able to get your Tablet PC connected to wired and wireless networks, as well as the Internet. Imagine yourself sitting in a meeting with wireless access to the company network, all on a machine scarcely much bigger or heavier than this book. Even better, imagine yourself surfing the Web on your Tablet PC while sipping a glass of wine in front of the fireplace.

In Part III, "Put Your Tablet PC to Work," you'll get to roll up your sleeves and put your machine to work with the utilities and applications that come on your Tablet PC. You'll revisit the applications you played with in Chapter 2, but this time you'll learn how to use them in your day-to-day work. You'll also get a tour of some great applications that were either modified to work better on the Tablet PC or written specifically for this new class of machine. Handwritten input and spoken input are the two aspects of the Tablet PC designed to make using the machine a more natural experience for us human beings. This is the part of the book where you really learn about handwriting and speech recognition, including lots of tips for getting the most from them in your work.

In Part IV, "Fix What Ails Your Tablet PC," we look at preventive maintenance on your new toy, as well as the all-important task of backing up your system. Think about it: A Tablet PC is meant to be used more often, in more places, and under more circumstances than any personal computer that came before it. Knowing how to back up, maintain, and fix your Tablet PC could come in very handy.

As I hope you can tell from this introduction, I've written this book in a casual, easy-to-read style. It's designed so that, to the extent possible, each chapter stands alone. You can certainly read the book cover to cover, and I encourage you to at least read the introduction to each chapter. But if you're looking for specific information, you can skip around without worry. To make the book more useful to you, I've included certain helpful design elements. They are:

- **How to sidebars**   How to sidebars provide step-by-step instructions on completing a particular task. They can be particularly important tasks, or just tasks that are related to a subject we're discussing in the chapter.

- **Did You Know sidebars**   Did You Know sidebars contain extra information. They're usually background info like historical notes or other interesting tidbits.

- ■ **Note icons**   Note icons provide helpful information related to the topic at hand. Be sure to read any Note you come across.

- ■ **Tip icons**   Tip icons describe ways to make better use of an application or feature, as well as anything else that might make things easier.

- ■ **Shortcut icons**   Shortcut icons provide quicker/easier ways to do things. They're good to read if you want to make the best use of your Tablet PC.

- ■ **Caution icons**   Caution icons flag things you need to be aware of. Always read these to avoid potential problems.

And with that, you're ready to learn how to do everything with your Tablet PC. If you have any thoughts on the book, or the Tablet PC in general, I would love to hear them. You can reach me by e-mail at: books@techforyou.com. Or you can visit my web site at: http://www.techforyou.com.

Part I

Get Acquainted with Your Tablet PC

Chapter 1

Meet Your Tablet PC

How to...

- Examine Your Tablet PC Hardware
- Turn Your Tablet PC On and Off
- Understand Docking, Undocking, and Converting Your Tablet PC
- Use the Pen to Control Your Tablet PC
- Work with the Windows Desktop
- Find Your Way Around Windows

The Tablet PC is a bid by Microsoft and its partners to evolve the notebook computer into something more usable, more practical, more natural than the machines most people use today. Since you're reading this book, you've probably bought yourself a Tablet PC, or had one provided to you by the IT department of your company. Whichever the case may be, I'm going to assume that you want to get the most out of your new toy (or burden, or tool) that you can.

Throughout the book, we'll explore the capabilities and benefits of the Tablet PC hardware and software. To do that, you'll need a basic understanding of your Tablet PC and the Windows XP Tablet PC Edition operating system that runs on it. So let's start at the beginning, by investigating that shiny new machine.

Examine Your Tablet PC Hardware

When you take your Tablet PC out of the box, spend a few minutes looking it over. Depending on the style of machine you have, your new Tablet PC may look like an ultralight notebook computer. Or it may look like nothing so much as a small flat-panel display that came off its stand. But whatever your new machine looks like, somewhere among all the accoutrements of a modern notebook computer— a spare battery, charger, cables, and whatnot—is a digital pen. This pen, and the digital ink that "flows" from it, are what make Tablet PCs unique. You'll learn the basics of how to use this pen later in this chapter, in the section, "Use the Pen to Control Your Tablet PC."

CAUTION

Throughout this book, when I refer to digital pen (or just pen), I always mean the digital pen that came with your Tablet PC or any other digital pen designed specifically to work with your Tablet PC. There are two types of Tablet PC pens, so the pen from someone else's machine might not work for yours. A regular ballpoint pen or even a stylus from your Pocket PC device definitely won't work with your Tablet PC. They can, however, make a mess of your machine's screen, so make sure you use the correct pen.

NOTE

Digital ink and using the pen to write with it are covered in Chapter 10.

Did you know?

Tablet PCs Come in Many Shapes and Sizes?

While the kinds of Tablet PCs we're talking about in this book all have to conform to certain requirements defined by Microsoft, those requirements leave room for a lot of variety. Tablet PCs come in two basic forms: convertibles and slates. A *convertible* Tablet PC, like the Acer TravelMate C100 shown next, has a built-in keyboard and can function like a regular notebook, as well as a tablet.

The *slate* machines, such as the ViewSonic V1100 shown next, which are sometimes also called *pure tablets*, don't have built-in keyboards.

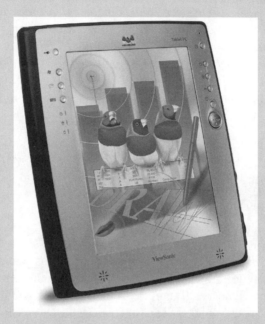

Some machines, like the Compaq Tablet PC TC1000 from Hewlett-Packard, are even more chameleon-like and can be used as both a slate and a convertible. Scattered throughout this book you'll find descriptions of still other styles of Tablet PCs, including machines designed for specialized uses or with other unique features.

A *docking station* is an add-on for many Tablet PCs. These docks support the Tablet PC when you are using it at your desk, usually providing additional disk drives and ports for connecting to a wired network or other peripherals. For slates, the dock can also provide connections to a keyboard and mouse.

Turn Your Tablet PC On and Off

It's time to turn on your Tablet PC. To do so, you must first provide power to the machine. If you bought the machine yourself, the package it came in should have instructions for providing power. If you are using a Tablet PC provided by the corporate IT department, the system should already be connected to power (and the battery likely already charged).

Your Tablet PC should also have instructions for turning it on. The location of a Tablet PC power switch isn't something that's specified by Microsoft, so you'll have to consult the documentation that came with your particular computer. Once you flip the switch, your Tablet PC will go through its startup procedure. While Tablet PCs are designed to resume from Standby mode in just a few seconds, starting from scratch usually takes a minute or two.

NOTE
If this is the first time anyone has turned on your Tablet PC, Windows will walk you through some setup procedures. Just follow the onscreen instructions and answer the questions and you should be done with that process in a short while. If you are required to enter a username and password, make sure you record this information so you can actually log onto your computer when the time comes.

Once you get past any initial setup steps, you're ready to log on to your computer. If Windows asks for it, enter your username and password. If the Windows Welcome Screen appears, use the pen that came with your Tablet PC to tap the icon that has your username. After a minute or two, you will see the Windows desktop.

NOTE
If your Tablet PC is connected to a corporate network, it may be set up to use a smart card for security. Your network administrators will need to provide you with information on how to use the smart card.

CAUTION
You should not try to turn off your Tablet PC by flipping the power switch, unplugging the machine from the wall, or anything like that. If you don't want to risk losing data and generally playing havoc with your system, you need to follow the proper procedure when you want to turn off your Tablet PC. This procedure is covered later in the chapter, in the section, "Turn Off Your Tablet PC."

Use the Pen to Control Your Tablet PC

In the previous section, I asked you to use the pen to tap an icon. That's the most basic way to use the Tablet PC pen. But you can use the pen to do more than just tap—it can completely replace the mouse.

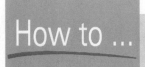

How to ... Find Out What Kind of Pen You Have

Now that you know there are two types of pens, you're probably wondering which kind your favorite Tablet PC has. If you're still shopping for a Tablet PC, your best bet is to ask. If you already have the Tablet PC, there are a few things you can do. The easiest is to see if your pen contains a battery. If it does, your pen (and the digitizer in the Tablet PC itself) is from FinePoint.

CAUTION *I usually recommend that people play with new hardware or software to get a feel for it, but not when it comes to using the Tablet PC pen. While it isn't hard to do, and the different actions soon seem perfectly natural, if you don't learn to use the pen the right way, right away, you'll have trouble using your Tablet PC.*

The best way to learn to use the pen as a mouse replacement is to work through one of the tutorials that come installed on Tablet PCs. The tutorial you'll use is named Get Going With Tablet PC, and you can run it by tapping Start | Get Going With Tablet PC. The icon for this tutorial is on the left side of the menu that appears when you tap Start, as shown next.

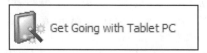
Get Going with Tablet PC

The first six screens of this tutorial are all you really need to go through to learn to use the pen instead of a mouse. Starting with tips for holding the pen (see Figure 1-1), the tutorial shows you how to *single-tap* (I'll call this tapping in this book), *double-tap*, and *right-tap* (also called *press and hold*). These actions correspond to left-clicking, double-clicking, and right-clicking with a mouse.

One additional mouse-like capability of the Tablet PC pen is the ability to *hover*. In Microsoft Windows XP, if you point the mouse at an icon on a toolbar without clicking or moving it, the mouse is said to be hovering over the icon. When the mouse pointer hovers over an icon, Windows can display a tooltip, or other descriptive information related to that icon.

For the Tablet PC pen, the equivalent of hovering the mouse pointer over an icon is hovering the pen tip over that icon. Because of the way they're designed,

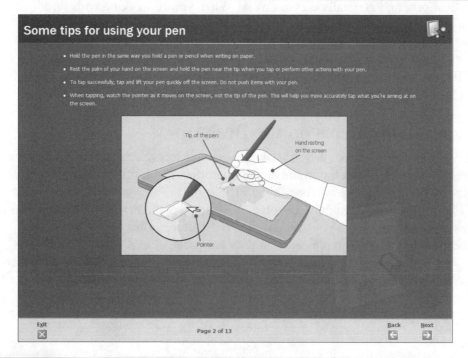

FIGURE 1-1   The Get Going with Tablet PC tutorial teaches you how to use the pen in place of a mouse.

Tablet PCs can detect their pens without the pen tip touching the screen. To make this happen, you just need to place the tip of the pen close to the screen without touching it.

 *Since the Tablet PC is sensitive to the pen and not to you, you can rest your hand on the screen while using the pen, making it much easier to hover.*

Now that you're trained in using the pen instead of a mouse, you're ready to start exploring Windows XP Tablet PC edition.

Work with the Windows Desktop

The Windows *desktop* occupies the majority of the screen and is designed to look a lot like a real-world desktop. It's a work space where you can open files, run applications, and generally do your work. When you're working with Windows, you can imagine that whatever you are working on is lying on top of the desk where you can get at it. Figure 1-2 shows what my Tablet PC screen looks like when I start my system. What you see will vary—each manufacturer sets things up a little differently. Also, I've been using my computer for some time, so I've made changes to the default layout and installed additional programs to suit my needs.

Examine the Items on the Desktop

On your Tablet PC desktop, you'll likely see a *window* (a rectangular area of the screen surrounded by a frame and containing information related to a specific activity) containing one or more Tablet PC tutorials. The window is in the center of Figure 1-2. You'll certainly see some *icons*, small pictures representing programs, files, or commands, that you can activate. The pictures often serve as a visual shorthand to give you an idea of what they represent.

For example, one icon you'll see on the desktop is the Recycle Bin. This icon looks like a little office trash can with a recycling symbol on its side. You can tell

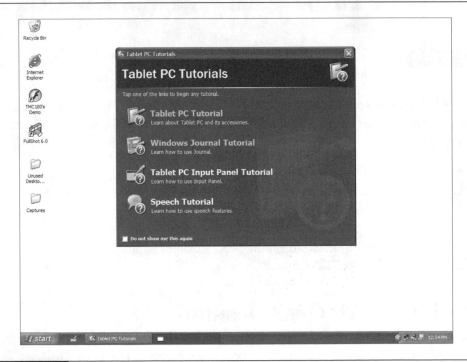

FIGURE 1-2   This Windows XP Tablet PC edition desktop shows some icons, the taskbar, and an open window.

at a glance, without reading the icon's title, that the Recycle Bin is a place to discard things. In Figure 1-2, all the icons are lined up along the left edge of the desktop, but they could be placed anywhere, as shown next.

The other thing you can see on the desktop in Figure 1-2 is the taskbar, which is covered in more detail later in the chapter, in the section, "Learn About the Taskbar."

Find Your Way Around Windows

Navigation around the Windows XP Tablet PC edition is virtually the same as with previous versions of Windows. The only difference is that you can navigate with the pen in addition to, or in place of, the mouse. With Windows XP Tablet PC edition, you can use the mouse and the pen interchangeably without any restrictions.

Having said all that, two aspects of Windows XP that you may not be familiar with are the taskbar and the Start menu.

Learn About the Taskbar

The Windows *taskbar* is one of the key components of the Windows XP user interface. The taskbar is a row of buttons and icons that appears in a bar along one side of the screen, usually the bottom. By default, your Tablet PC should start out with the taskbar visible at the bottom of the screen. Figure 1-3 shows the taskbar. Proceeding from left to right, the taskbar is divided into five sections: the Start button, the Tablet PC Input Panel icon, the Quick Launch toolbar, an area holding buttons for each running application, and the notification area.

- ■ **Start button**   The Start button opens the Start menu and is covered in detail in the "Learn About the Start Menu" section later in this chapter.

- ■ **Tablet PC Input Panel icon**   This icon activates the Tablet PC Input Panel (a tool that allows you to enter text into Windows applications by writing or speaking it instead of typing it), which is covered in more detail in Chapters 2, 10, and 15.

- ■ **Quick Launch toolbar**   The Quick Launch toolbar is an area containing icons for applications that you can start with a single tap of the pen. This

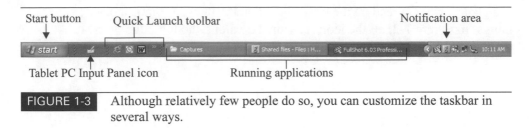

Start button   Quick Launch toolbar   Notification area

Tablet PC Input Panel icon   Running applications

FIGURE 1-3   Although relatively few people do so, you can customize the taskbar in several ways.

area is not normally visible on the taskbar, but I recommend you activate it. It's a quick way to start the programs you use frequently.

- **Application buttons**   The area to the right of the Quick Launch toolbar contains buttons representing each program that's running. Tap a button to bring the corresponding program into view. If you have several instances of a particular program running simultaneously, Windows will group them under a single button for easier handling. When you tap this button, Windows displays a small menu you can use to choose which of the grouped instances of the program you want to see.

- **Notification area**   At the end of the taskbar is the Notification area, a place where Windows can provide information on the status of your computer.

Learn About the Start Menu

The *Start menu* is the launching point for most programs on any PC running Windows XP. The Start menu is the menu that appears when you tap the Start button on the Windows taskbar. This menu, which looks something like Figure 1-4, is divided into two columns. The left column contains icons that start specific programs and the All Programs menu (the Program menu), while the right column contains icons that open specific folders, as well as special tools like the Control Panel, Help and Support (online help), Search, and the DOS Command Line.

NOTE   *If you've customized your Start menu, it may look significantly different than the one shown in Figure 1-4, and therefore, it may function somewhat differently.*

The eight Start menu sections shown in Figure 1-4 are listed here:

- **Pinned item list**   The *pinned item list* appears at the top of the left column. It contains program icons (*pinned items*) that remain in place unless you explicitly move them.

FIGURE 1-4   The Start menu gives you access to your applications and folders.

- **Most frequently used programs list**   The *most frequently used programs list* appears beneath the pinned item list. Windows automatically adds programs to this list, based on how often you use them. That means this list changes as the way you work with your Tablet PC changes.

- **All Programs**   *All Programs* appears beneath the most frequently used programs list and displays a menu of the programs you can run.

- **Special folders**   At the top of the right column is a list of special folders. Tap one of these to quickly open that folder.

■ **Control Panel** The *Control Panel* appears below the special folders. As you've seen earlier in this chapter, the Control Panel is one of the primary locations for configuring your Tablet PC.

■ **Help and Support** *Help and Support* displays the online help system, which is covered in Chapter 4.

■ **Search** *Search* lets you search your Tablet PC for files and other information. Its use is also covered in Chapter 4.

■ **Run** *Run* opens the Run dialog box, where you can execute programs by typing their name and location.

NOTE *You can open the Start menu by tapping the Start button. You can also open the menu by pressing the* WINDOWS *key or* CTRL-ESC *(assuming, of course, that you have access to a keyboard). The Input Panel, a new feature of Windows XP Tablet PC edition, includes a virtual keyboard complete with a* WINDOWS *key.*

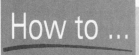

How to ... Turn Off Your Tablet PC

As I mentioned earlier in the chapter, there's a correct process for turning off your Tablet PC. Although I've probably made it sound complex to you, it isn't really. Here's how you do it:

1. Tap Start.

2. Tap the Turn Off Computer icon (it's in the lower-right corner of the Start menu).

3. In the Turn Off Computer window that appears, tap Turn Off to shut down your computer completely.

After a moment or two of whirring and chugging, your Tablet PC turns itself off. That's all there is to it.

Chapter 2

Explore Your Tablet PC

How to...

- Take Notes with Your Tablet PC
- Enter Text with the Pen
- Change the Screen Orientation for Comfort and Usability
- Post a Handwritten Reminder on the Screen
- Draw Pictures on the Screen
- Try Out the Enhanced Microsoft Reader
- Play a Game on Your Tablet PC Using the Pen

In Chapter 1, you accomplished the work needed to get your new Tablet PC up and running. Although there's still plenty you can do to configure, customize, and optimize your new machine, you're probably itching to explore some of the unique capabilities of your Tablet PC. If so, you're reading the right chapter.

This chapter takes you on a whirlwind tour of some of the unique benefits of a Tablet PC. For now, you'll stick with pen input only. Voice takes more effort to set up, and is covered in detail starting in Chapter 15. Grab your pen, and let's give this thing a workout.

> **TIP** *If you have a convertible Tablet PC, like the Acer TravelMate, you'll find it easier to follow along if you convert to tablet mode before going any further.*

Take Notes with Your Tablet PC

One of the most commonly cited benefits of the Tablet PC is that it can replace a pad and paper for taking notes in meetings. Windows Journal is the application that comes with every Tablet PC that is specifically designed for note taking. When you're working with Windows Journal, it's almost as if you were writing on an endless pad of paper. But it *is* an endless pad of paper that can do all sorts of things no real pad of paper can do. Let's give this a try right now.

To start Windows Journal, tap Start | All Programs | Windows Journal. Windows Journal opens with a new blank page ready for writing, as shown in Figure 2-1.

With Windows Journal open, take your digital pen and start writing on the Tablet PC screen. Or start drawing. Or graphing. Or just plain old doodling. Anything you can write on a piece of paper, you can write in the Windows Journal.

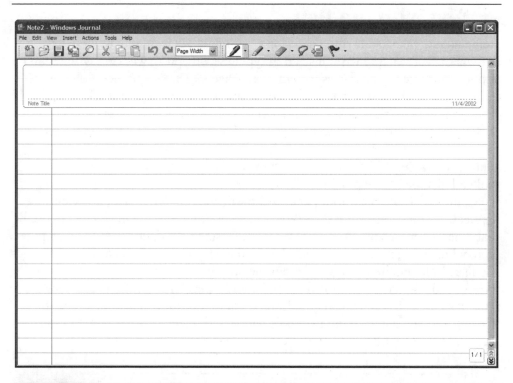

FIGURE 2-1   Windows Journal acts like an almost inexhaustible notebook filled with searchable, modifiable paper.

If you wanted to save your note, you could write a title in the box at the top of the page and tap the Save icon on the Windows Journal toolbar. Although you can do that now, you'll get the chance to work with Windows Journal in much more detail in Chapter 13. There, you'll get to experience the full power of Windows Journal, including its ability to handle these tasks:

- Organize and search notes

- Modify notes by adding space, even dragging text around the page

- Convert notes to text you can use in other applications

- Mark up images of documents as if they were hard copies

- Share notes with others, even if they don't use Windows Journal

For now, just get the feeling of taking notes.

Enter Text with the Pen

Being able to take handwritten notes on your Tablet PC is undoubtedly useful, but what if you want to write instead of typing when you're working with regular applications like word processors and spreadsheets? That's a particularly crucial question if you have a true tablet-style Tablet PC. When you're working away from your Tablet PC's docking station, you won't have access to a real keyboard. Although an onscreen keyboard works fine for short bits of text, tapping in characters with the pen isn't very productive for writing something substantial. Well, your Tablet PC has this contingency covered too, thanks to a nifty little tool called Tablet PC Input Panel.

Using the Tablet PC Input Panel is the way you get handwritten text into applications that don't work directly with handwriting. Input Panel is so important that it has a permanent icon on the Windows Taskbar. To open Input Panel, tap its icon, which is right next to the Start button on the Windows Taskbar.

The Tablet PC Input Panel includes the onscreen keyboard, as well as a writing pad. Tablet PC Input Panel also handles speech recognition (covered later in Chapter 15) and the very helpful Text Preview tool shown next. Tap the Writing Pad tab, and then tap the Tools button and select Text Preview to see the Tablet PC Input Panel's handwriting recognition abilities for yourself.

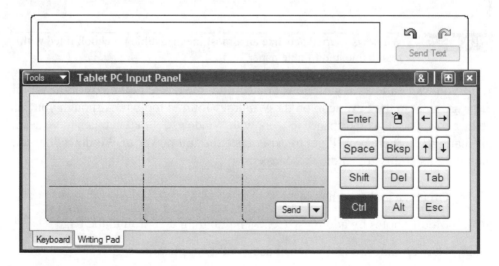

Write something on the Input Panel Writing Pad. You can print, write in cursive, or both. Then wait a few seconds while your Tablet PC tries to recognize

Did you know?

You Can Talk to Input Panel?

Input Panel not only handles handwriting recognition for the Tablet PC, but it handles speech recognition too. This tool is clearly a key to working with your Tablet PC, and clearly merits its special spot on the Windows Taskbar. You'll learn how to talk to Input Panel in Chapter 15.

what you wrote. Don't worry if Input Panel has trouble with your handwriting. Chapter 10 will help you understand the issues involved in handwriting recognition, and will give you tips to increase the recognition accuracy.

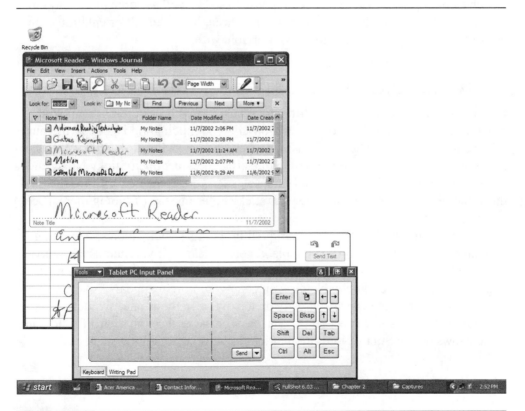

FIGURE 2-2   The Tablet PC screen is wider than it is tall in landscape mode.

Change the Screen Orientation for Comfort and Usability

One of the design requirements for Tablet PCs is that you be able to change the screen orientation to match the way you are working with the device. In other words, you can change the display on your Tablet PC so it is readable no matter how you're holding the device. The easiest way to understand this is to try it out for yourself.

To change the screen orientation, tap the Tablet And Pen Settings icon in the notification area. The icon looks like a Tablet PC with a stylus. In the menu that appears, tap Change Screen Orientation. The screen orientation changes to the next of four possible orientations, two each of landscape mode (Figure 2-2) and portrait mode (Figure 2-3).

In Chapter 3, you'll learn how to control which orientations your Tablet PC will switch through and the order in which it will do so, as well as some other ways to trigger the change. But for now, just continue through the default orientation order until you get to the one you're most comfortable with.

Post a Handwritten Reminder on the Screen

Chances are good that you've got little notes stuck to your desk, wall, even your monitor. I certainly do. But your notes won't do you much good if they're in your office and you're somewhere else. That's where the new Microsoft Sticky Notes come in. Now when you need to write yourself a note, just open Sticky Notes and write it. Windows will keep track of your notes for you. Even better, since this is the Tablet PC, you get to handwrite your sticky notes instead of typing them. (See Figure 2-4.)

Try creating a sticky note. Tap Start | All Programs | Sticky Notes. Assuming you haven't tried Sticky Notes yet, a blank note appears. (If you had used Sticky Notes before, your last note would appear instead.) Write something in the note, and then close it. Open Sticky Notes again, and your note reappears. Now tap New Note. A new blank note appears directly on top of the previous one. Windows keeps all your sticky notes in a stack so you can easily browse through them. The left and right arrows on the Sticky Notes toolbar let you scroll through the stack easily.

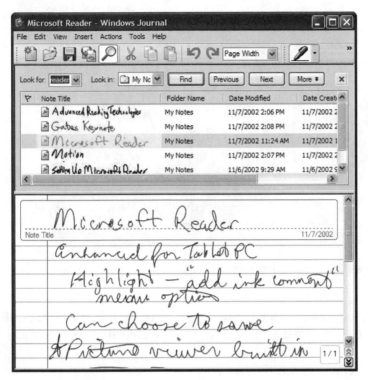

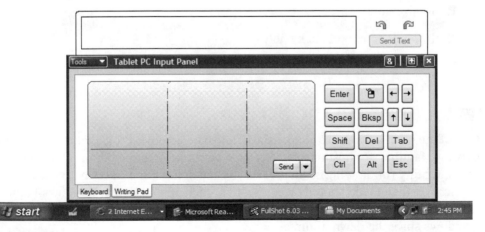

FIGURE 2-3   The Tablet PC screen is taller than it is wide in portrait mode.

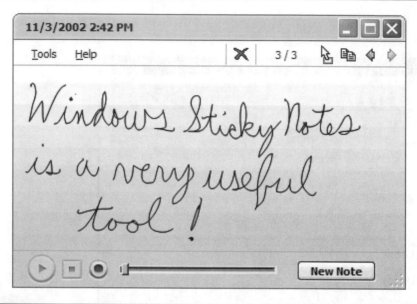

FIGURE 2-4   Windows Sticky Notes lets you replace your paper sticky notes with the digital equivalent.

Sticky Notes is not only convenient, but it's much more flexible than a stack of paper notes. Because the notes are digital, you can perform tasks like the following:

- Scratch out material you don't want
- Resize notes
- Import and export sticky notes
- Record voice notes

Draw Pictures on the Screen

One of the great advantages about using the pen on a Tablet PC is that it works with existing, familiar applications, not just new ones like Windows Journal. In some cases, writing (or drawing) with the pen is a much more natural way to use an application than the keyboard or mouse. One such application is Windows Paint (shown in Figure 2-5), the paint program that has come with every version of Windows since the dawn of time.

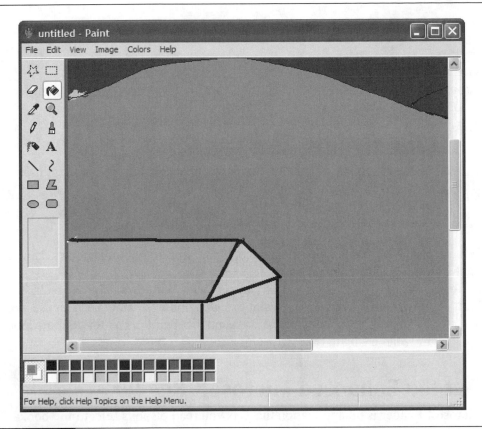

FIGURE 2-5   When you can draw with a digital pen instead of a mouse, Windows Paint
becomes a much more capable application.

If you've ever used Windows Paint on a conventional PC, you know that a mouse
is a clumsy tool for drawing. On a Tablet PC, Windows Paint is a much better tool
because you can now use the pen on the screen to draw instead of the mouse on

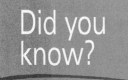

Corel Grafigo Brings Collaborative Drawing to Tablet PC?

Corel's Grafigo application is a new sketching and drawing tool for the
Tablet PC. It offers features like handwritten input, shape recognition, and
group collaboration on designs. See Chapter 12 for more information on
this and other applications specifically designed for your Tablet PC.

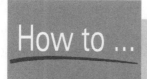 **Resize the Windows Paint Background**

You can easily resize the Windows Paint background to give yourself plenty of room to draw. Here's how:

1. On the Windows Paint toolbar, tap Image | Attributes.

2. In the Attributes dialog box, set the width and height you want to use.

3. Tap OK.

a mouse pad. With your computer in tablet mode, working with Windows Paint is much like using a sketchbook.

To see what I mean, take a minute and play with Windows Paint yourself. Tap Start | All Programs | Accessories | Paint to start Windows Paint. You can use your pen to draw anywhere on the white background that Paint opens for you. It's much more natural than trying to draw with a mouse.

Try Out the Enhanced Microsoft Reader

Microsoft Reader is an application that lets you read eBooks (electronic books formatted for viewing with Microsoft Reader) on your PC. Reader has been around for a while now and can be used on traditional PCs and laptops. The version of Reader that comes on your Tablet PC has been enhanced with the ability to display eBooks in portrait mode, add handwritten notes to eBooks, and more. With Microsoft Reader, a Tablet PC is a great way to read eBooks.

If you would like to give Microsoft Reader a try, I suggest you start with your screen oriented in portrait mode. Then tap Start | All Programs | Microsoft Reader to launch Microsoft Reader. When the License Agreement window pops up, read the agreement, and then signal your acceptance of it by tapping I Accept The Terms In The License Agreement. Tap OK to start Microsoft Reader.

Microsoft Reader opens to the Library, which contains all your eBooks. Tap Microsoft Reader Help to open the help system. This brings you to the cover page of the Microsoft Reader Help eBook. Tap Microsoft Reader Help again to open the table of contents of this eBook. Now right-tap the word Asked in the first line of the table of contents. In the shortcut menu that appears, tap Add Ink Comment. You can now make handwritten comments like the one in Figure 2-6. Tap Exit on

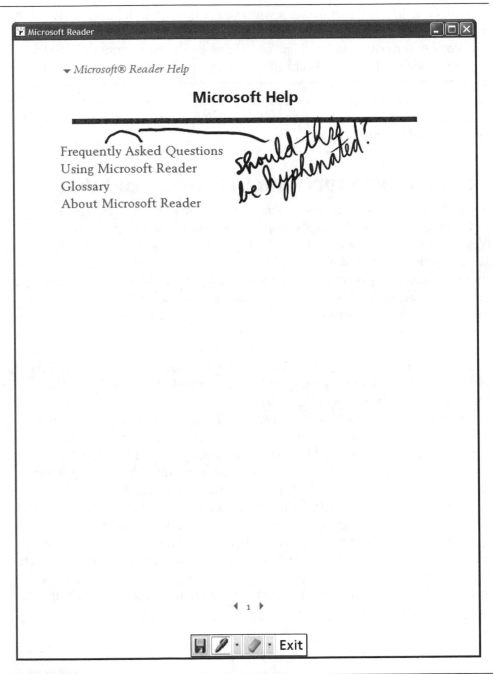

FIGURE 2-6 With the Tablet PC version of Microsoft Reader, you can write in your eBooks like you might do in a printed book.

the toolbar at the bottom of the page when you're done. You'll have the option to save your comments or discard them. If you do save your comments, they stay with your copy of the eBook and will reappear the next time you open to that page.

To go much further with Microsoft Reader, you'll need to configure some of the Tablet PC buttons and download some new eBooks. For now, just note how nicely the Microsoft Reader eBook pages match up to the display in portrait mode and how nice the text looks, thanks to the Clear Type font technology used by the Tablet PC and Microsoft Reader.

Play a Game on Your Tablet PC Using the Pen

Games have always been a part of Windows. They're a fun, nonthreatening way for beginners to get comfortable with their computer and show off new capabilities. Windows XP for Tablet PC comes with a few new games, including InkBall. Despite its name, InkBall isn't a digital simulation of Paint Ball (a game where people go out in the woods and shoot each other with paint pellets). In InkBall, you use your pen to draw ink strokes on the playing surface and direct bouncing balls into the appropriate holes. It's surprisingly fun and a good way to get comfortable with the pen (at least that's what I tell my wife).

To start InkBall, tap Start | All Programs | Games | InkBall. A playing area similar to the one shown in Figure 2-7 will appear. The exact appearance of the screen varies from round to round, getting more complicated as you go. The figure also shows two balls in play.

The balls bounce around the playing area according to the laws of physics. If that's all that happened, InkBall might make a nice screen saver but wouldn't be much of a game. You play by making marks on the screen with the pen. When a ball hits one of your marks, it bounces off the mark at an angle and velocity determined by the angle of impact. The objective is to get all the balls to go into the holes of the same color. If a ball goes into a hole of a different color, you lose.

At first, the game seems pretty trivial. You could continue to draw lines around a particular area to corral the balls into the right holes. However, when a ball strikes one of your marks, the mark disappears, making that strategy much harder to execute. The arc near the center of the figure and the small dot to the lower left of the arc are the only marks remaining of the ten or so I had already made to help direct the balls.

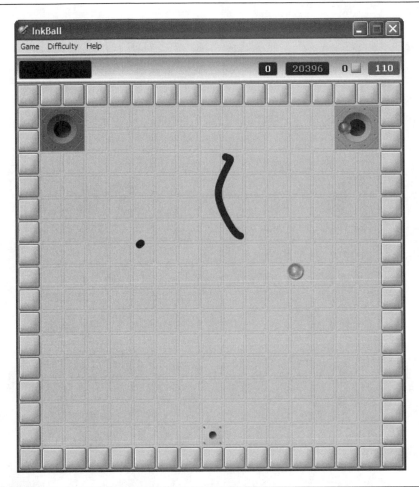

FIGURE 2-7   Sharpen your digital pen skills and take a break at the same time
with InkBall.

That's basic InkBall. But things quickly get more complicated, with disappearing
walls, walls that change the color of the ball, one-way color-filter walls, ramps,
and assorted other twists on the basic pattern. Have fun.

Part II

Set Up Your Tablet PC

Chapter 3

Configure the Tablet PC for Your Needs

How to...

- Import Your Old Files and Settings
- Configure the Windows Interface
- Configure Your Tablet PC Hardware

Now that you've had a chance to explore your Tablet PC a bit, it's time to get down to serious business. In this chapter, you'll learn how to configure your Tablet PC to suit your needs. Windows XP Tablet PC edition has new controls and settings to go with its new features and the new capabilities of the Tablet PC hardware. So even if you have lots of experience setting up PCs and laptops, you'll find some interesting new settings to play with.

Import Your Old Files and Settings

The most important step in configuring your Tablet PC is to get your old files and settings onto the device. You spent a lot of time working on your old machine and getting it configured to meet your needs, so why not take advantage of all that work? Microsoft has made this usually painful task a lot easier for people who use Windows XP, a group that includes Tablet PC owners. The new Files And Settings Transfer Wizard (see Figure 3-1) can do most of the work for you. But first, you need to come up with a file transfer strategy.

> **TIP** *If you plan to use your Tablet PC as a second computer, and you will continue to use your old PC as your main computer, you don't need to import your old files and settings. All you need to do is install the right applications on your Tablet PC.*

Decide How You Will Transfer Your Files and Settings

Because your old files and settings could amount to hundreds of megabytes, even gigabytes of information, you need to have a plan for transferring them from your old PC to your Tablet PC. Moving the information by floppy disk isn't a viable option, considering that it would likely take hundreds of floppy disks to hold everything, and I can't think of a brand of Tablet PC that comes with a floppy drive.

If you have a Zip drive or a similar high-density removable storage device, you can use that to transfer the information. However, using the Files And Settings Transfer Wizard makes the most sense when you can connect the old PC to the

FIGURE 3-1   Follow the Files and Settings Transfer Wizard onscreen instructions to transfer much of your personal information from your old computer to your Tablet PC.

Tablet PC through a network. If you can have both machines on the network simultaneously, the wizard will make short work of the transfer. A direct connection between the two machines will also work, but using an existing network is much easier.

Other factors to consider include the following:

■ The Files And Settings Transfer Wizard primarily transfers settings from Microsoft applications like Outlook Express and Internet Explorer, as well as a few third-party applications. That means you'll still need to change some settings manually on your Tablet PC.

■ The wizard can transfer settings only for applications that are already installed on the new machine. That means you'll need to install the applications you want to use before you run the wizard.

Put the Files and Settings Transfer Wizard to Work

Assuming that you have already installed your applications on the Tablet PC, putting the Files And Settings Transfer Wizard to work is pretty easy. You start by running the wizard on your new computer.

 *You must make sure the hard disk of the old computer is shared with your Tablet PC if you're transferring the files and settings across the network.*

To start the wizard on the Tablet PC, tap Start | All Programs | Accessories | System Tools | Files And Settings Transfer Wizard. Follow the step-by-step instructions and answer the questions that appear (see Figure 3-2) to complete the transfer. If you're using Zip disks or other removable storage to transfer the files, the wizard will calculate how much information it needs to transfer and will prompt you to provide fresh disks as necessary.

Once you finish transferring the files and settings to your Tablet PC, you are ready to configure the Windows interface on your Tablet PC.

Configure the Windows Interface

Once you have your important files and settings transferred to the Tablet PC, it's time to start configuring your new machine. Windows XP Tablet PC edition and the Tablet PC hardware are both highly configurable. This makes sense because the Tablet PC is probably the most *personal* personal computer you've ever used.

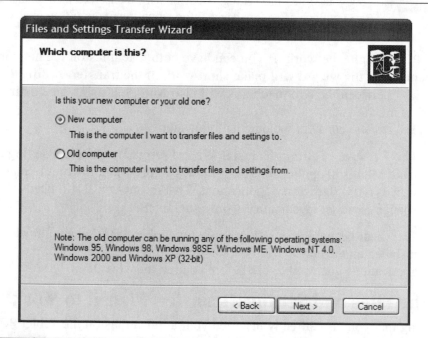

FIGURE 3-2   Its clear onscreen instructions make using the Files And Settings Transfer Wizard a straightforward, if possibly time-consuming, task.

One of the main goals Microsoft had in developing the Tablet PC was to create a personal computer that you would use more of the time, in more ways, and in more places than ever before. The more you use something, the more you want to make it work exactly the way you want it to.

The following sections address the major areas where you can configure the Windows interface on your Tablet PC. You can also configure various elements of the Tablet PC hardware. These elements are covered later in this chapter, in the section "Configure Your Tablet PC Hardware."

Configure Accessibility Options

Recent versions of Microsoft Windows have included tools to make PCs easier to use for people with disabilities. Windows XP is no exception. The tools included with Windows XP Tablet PC edition are the same as those included in Windows XP Home and Professional.

Tap Start | All Programs | Accessories | Accessibility to see the five accessibility tools included with Windows XP Tablet PC edition. Unless you know exactly which accessibility settings you would like to use, I suggest you open the Accessibility Wizard and let it guide you in adjusting the Windows interface to meet your needs.

Work your way through the wizard by reading the onscreen instructions and selecting the vision options (shown in Figure 3-3), as well as hearing and mobility options that work for you.

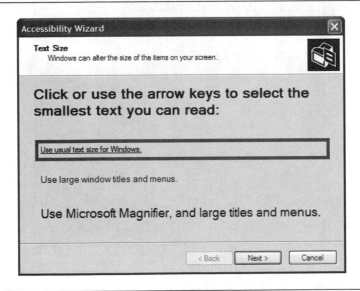

FIGURE 3-3   The Accessibility Wizard can help you adjust the Windows interface to meet your unique needs.

Configure Language and Regional Options

Windows XP supports multiple languages. It can also customize the display of certain types of information to correspond to the standards of particular regions of the world. To configure these options, tap Start | Control Panel | Date, Time, Language, And Regional Options. When the Pick A Task screen appears, tap Regional And Language Options to open the Regional And Language Options dialog box shown in Figure 3-4. This dialog box provides options on three tabs.

■ **Regional**   The Regional tab keeps the current language, but allows you to adjust the way numbers, currencies, dates, and times appear on the screen. Some services provide localized news and information based on the location listed here. Set the region to your current location if you want services that use this information to know where you are in the world.

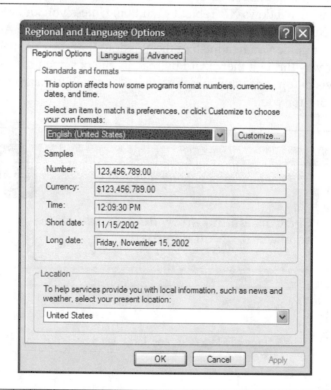

FIGURE 3-4   Configure your Tablet PC for your region and language to make yourself more productive.

- **Languages**   The Languages tab lets you configure Windows to display information in the language you select. Most of the programs you use will automatically adapt to match the language you select, although a few third-party applications might not work in anything but the default language installed on the Tablet PC.

- **Advanced**   The Advanced tab allows you to adjust the behavior of non-Unicode applications. (These are applications that won't automatically switch to a new language when Windows does.) By selecting the correct code tab conversion tables, you can get some non-Unicode programs to display their menus and dialog boxes in the correct language.

If you need to choose code tabs to make a non-Unicode application work the way you want it to, I suggest you contact the manufacturer of the application causing the problem. They may be able to give you useful advice or information on how to address the problem. They may even have a new version that works properly with Windows XP Tablet PC edition.

Configure the Windows Desktop

The Windows desktop is the workspace on your Tablet PC screen. Applications like Windows Journal, your word processor, and similar programs appear on the Windows desktop. You can adjust many of the characteristics of the Windows desktop to suit your own needs and tastes, using the Display Properties dialog box, which appears in Figure 3-5.

Like the Display Properties dialog box, the Accessibility Wizard (covered in the "Configure Accessibility Options" section) can change some Windows desktop characteristics.

In this section, you'll learn to configure the options on four of the five tabs of the Display Properties dialog box. The fifth tab, Settings, deals with hardware display options like the screen resolution, and is covered in the "Configure Your Tablet PC Hardware" section of this chapter.

The four tabs you will work with now are called Themes, Desktop, Screen Saver, and Appearance.

Choose Windows Themes

A *theme* is a group of visual elements that you can select with a single click. A theme specifies the Windows background, icons, sounds, and other elements of the

FIGURE 3-5   You can significantly change the look of the Windows desktop with the options in the Display Properties dialog box.

Windows desktop and interface. You can use the Themes tab to change your theme. You can use the themes that came with your Tablet PC, save your current Windows desktop settings as a theme, or buy additional themes as part of Plus! for Windows XP—a set of graphics, games, and multimedia tools published by Microsoft.

Customize the Desktop

Use the Desktop tab to change the Windows background. You can choose from dozens of included backgrounds, or tap Browse to find images on your hard disk that you can use as backgrounds. The Position button lets you control how Windows displays background images that are smaller than the background, while the Color list lets you select the color of the portions of the background that aren't covered by background images.

Tap Customize Desktop to customize the desktop even further. On the General tab, you can control which icons appear on the desktop, change their appearance, and control the Desktop Cleanup Wizard. This wizard can automatically gather desktop icons that you haven't used recently and put them in a folder so they're not cluttering your system.

The Web tab of the Customize Desktop dialog box lets you display web pages on your Windows desktop. Select your current home page by tapping the check box next to it in the Web Tabs list, or choose one or more additional pages by tapping New and entering the appropriate URL.

To control how often the information on your desktop web pages gets updated, select a page in the Web Pages list, and then tap Properties | Schedule and create a synchronization schedule. To control which content gets synchronized, tap the Download tab and set the options you want to use in the Content To Download section of the tab.

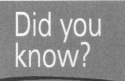

That Choosing the Right Link Depth Is Important?

One of the options on the Download page has the somewhat confusing title, "Download Pages X Links Deep From This Page," where X is a number from zero to three. This option has a direct but nonobvious effect on how much work your Tablet PC must do when it synchronizes the web content. By default, X is 0, which means Windows downloads only the page you specified. If you set X to 1, Windows downloads the page you specified, as well as every other page on the same site the original page links to. So if the original page linked to five additional pages at the same site, Windows would download the original page and the five pages to which it links.

If you set X to 2, Windows downloads the original page, all the pages at that site to which the original page links, and all the pages at the original site to which those pages link. If your original page and every page at the original page's web site link to five other pages on the site, you get a situation like this:

- With X set to 0, Windows downloads the original page.

- With X set to 1, Windows downloads the original page, plus the five pages it links to, for a total of six.

- With X set to 2, Windows downloads the original page, plus the five pages it links to, plus the 25 pages to which those five link, for a total of 31.

■ With X set to 3, Windows downloads the original page, plus the five pages it links to, plus the 25 pages those five link to, plus the 125 pages the previous 25 link to, for a total of 156.

The situation gets even worse if you set the option Follow Links Outside Of This Page's Web Site. That allows Windows to download pages that aren't on the site of the original page, as well as those that are on the site. Imagine if one of those offsite links leads to an index site like Yahoo! There could be dozens, even hundreds of links to follow on such an index page.

As I've shown, the situation can quickly get out of hand if you set a link depth greater than absolutely necessary. That's why another option here is to set a limit on how much hard disk space Windows will allow a single page (and the pages to which it is linked) to consume. The best approach is to limit the number of web pages you display on your desktop, and limit the link depth as much as you can.

In addition to controlling which content gets downloaded and when, you can use the Web tab to have Windows send e-mail whenever it detects that the selected web content has changed. This feature is useful because it saves you from having to constantly scan the sites for changes yourself. Finally, if the web content to be displayed on your Windows desktop requires a user name and password, tap Login to provide Windows with that information.

Choose and Customize Screen Savers

The Screen Saver tab allows you to control what happens on your Tablet PC display when you're not actively using it. This tab also gives you access to the full range of Tablet PC power schemes—which, among other things, determine when to turn off the display to save power.

 *I cover Tablet PC power settings in the "Configure Your Tablet PC Hardware" section of this chapter, so we'll concentrate on screen savers here.*

Screen savers are usually some sort of animation that appears on the screen when you haven't used the computer for a certain amount of time. Windows XP comes with a collection of screen savers, ranging from a simple blank screen to elaborate, ever-changing 3-D images, to text or images that you create. The manufacturer of your Tablet PC also likely included their own screen saver.

To choose a screen saver, select the name of one from the Screen Saver list on this tab. To see what that screen saver does, tap Preview. This activates the screen saver immediately so you can see how it looks. To end the preview, as well as to stop a running screen saver, you need only move the cursor or type a keystroke. Make sure you remove the pen tip from the screen once you tap Preview, or you'll likely twitch your hand enough to end the preview almost instantly.

Many screen savers have options you can adjust. With the screen saver you're interested in selected, tap Settings to see the options for that specific screen saver. Make your changes, and then use Preview to see what effect they have. To control how long it takes the screen saver to pop up when there is no activity on the Tablet PC, set the number of minutes in the Wait list.

You can use screen savers as a basic form of security on your computer by selecting the On Resume, Password Protect check box. If you do this, you'll need to enter your normal login password to end the screen saver.

An important point to remember about screen savers is that any kind of action on the display consumes more power than simply turning the display off when you're not using it. You'll learn how to do this when we reach the Power Options Properties dialog box in the "Configure Your Tablet PC Hardware" section of this chapter.

Change the Appearance of the Desktop

If you're interested in customizing the look of your Windows desktop, you'll really love the Appearance tab shown in Figure 3-6. Using this tab, you can change the style of your desktop, select a default color scheme, and even change the size of the fonts Windows uses for things like dialog box and button titles. The related Effects and Advanced Appearance dialog boxes give you even more precise control.

Visual elements of Windows XP (buttons and windows) normally have rounded corners, and an overall look that is distinct from earlier versions of Windows. Using the Appearance tab, you can switch between the Windows XP style and the Classic (old) style. Just choose the style you want in the Windows And Buttons list. Tap Apply to make the change go into effect. This will take a short while, and your computer will be unresponsive while Windows reworks everything.

Windows XP comes with three predefined color schemes: Default (a blue scheme), Olive Green, and Silver. Choose a scheme from the Color Scheme list and tap Apply to switch. As with choosing a style, Windows will be unavailable for a moment as it reworks everything to match the new color scheme.

Changing the font size works the same way as changing the styles and schemes. Choose a size from the Font Size list and click Apply. Then wait while Windows reworks everything.

FIGURE 3-6   Use the Appearance tab and its associated dialog boxes to customize the look of Windows XP on your Tablet PC.

Tapping the Effects button opens the Effects dialog box, where you can configure several of the special effects that Windows uses. To change the way menus and tooltips appear, you can select the Fade effect or the Scroll effect. To eliminate these transitional special effects altogether, clear the Transition Effect check box.

The next option controls how Windows smoothes the edges of screen fonts. By default, your Tablet PC should be set to use ClearType, a technology that takes advantage of the physical design of your Tablet PC liquid crystal display (LCD) screen. Choose one of the two methods in the list, or turn off font smoothing altogether by clearing the Smooth Edges check box. You have to trade off between processing power expended on font smoothing and an easier-to-read display. ClearType gives the best visual results, but it uses the most processing power. Clearing the check box means no processing power is expended on font smoothing, but the display is less pleasant to look at and slightly harder to read than with either of the smoothing methods.

3

Did you know?

Did You Know How Screen Font Smoothing Works?

Windows XP has two different methods for smoothing the fonts you see on the screen. Without going too far into the technical details, the standard method smooths fonts by adjusting the colors of pixels adjacent to the pixels that make up the font. By setting the color of the adjacent pixels to intermediate values, Windows makes the fonts look smoother, at the expense of making them slightly fuzzier.

The ClearType method takes advantage of the fact that physically, each of the pixels on the Tablet PC LCD screen is made up of red, green, and blue elements side by side. ClearType manipulates the brightness of each of these elements to smooth the fonts. Because ClearType can control each of the three elements of each pixel individually, it can, in effect, use as little as a third of a pixel for smoothing. This results in much smoother fonts on LCD displays like the one on your Tablet PC. Unfortunately, ClearType can do its magic only for one set of screen orientations. Because it relies on the horizontal layout of the elements of pixels, ClearType can't work when the orientation of the screen is rotated 90 degrees, because this in effect makes the layout of the elements vertical. You'll need to experiment with these settings and choose the one that works best for you.

The other four options in the Effects dialog box are aesthetic choices that you can use or not, remembering always that every effect you select consumes a tiny bit of processing power and adds a bit to the drain on your battery.

The final dialog box associated with the Appearance tab is Advanced Appearance. Tap the Advanced button on the Appearance tab to open the Advanced Appearance dialog box. Here, you can adjust 18 different items on the Windows desktop, everything from the color of the active title bar, to the size of message box text, to the distance between icons. To do this, select an item from the Item list, and then adjust its settings using the controls to the right of the list. Many of the changes you make will be immediately visible in the example window at the top of this dialog box, but for the rest, you'll need to tap OK | Apply and actually make the changes to see their effects. If you change the Windows And Buttons style to anything other than Windows Classic, that change will override the changes you make here.

Customize the Taskbar

By default, your Tablet PC should start out with the taskbar visible at the bottom of the screen. The taskbar is shown next. Proceeding from left to right, the taskbar is divided into several sections: the Start button, the Tablet PC Input Panel icon, the Quick Launch toolbar, an area holding buttons for each running application, and the notification area.

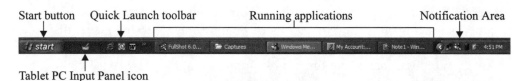

Start button   Quick Launch toolbar   Running applications   Notification Area

Tablet PC Input Panel icon

Although relatively few people do so, you can customize the taskbar in several ways. You can move it, resize it, add toolbars and shortcuts to it, and change its properties. Before you can perform most of those tasks, however, you need to enable taskbar changes.

The taskbar is normally locked to prevent any changes other than which toolbars the taskbar shows. You unlock the taskbar by right-tapping an empty area of the taskbar to open the taskbar shortcut menu. Once the menu appears, shown next, clear the Lock The Taskbar option by tapping it.

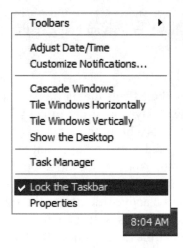

You can always find some unused space next to the time display in the notification area.

With the taskbar unlocked, you can start customizing it. You can move the taskbar to another edge of the screen by simply dragging it there and dropping it. Placing the taskbar along one of the sides of the screen allows it to show many more application buttons than it would normally (and looks pretty cool), but it occupies a lot more of the screen.

You can change the size of the taskbar by dragging the edge of the taskbar closest to the Windows desktop. A larger taskbar allows for more information on each application button but occupies more of the screen.

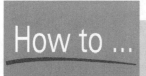

How to ... Find the Taskbar When It Isn't Visible

Although Tablet PCs normally come configured so that the taskbar is always visible, two settings can cause the taskbar to be hidden. One setting allows windows on the desktop to cover the taskbar, and the other hides the taskbar when it isn't needed. Follow these steps to find the taskbar when it is missing in action:

1. Minimize any open windows in case they are covering the taskbar.

2. Drag the cursor to the bottom of the screen. If the taskbar is set to hide itself, this can cause it to appear.

3. If the taskbar still isn't visible, use your Tablet PC mouse, touch pad, or other nonpen pointing device to drag the cursor to the bottom of the screen. Using the pen, it can be difficult to bring the cursor close enough to the bottom of the screen to cause the taskbar to appear.

4. Adjust the taskbar settings to force it to stay visible. Tap Start | Control Panel | Appearance And Themes | Taskbar And Start Menu. On the Taskbar tab, make sure that Auto-Hide The Taskbar is cleared and that Keep The Taskbar On Top Of Other Windows is selected. Then tap OK. This should bring the taskbar into view.

Using this technique, you can reduce your taskbar to a thin strip along the edge of the screen, which can be very hard to work with, particularly using the pen. If this happens, you may need to use your mouse to drag the taskbar back to a usable size, or press the Windows key on the keyboard.

Other changes you may wish to make to the taskbar require you to use the Taskbar And Start Menu dialog box. Tap Start | Control Panel | Appearance And Themes | Taskbar And Start Menu to open this dialog box. On the Taskbar tab, shown in Figure 3-7, you can change the appearance of both the main taskbar and the notification area. Select the options you want to use and tap OK to put them into effect.

■ **Auto-Hide The Taskbar**   This option makes the taskbar disappear when it isn't needed, freeing the area of the screen that would otherwise be occupied by the taskbar. When the taskbar is hidden, you can make it reappear by dragging the cursor to the screen edge on which the taskbar is located.

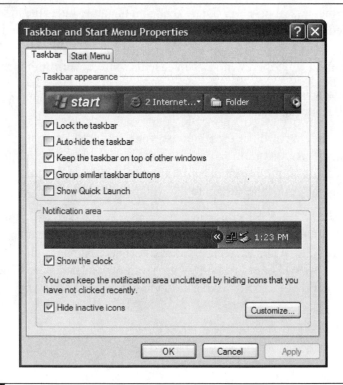

FIGURE 3-7   Use the Taskbar tab of the Taskbar And Start Menu dialog box if you want to change key aspects of the taskbar.

TIP   *If you select Auto-Hide The Taskbar and are using the pen, you may find it very hard to drag the cursor close enough to the edge to make the taskbar reappear. I strongly recommend that you do not auto-hide the taskbar on your Tablet PC.*

- **Group Similar Taskbar Buttons**   This option, which is set by default, allows Windows to combine all your active instances of say, Microsoft Word, into a single application button. This reduces the number of application buttons on the taskbar and makes it easier to read the titles of each.

- **Show Quick Launch**   This option adds an area to the taskbar where you can place shortcuts to the applications you want to be able to launch quickly. When this option is selected, you can place the icons of your favorite applications on the taskbar just to the right of the icon that starts the Tablet PC Input Panel. This is the one change I make to the standard taskbar setup. I add applications that I frequently use to the Quick Launch toolbar so I can start them with a single click.

- **Hide Inactive Icons**   This option conserves space on the taskbar by hiding notification icons when they're not active. This leaves more space on the taskbar for other information. You can control which notification icons are hidden by tapping Customize and following the directions in the Customize Notifications dialog box.

The final configuration option for the taskbar is to add additional toolbars to it. The Quick Launch area is actually a predefined toolbar. You can add a toolbar that represents a folder, a drive, or even an Internet address. To add a toolbar to the taskbar, right-tap an open area on the taskbar, and in the shortcut menu, tap Toolbars | New Toolbar. Browse to the folder, drive, or Internet address you want to include, and tap OK to add it to the taskbar. Adding toolbars to the taskbar can be a good idea when you need quick access to the information stored on that toolbar.

Configure the Start Menu

You can customize the Start menu by right-tapping the Start button to open the shortcut menu, and then tapping Properties | Start Menu | Customize. The General tab of the Customize Start Menu dialog box (Figure 3-8) lets you control which application shortcuts appear in the menu and how large they are. It also allows you to specify a web browser and e-mail program that will appear in the Pinned Item list, as well as the number of programs that will appear in the Most Frequently Used Programs list.

Use the Customize Start Menu dialog box to control what appears on the Start Menu.

On the Advanced tab, you can go further in controlling which applications appear in the menu. This is also the place to activate the Most Recently Used Documents list, as well as set submenus to appear automatically when you hover the pen over the main menu. Both of these options are useful in making you more productive.

Change Folder Views

You can change the way Windows displays the contents of folders to accommodate the way you use the contents of those folders. As you learned in Chapter 1, most folders are document folders. Windows comes with a total of seven *folder templates*: Documents, Pictures, Photo Albums, Music, Music Artist, Music Album, and Videos.

Each template has specialized properties that are appropriate for the kind of content Windows expects you to store in them. To change the template used with a particular folder, you need to right-tap the folder's icon; then in the shortcut menu that appears, tap Properties | Customize. Select the template you want to use in the Use This Folder Type As A Template list. If all the subfolders of this folder are the same type as this folder, set the Also Apply This Template To All Subfolders option.

NOTE   *If the Properties dialog box for a folder doesn't have a Customize tab, you cannot change the template it uses.*

You can also customize a folder without changing its template. To do so, open the folder you want to customize. Tap View, and then select your options from the View menu that appears. The first section of this menu allows you to adjust the toolbars and other bars that appear at the top of the folder.

The second section of the View menu lists basic styles that the folder can use when displaying its contents. I suggest you try the styles yourself to get an idea of what works best for you. Folders that use the Pictures template have an additional style, Filmstrip, which arranges the pictures in a strip along the bottom of the window and displays the selected picture in the upper part of the folder.

The third section allows you to change the order of the contents. You can choose to arrange them by size, date, or other characteristics. Although the menu option says Arrange Icons By, it really applies to whichever form the folder content is displayed in.

In the fourth section, the Choose Details option controls which properties are displayed for each item in the folder, when you view the folder in the Detail style. As I said before, your best bet here is to try different options for your folders over time. You'll likely evolve your own preferences for the folders you use frequently, just as I have.

Another way you can customize folders is by changing around the menu bars and toolbars that appear in each folder. You can not only control the positions in which they appear, but you can also decide which ones will appear.

To change the positions of the bars, you must first unlock them. Tap View | Toolbars, and make sure the Lock The Toolbars option is cleared. If the bars are unlocked, they'll have a column of dots near the left end. To actually move the bars, point to that column of dots, and use it to drag the column to a new location. You may have to fool around with the bars for a bit to get them where you want them, so just keep at it.

To change which bars appear in the folder, tap View | Toolbars; then select the ones you want from the menu that appears. The exact contents of this menu vary depending on the applications installed on your Tablet PC. For example, I have Norton AntiVirus installed on my Tablet PC, and my Toolbars menus include the option to display a Norton AntiVirus toolbar.

Configure the Explorer Bar

You can make the Explorer bar appear in place of the Task pane. The Explorer bar can contain various types of information and tools, including the following:

- **Search** Provides the Windows XP search tool.

- **Favorites** Provides a collection of shortcuts to your favorite folders, web sites, and other items. Favorites are covered in Chapter 7.

- **Media** Gives you direct access to the Windows Media Player. Windows Media Player is covered in Chapter 12.

- **History**   Shows a day-by-day list of the files you've opened recently in Windows Explorer or Internet Explorer. Internet Explorer is covered in Chapter 7.

- **Folders**   Displays the folder tree.

To display the Explorer bar in a folder, tap View | Explorer Bar, and then select the type of Explorer bar you want to use. Figure 3-9 shows the Search Explorer bar in the My Documents folder. To close the Explorer bar once it is visible, you must tap the Close button in the upper right-hand corner of the Explorer bar. You cannot close the bar from the Explorer Bar menu.

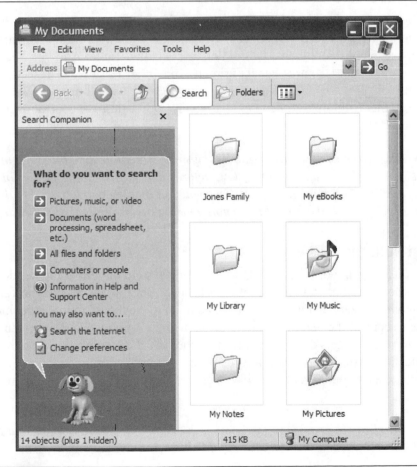

FIGURE 3-9   Search is one of the Explorer bar options you can choose for a particular folder.

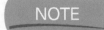 *Tip Of The Day and Discuss are not Explorer bar options, even though they appear on this menu. Tip Of The Day displays a daily tip at the bottom of the folder window, whereas Discuss attempts to activate a discussion of the selected item. This is not a topic we will cover in this book.*

Configure Your Tablet PC Hardware

In keeping with the more personal nature of a Tablet PC, its hardware is configurable. The rest of this chapter addresses the main hardware areas you can configure: the pen and tablet, the keyboard, the mouse, and the display.

Configure the Tablet and Pen

Because the tablet and pen are a new way to interact with your Tablet PC, it's no surprise that Windows XP Tablet PC edition includes a new Control Panel applet you can use to configure them. This dialog box is called Tablet And Pen Settings. To open it, tap Start | Control Panel | Printers And Other Hardware | Tablet And Pen Settings. This dialog box, shown in Figure 3-10, uses four tabs (Settings, Display, Tablet Buttons, and Pen Options) to give you extensive control over the behavior of the pen and tablet.

NOTE *Aside from the options on the Settings tab, I recommend you use your Tablet PC for at least a few days before changing anything in the Tablet And Pen Settings dialog box. Give yourself a chance to get used to the different feel of a Tablet PC before making other pen and tablet changes.*

Adjust Settings

When you are typing on a keyboard, the operating system of your computer doesn't need to know whether you are left- or right-handed. But for devices like the Tablet PC—which use pen input instead of, or in addition to, keyboard input—which hand you use to control the pen makes a big difference. Left-handed and right-handed people form characters differently, affecting the way the handwriting recognition software should function. Also, the area of the screen that's covered by your hand when you use the pen is different if you are left-handed than it is if you are right-handed.

NOTE *Handedness and Menu Location aren't really hardware options, but I've covered them here with the rest of Tablet And Pen Settings options.*

3

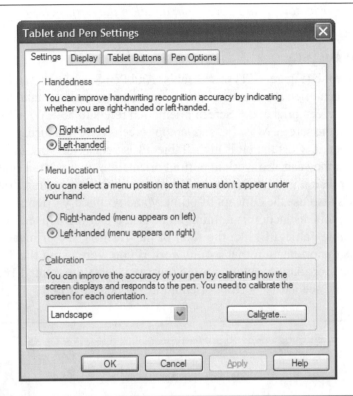

FIGURE 3-10   Use the Tablet And Pen Settings dialog box to configure these new Tablet PC components.

In the Handedness section of the Settings tab, select the hand you use to hold the pen. You won't detect any visible changes, but the Tablet PC handwriting recognition should work somewhat better than it would otherwise.

In the Menu Location section of the tab, you should also select the option that corresponds to the hand you use. If you select for right-handedness, it does produce a visible difference, but only when Windows is showing a submenu. In this situation, if there is enough room to the left of the main menu, the submenu will appear on the left instead of the right, where it would normally be. Putting the menu on the left keeps it from being hidden beneath your hand if you are right-handed.

Pen-sensitive displays like those found on Tablet PCs and personal digital assistants (PDAs) sometimes require calibration to ensure that the computer is accurately interpreting the position of the pen. The Calibration section of the Settings tab lets you calibrate the accuracy of pen positioning for each of the screen orientations you use.

Screen orientations are covered in detail in the next section.

Adjust the Display

On the Display tab (Figure 3-11) of the Tablet And Pen Settings dialog box, you can change the screen orientation, control the sequence of screen orientation changes, and adjust the screen brightness. Screen orientation refers to how Windows displays information on the screen. Most PC and laptop screens have a landscape orientation, where the screen is wider than it is high. Tablet PC screens can work in landscape orientation, but they can also work in portrait orientation. In a portrait orientation, the screen is taller than it is wide. Paper and books usually have a portrait orientation.

Tablet PCs also use the concept of primary and secondary orientations. To a certain extent, this distinction is nothing more than a naming convenience. If you use a convertible Tablet PC, like the Acer or the Toshiba, the primary landscape orientation is the orientation that would work if you were using the Tablet PC keyboard. The secondary orientation is the primary orientation rotated 180 degrees. The primary and secondary portrait orientations work similarly.

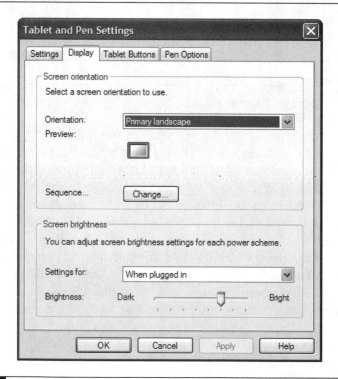

FIGURE 3-11 Use the Display tab to adjust screen orientation and brightness.

How to ... **Calibrate the Screen**

To calibrate the screen, you need to start with the Settings tab of the Tablet And Pen Settings dialog box.

1. In the Calibration section of the tab, select a screen orientation.

2. Tap Calibrate. The display changes to a blank background with some instructions in the center and a cross hair (a cross with a small empty space in the center) in the upper-left corner of the display.

3. Hold the pen as you normally would for writing on the screen in this orientation, and tap the center of the cross hair.

4. The cross hair appears in another corner of the screen. While holding the pen naturally, keep tapping the center of the cross hair until it has appeared in all four corners of the display.

5. When the OK button appears near the center of the screen, the calibration is complete. Tap OK to return to the normal display.

6. Repeat steps 1 through 5 for each screen orientation you want to calibrate. The Tablet PC automatically adjusts the screen orientation to match the one you selected, then restores the original orientation once you are done calibrating.

In the Screen Orientation section of the Display tab, you can change the screen orientation by selecting an orientation from the Orientation list and tapping OK or Apply.

NOTE *You can also change the screen orientation by using the Change Tablet And Pen Settings icon in the Notification Area, as well as using the Tablet buttons.*

Your Tablet PC allows you to select each of the four possible screen orientations one after the other. You can change the screen orientation with the Hardware button assigned to screen orientation on your Tablet PC. This gives you a quick way to adjust the orientation to match the way you're using the computer at the moment. However, most people find that they use only one or two orientations. By tapping Change, you can use the Orientation Sequence Settings dialog box to modify the screen orientation sequence, including removing those orientations you don't use.

In the Screen Brightness section of the Display tab, you can tell the Tablet PC which screen brightness to use when the system is running on batteries and when it is plugged in. Select the situation you want to work on and adjust the Brightness slider. If you're interested in extending your battery life, choose the lowest brightness you can comfortably use.

Configure Tablet Buttons

Use the Tablet Buttons tab to configure the Tablet buttons. Tablet buttons are physical buttons (often called Hardware buttons) on the face of your Tablet PC. You can configure these buttons for performing common tasks like changing the screen orientation, starting an application, or activating the Input Panel.

NOTE   *Consult the documentation that came with your Tablet PC to find the names and locations of the Tablet buttons on your particular system.*

The Tablet buttons on your Tablet PC were set to certain functions when you received it. You can find out what those settings are by looking at the list of Tablet buttons and actions on the Tablet Buttons tab. This list contains the names of all the Tablet buttons you can customize. Other buttons, like the Security button, have fixed functions that you cannot change.

To customize a Tablet button, select it in the list, tap Change, and select a function from the dialog box that appears. If you are unhappy with the changes you've made, tap Reset to return to the defaults.

Set Pen Options

You use the Pen Options tab to control how the pen and the screen interact. The Pen Actions section of the tab seems like it should be similar to configuring Tablet buttons, but it's not. Here, the relationship between pen and mouse actions is fixed. What you can do is modify how each action works a bit. For example, if you select Press And Hold in the list, and then tap Settings, you can change the length of time you need to press and hold before the Tablet PC recognizes a right-click, as well as how long you have to actually complete the action. I haven't found it necessary to change any of these options, but you may find doing so to be helpful.

Configure the Keyboard

You may not have even realized that there was anything to configure on your keyboard, but there is. Specifically, you can use the Speed tab in the Keyboard

Properties dialog box (see Figure 3-12) to adjust the amount of time that you can hold down a key before the Tablet PC starts repeating the character. To open the Keyboard Properties dialog box, tap Start | Control Panel | Printers And Other Hardware | Keyboard.

NOTE *Details of the Keyboard Properties dialog box may vary from one model of Tablet PC to the next.*

3

From the Speed tab, you can control how fast the tablet PC repeats the character once it has started doing so. You can also adjust how fast the cursor blinks when you are entering text into a word processor or other program that isn't using ink.

The Hardware tab is primarily useful for fixing keyboard problems, and is covered in Chapter 18.

FIGURE 3-12   Use the Keyboard Properties dialog box to adjust some basic keyboard characteristics.

Configure the Mouse

Configuring the mouse may seem like an odd activity to undertake on a Tablet PC, but every Tablet PC can be connected to a keyboard and a mouse. Plus, convertible machines like the Acer and Toshiba include a touch pad that can take the place of a mouse. I've even seen a few Tablet PCs with hardware that emulates a mouse attached to the tablet instead of the keyboard, so it can be used independently of the keyboard.

The basic components you can adjust for any mouse or mouse work-alike are the buttons and the pointers used to indicate where the mouse is pointing on the screen. You'll also find a Hardware tab similar to the one for keyboards. And like that tab, the mouse Hardware tab is covered in Chapter 19.

To open the Mouse Properties dialog box, tap Start | Control Panel | Printers And Other Hardware | Mouse. You will likely see quite a number of tabs related to the mouse and mouse-like gizmos that come with your model of Tablet PC. Figure 3-13 shows the crowd of tabs in my Mouse Properties dialog box. Most of these should be self-explanatory, but for those that are not, you'll need to consult the documentation that came with your Tablet PC.

Configure Your Display

Because your Tablet PC probably runs on batteries much of the time, managing its power use is very important. One of the best ways to do that is to turn off components of the machine when you're not using them. You can set up *power schemes* on your Tablet PC that determine when (if ever) to turn off the display and the hard disk, as well as when the Tablet PC should go into standby or hibernate.

When in *standby,* the Tablet PC is just idling along, running in a minimal power use state that can significantly prolong the battery life. According to the specifications from Microsoft, a Tablet PC must return to full functionality from standby in around 5 seconds.

When in *hibernation,* the Tablet PC is fully shut down. Before it hibernates, your machine copies the contents of its memory to the hard disk, allowing it to restore Windows and all your applications to the state they were in before the hibernation. If you have three applications open when the Tablet PC hibernates, you'll have those three applications open when the computer returns from hibernation. When hibernating, the Tablet PC consumes no power. Unfortunately, it can take 30 seconds or more for the machine to wake up from hibernation, so this isn't something you want to have happen while you're in the middle of working on something.

3

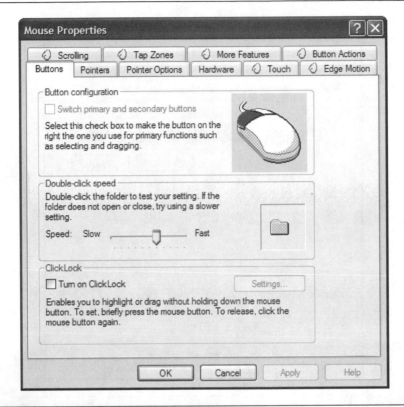

FIGURE 3-13   The Mouse Properties dialog box can get quite busy with mouse and mouse-like hardware options.

CAUTION   *Some hardware may not work properly after hibernation, and it may need to be disconnected and reconnected before it functions properly again. In some cases, you may have to reboot the Tablet PC to clear up the problem.*

You control the power schemes with the Power Options Properties dialog box. To open this dialog box, right-tap an empty spot on the desktop. When the shortcut menu appears, tap Properties | Screen Saver | Power | Power Schemes. (See Figure 3-14.)

As Figure 3-14 shows, there's a menu of power schemes in the dialog box. When you select a scheme, the settings it includes appear at the bottom of the dialog box. Notice that there are settings for both when the Tablet PC is plugged in and when it is running on batteries.

Windows comes with a large set of predefined schemes, but you may want to do as I did and define your own by putting your own values into the settings fields and then saving those settings as a new power scheme.

FIGURE 3-14   Use the Power Options Properties dialog box to manage power use on your Tablet PC.

The exact values you should choose for the settings depend on the way you work.

If you seldom spend long periods using your Tablet PC away from your desk, you'll probably want to keep everything running as much as possible. On the other hand, if you spend a lot of time running on batteries, you'll want to consider turning off the screen after just a minute or two and the hard disk shortly after that. The screen takes almost no time to come back on, so turning it off as much as possible will save you power without affecting your work.

If your work involves significant periods of thought interspersed with short bursts of computer use, you'll want to delay hibernation and perhaps standby enough to avoid having the machine go to sleep just when you need it.

In addition to the power options you just learned about, we've already looked at some settings you can change for the display (see the "Adjust the Display" section

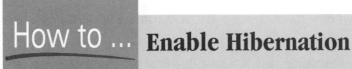

Enable Hibernation

Your Tablet PC may not have come with hibernation enabled. Here's how you can enable (or disable) hibernation. First, you need to figure out if hibernation is enabled already, which is easy. Just look at the Power Schemes tab in the Power Options Properties dialog box. If the tab doesn't include any boxes called System Hibernates, hibernation is turned off.

To enable hibernation, follow these steps:

1. Tap the Hibernate tab while you're in the Power Options Properties dialog box.

2. Look at the amount of disk space you have available and the amount of disk space required to hibernate in the Disk Space For Hibernation area of the dialog box.

3. Assuming you have significantly more disk space available than is needed to hibernate, tap Enable Hibernation, and then Apply.

4. Go back to the Power Schemes tab. If you see the System Hibernates boxes, you've successfully enabled hibernation on your Tablet PC.

earlier in this chapter), but you can adjust another whole set of options. These have to do with the display resolution, the screen refresh rate, and similar settings.

However, you don't really want to do anything with these settings. Remember, your Tablet PC comes with a built-in display. You can be sure that the manufacturer adjusted the display settings to work properly with the installed display. My best advice for you is to leave these settings as they are.

Take Advantage of Other Power Options

The Power Options Properties dialog box has a few other tabs you might want to configure.

■ **Alarms**   Lets you set the battery power levels that will cause Windows to set off alarms, and decide what form those alarms will take.

- **Power Meter**   Shows how much power is left in the Tablet PC battery or batteries.

- **Advanced**   Among other things, lets you set a Power Meter icon to appear in the notification area so you can easily check power levels. There's an option to require a password when resuming from standby, but this doesn't make much sense for a Tablet PC. They're designed to resume from standby within seconds, and requiring a password each time runs counter to that fast recovery requirement.

Chapter 4

Use Windows XP Tablet PC Edition

How to...

- Create and Manage User Accounts
- Manage Files and Folders
- Manage Programs and Components
- Find Stuff with the Search Companion
- Work with the Recycle Bin

Although you can accomplish all sorts of tasks on your Tablet PC with just the skills you've learned so far in the book, to make full use of your machine, you need to learn about a few more topics. You can share your Tablet PC with others, and Windows XP Tablet PC edition lets you do so safely by managing user accounts. Just as you can add and manage user accounts, Windows XP allows you to add and manage files, folders, entire programs, and even individual Windows components. This chapter walks you through all those topics, as well as the use of the Recycle Bin.

Create and Manage User Accounts

A *user account* contains Windows settings and other information relevant to a particular user. If everybody who uses your Tablet PC has their own user account, then they can configure the computer to work the way they want when they are using it. Each user account can have the following individual settings:

- Screen settings
- Web favorites and recently visited sites list
- Password protection of important or personal information

Windows XP Tablet PC edition supports four types of user accounts. Each has different capabilities and is suitable for different kinds of users. The following list describes the four types of user accounts:

- **Computer Administrator account**   A *Computer Administrator account* allows users to make any modifications to the computer they want, including viewing and modifying the files and information in other accounts. There must always be at least one Computer Administrator account. Windows will not let you remove the last such account, or change the last such account into another type of account. If you have set up your Tablet PC yourself, your personal account should be a Computer Administrator account.

- **Standard account**   A *Standard account* is available only if the user is a member of a domain on a network.

- **Limited account**   A *Limited account* is exactly that: a user with a limited account has only a limited ability to make changes to the computer. Holders of limited accounts can change only their password and change the picture associated with their account.

- **Guest account**   You can enable a single *Guest account* if you want to allow people who don't have their own account to use your computer. A Guest account is even more limited than a Limited account. The only task the user can perform is run programs that are installed on the Tablet PC.

Enabling a Guest account can compromise the security of your Tablet PC because it does give anyone who picks up your computer some access to its resources.

Modify Existing Accounts and Create New Ones

The User Accounts window is the place to start when you want to modify existing user accounts or create new ones. To open the User Accounts window, tap Start | Control Panel | User Accounts.

The Computer Management console is another place where you can make changes to user accounts. The changes you make there are primarily related to using the Tablet PC on a network, so the Computer Management console is covered in Chapter 8.

If you are using a Computer Administrator account, you should see something like Figure 4-1. In this case, the window contains shortcuts to common tasks you can perform on user accounts, a list of accounts you can change, and links to information about various user account topics.

If you are using a Standard or Limited account, you should see something like Figure 4-2. Note that the window doesn't show any other accounts, because only Computer Administrator accounts have the right to modify other accounts.

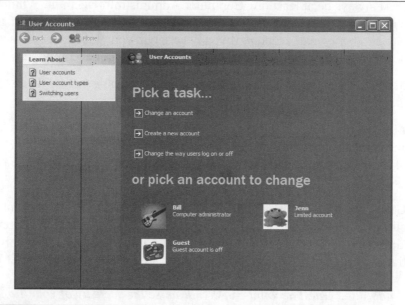

FIGURE 4-1 The User Accounts window for Computer Administrators is where you create new accounts and modify existing ones.

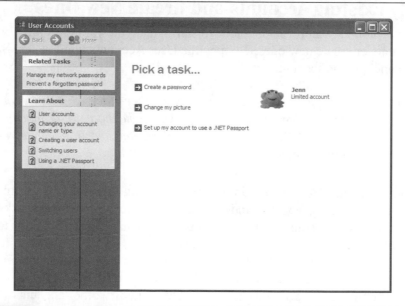

FIGURE 4-2 The User Accounts window for Standard or Limited accounts has fewer capabilities than the one for Computer Administrators.

Change a User Account

You can always make changes to your own account (unless you're using a Guest account). For the rest of this section, I'll assume you are using a Computer Administrator account. If you're not, your options are pretty limited and clearly visible from the User Accounts window.

To modify an account, tap the Change An Account link. Windows displays a new window showing all the accounts you can change. Tap the icon for the account you want to change. The window that appears next lists all the changes you can make to the account, as well as a collection of shortcuts to related tasks and more information in case you're unsure what to do next. The contents of this window will be similar to the one shown in Figure 4-3.

Tap the link for the change you would like to make, and then follow the onscreen instructions to make the change.

CAUTION *If you want to add a password to your account for protection, please read the section "Add Password Protection for User Accounts" later in this chapter before doing so. This section provides additional information, including instructions on how to recover if you forget your password.*

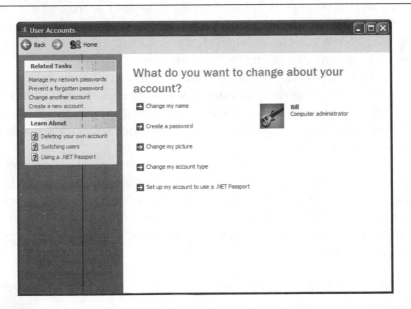

FIGURE 4-3 Use this window to change characteristics of a user account.

Create a New User Account (Computer Administrators Only)

To create a new account, you begin at the main User Accounts window. (Tap Start | Control Panel | User Accounts to get there.) Under Pick A task, tap Create A New Account, and then follow the instructions and fill in the fields to create the account. If you're unsure what to do at any point in the process, consult the information listed in the Learn About box on the left side of the window.

Remember that Computer Administrator accounts provide full control over your computer. If you give someone a Computer Administrator account, that person can even delete all other administrator accounts on your computer and lock you out of your own Tablet PC. Unless someone specifically needs to install hardware and software on your computer, or needs one of the other rights reserved for Computer Administrator accounts, you should create only Limited or Standard accounts for other people on your Tablet PC.

Add Password Protection for User Accounts

Adding a password to a user account is easy to do, but there are ramifications to doing so, particularly on a Tablet PC. This section covers the issues you should understand before you add password protection to a user account.

In general, adding password protection to a user account is a good idea. Doing so prevents unauthorized persons from logging in as you and making changes to your account. You can also apply your password to all your files, using the *Encrypting File System* (EFS). When files are encrypted with EFS, even people with valid accounts on your computer cannot look at your files.

There are two drawbacks to adding a password to your user account. The first is that you must remember that password. If you don't remember the password, you can't log in to your account. Forgetting a password is such a common cause of problems for computer users that Microsoft has included some ways to address the problem in Windows XP.

If you can log in to the computer using a Computer Administrator account for which you do know the password, you can reset the forgotten password. However, there is a potential disaster here. If the user account with the forgotten password has files protected with EFS, resetting the password could result in the permanent loss of all the encrypted files. As Figure 4-4 shows, the range of files that could be lost is quite extensive.

 *Do not reset a password unless you have no other choice. Permanent loss of data may result.*

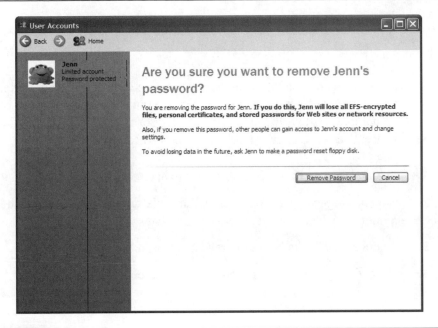

4

FIGURE 4-4   Resetting passwords should be a last resort because doing so can result in significant data loss.

The second problem with adding a password to a user account isn't potential data loss. It is a usability problem. One of the key design goals for Tablet PCs is the ability to resume working quickly when the computer has been in standby mode. Because Tablet PCs are expected to be in use throughout the day, they may well go into and out of standby mode several times a day. Adding a password to your account makes resuming from standby a much slower and clumsier affair. You'll have to balance the need for security with the need for usability.

Another approach to this problem is to create a *password reset disk*. Then you can store it in a secure location and use it to log in to your computer if you've forgotten the password.

If your Tablet PC doesn't have a removable disk drive (in the computer itself or in the dock), you cannot create a password reset disk. If a password reset disk is important to you, you may wish to invest in a USB floppy disk drive.

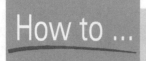 **Create a Password Reset Disk**

The steps needed to create a Password Reset Disk are different if your Tablet PC is part of a network domain than if it is not. If your computer is part of a network domain, consult with your IT department for instructions on creating a Password Reset Disk. Otherwise, follow these instructions:

1. Tap Start | Control Panel | User Accounts to open the User Accounts window.

2. If you are logged on as a Computer Administrator, tap the icon of the account for which you want to create the Password Reset Disk.

3. In the Related Tasks box, tap Prevent A Forgotten Password.

4. Follow the instructions that appear on the screen to create the disk.

If you still want to add a password to a user account, tap Start | Control Panel | User Accounts, and then tap the icon representing the account to which you want to add a password. Then fill in the fields and follow the directions to complete the task and add the password.

The process for removing a password from a user account is also simple (but remember the possibility of losing encrypted data). Tap Start | Control Panel | User Accounts, and then tap the icon representing the account you want to reset. Tap Remove The Password | Remove Password, and you're done.

Easily Share Your Tablet PC with Fast User Switching

Fast User Switching is a feature of Windows XP that allows you to switch from one user account to another without closing your applications or logging off the computer.

With earlier versions of Windows, if you were working on something, say a book, and your daughter wanted to use the computer for a few minutes to play Spider Solitaire, you would have two choices. One, you could let your daughter play the game and hope she doesn't do anything to mess up your work while she's at it. Two, you could close everything you were working on, log off the computer, and let your daughter log on using her own account. That would protect your work, but at the cost of several minutes at each end of the session to switch accounts and get the right applications running. If Fast User Switching is enabled on your

Tablet PC, this process becomes much easier. Your daughter can just switch to her account without you having to close anything or turn off your computer.

To switch user accounts, tap Start | Log Off | Switch User. When the Welcome screen appears, tap the icon belonging to the next person who will use the computer.

When you switch back to the first user account, you will find that everything is the way you left it. However, there are two drawbacks to activating Fast User Switching. The first is that turning off the computer while another user is logged

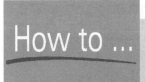 **Turn On Fast User Switching**

Before you can use Fast User Switching, it must be turned on. You need to be using an account with administrator privileges to turn Fast User Switching on or off, and your computer cannot be part of a network domain. If you meet these criteria, here's how you can turn Fast User Switching on or off.

1. Tap Start | Control Panel, and double-tap User Accounts.

2. In the User Accounts window, tap Change The Way Users Log On Or Off.

3. In the Select Logon And Logoff Options window, set or clear the Use Fast User Switching option.

4. Tap Apply Options to put the new settings into effect.

CAUTION *If you turn on Fast User Switching, the Serial Keys accessibility option will not work. If you control your computer with puff and sip or other alternative input devices, you shouldn't turn on Fast User Switching. Other features and devices, including ActiveSync and offline files, will also be affected by Fast User Switching.*

on could cause that user to lose data. The second is that each user session uses some computer processing power, slowing down other activities on the Tablet PC. So if several other users are logged on to your machine, you may find your work slowed to a crawl and your computer's ability to recognize handwriting compromised.

Manage Files and Folders

Although I've used the term "file" numerous times in this book, I've never defined it. A *file* is a collection of information grouped together with a single name and stored on a disk. Programs are stored as files. So are music and video clips, spreadsheets, word processor documents, saved searches, Windows settings, and so on. A *folder* is a container for files and other folders. They're useful for organizing your files. Once a computer has been in use for a while, you're likely to find that its hard disk contains dozens of folders and thousands or tens of thousands of files.

Your Tablet PC hard disk contains many files and folders created for use by Windows and by the various programs installed on the machine. You can also create new folders, as well as rename, copy, move, delete, and compress them. If your Tablet PC connects to a network, you can share your folders, making them accessible to other computers on the network.

Understand File and Folder Properties

Like most things in Windows XP, files and folders have properties. Although files and folders can have a wide range of properties, they do have certain properties in common. These include the following:

- A name
- A location
- The date and time they were created, modified, and last accessed
- The size of the file or folder and the amount of space it takes up on the disk

You can view properties without opening the folder or file to which they belong. Figure 4-5 shows the General tab for the My Documents folder on my Acer, along with the General tab for one of the files stored in the My Documents folder.

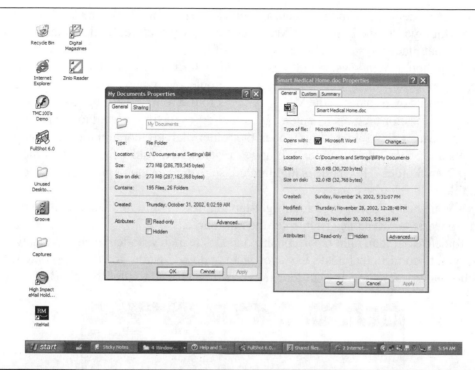

4

FIGURE 4-5   Files and folders can have many different properties, but they also have several basic properties in common.

NOTE   *As you'll see in the section titled "Find Stuff with the Search Companion," you can search for files or folders using these properties as search criteria, which makes for fast and efficient searching.*

Under most circumstances, you won't have to worry about file and folder properties because Windows XP will handle them for you, so we won't go into more depth on them. Instead, let's look at how you can manage your files and folders.

Manage Your Folders

When Windows XP Tablet PC edition was installed on your computer, part of the process involved creating a number of folders on your hard disk. These include a bunch of folders that Windows uses, as well as a set of folders for the kinds of files with which you're likely to work. My Documents, My Pictures, and similar folders make great places to store the relevant types of files.

Even though Windows provides useful folders for you, you are likely to need to create your own folders sooner or later. For example, every book or magazine article I write has its own folder in the My Documents folder. Within each of those folders are subfolders for pictures, chapters, and other types of files related to the project.

To create a new folder, simply open the folder that will contain the new folder, and then tap File | New | Folder. Windows creates a new folder for you with the name New Folder. This name is highlighted, so just enter the name you want for the folder and you're done.

If you want to rename a folder, right-tap that folder, and in the shortcut menu that appears, tap Rename. Then enter the new name.

To delete a folder, right-tap it, and then tap Delete in the shortcut menu. Windows asks you to confirm that this is what you want to do and warns you that the contents of the folder (including any subfolders) will all be moved to the Recycle Bin.

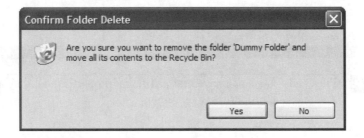

Most of the menu options for folders are self-explanatory.

We should, however, spend a few minutes on the View menu. It lets you change the way Windows displays the contents of folders to accommodate the way you use the contents of those folders. Windows XP provides six *folder templates,* which provide specific views of the contents of a folder. Most folders are *document folders,* which are folders designed to hold any kind of content. Figure 4-6 is a typical document folder.

Windows has five other folder templates, each of which is designed to hold a certain type of content and display it in a particular way. The My Pictures folder (see Figure 4-7) uses the Pictures template to display its contents in a particular way, with specific Picture Tasks options like Order Prints Online, available right in the folder.

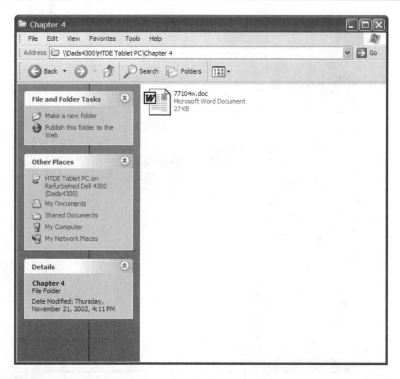

FIGURE 4-6   Document folders like this one are the most versatile type of folder for most uses.

To change the folder template, tap View | Customize This Folder, and then select the template you want to use from the list provided. Within the bounds of the selected folder template, you can change how the folder's contents appear in the right-hand pane. Tap View, and then select among the options available.

NOTE   *You cannot change the template for special folders like My Documents and My Pictures.*

For folders that you expect to use frequently, you may want to experiment with different View menu options to decide which ones work best for that folder. I find myself frequently adjusting the view of folders like My Documents to meet the needs of the moment. So don't be afraid to experiment. Remember that when you use the View menu, you're just changing the way the folder displays its contents. You're not changing the properties of those contents, so you can't hurt anything.

FIGURE 4-7   Windows can also present specialized folders designed for specific types of content.

TIP *Before you start creating lots of folders, think about a strategy for storing information on your computer. One approach is to put all your picture folders in My Pictures, music folders in My Music, and so on. But if you do lots of projects that involve different types of files, consider creating project folders in My Documents, and putting all the files and folders for a project in that project folder. This approach lets you easily find everything related to a particular project.*

Manage Your Files

Although your Tablet PC may have tens of thousands of files on its hard disk, managing those files is relatively simple. You don't create files like you create folders. Programs create files in the course of their operation. When you're using an application like Microsoft Word, the program creates files for you and saves them where you tell it to, so you don't really have to worry too much about that aspect of managing files. You can usually use an application to delete and rename the files it works with, so that's easy too.

You can delete, rename, and move files without the help of the program with which they're associated. You delete or rename them by right-tapping their icons and selecting the appropriate option in the shortcut menu. You move them by dragging them from their old location to the new one.

4

Manage Programs and Components

Programs are sets of software instructions that tell your computer what to do. Certain types of programs go by different names: a *utility* is generally a small program that performs specific functions like defragmenting the hard disk or scanning for viruses. An *application* is a program you use for getting your work done, such as a word processor or spreadsheet. And *games,* well, they're games you play on your computer. But whatever the name for the particular category, they're all still programs.

Windows *components* are also programs. But these programs are optional parts of the Windows XP Tablet PC edition operating system. Windows XP is itself a very large and complex program.

You install programs on your Tablet PC to allow it to perform tasks it couldn't do before, or so it can perform those tasks better than it did before. For example, Windows XP doesn't include its own antivirus program. By adding one, you give your Tablet PC the ability to do something it couldn't do before.

To reduce the amount of memory, disk space, and processor time Windows uses, some less-frequently used components of Windows are not installed automatically when Windows is installed on a computer. You treat Windows components very similarly to other programs when it comes to installing them on your computer and removing them.

Just as you can install programs or components when you need them, you can uninstall (remove) them when you no longer need them. The next two sections show you how to install and remove programs and components when your Tablet PC has either a built-in CD-ROM drive or one that connects directly to it through a dock or a cable.

You can also install programs by downloading them from the Internet or installing them from another computer on a network. Downloading from the Internet is covered in Chapter 7, where we connect your Tablet PC to the Internet.

Get Your CD-ROM Drive Connected

Most programs that you will want to install on your Tablet PC come on a CD-ROM. Similarly, you'll install Windows components from the Windows CD-ROM that came with your Tablet PC. Your computer may have a built-in CD-ROM drive, it may have a drive in the docking station, or it may have an external drive that connects to the Tablet PC through a cable. In all cases, the documentation that came with your computer tells you what, if anything, you need to do to connect your CD-ROM drive to your Tablet PC. Once they're connected, the way they're connected is irrelevant when it comes to installing and removing programs.

Install Programs

Make sure your CD-ROM drive is turned on, and then insert the CD-ROM containing the program into the drive. Normally the CD-ROM will start spinning, and Windows will display a dialog box asking if you want to install the program. If that happens, all you need to do is follow the onscreen instructions and Windows will install the program.

If you put the CD-ROM in the drive and nothing happens, first make sure the CD-ROM drive has power and is connected to the Tablet PC properly. Consult the documentation that came with your system if necessary to ensure that the CD-ROM drive is on and connected to the computer. If everything seems to be connected and powered properly, tap Start | My Computer, and look for an icon that represents the CD-ROM drive. Figure 4-8 shows that icon under the heading Devices With Removable Storage. If you don't see the icon, the CD-ROM drive still isn't connected properly, or isn't turned on. (Or the drive is in the dock, and the Tablet PC is in your hands. Although your Tablet PC has wireless capabilities, it needs to be physically connected to the CD-ROM drive for this procedure to work.)

If you do see the icon, right-tap it. In the shortcut menu that appears, tap either Install or AutoPlay to start installing the program. Follow the installation instructions that appear.

Install Components

You install Windows components with the Add Or Remove Programs window. To open the window, tap Start | Control Panel | Add Or Remove Programs. The window opens with a list of all the programs currently installed on your Tablet PC. On the left side of the window, tap Add/Remove Windows Components to open the Windows Components Wizard shown in Figure 4-9.

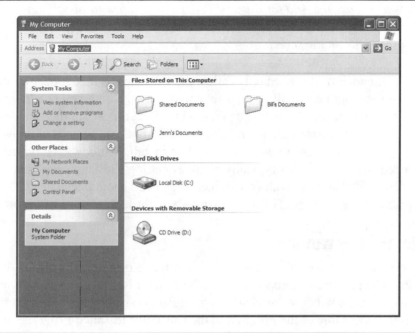

FIGURE 4-8   If you don't see an icon for the CD-ROM drive in the My Computers window, the drive isn't connected properly or isn't turned on.

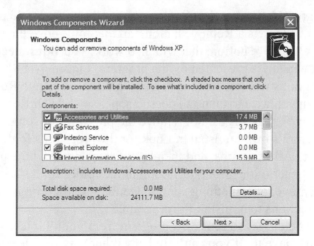

FIGURE 4-9   The Windows Components Wizard makes it easy to install or remove optional components.

 *You can use the Add Or Remove Programs window to install new programs if you wish. Tap Add New Programs and then follow the directions on the screen.*

To use the wizard, you need only follow the instructions that appear on the screen. Some components will contain subcomponents, which you can learn more about by tapping Details. Every time you tap Details, you get another window, which looks very similar to the main Windows Components Wizard window.

Once you select the components you wish to install, Windows XP figures out what it needs to do next. This typically involves getting files and programs from the Windows CD that came with your Tablet PC, so you should have that CD-ROM in the drive or have it handy. The wizard guides you through the rest of the process.

Remove Programs

When you no longer need a program, you can remove or uninstall it from your Tablet PC. The preferred approach is to use the Add Or Remove Programs window. To do this, open the window (tap Start | Control Panel | Add Or Remove Programs), and then find the name of the program in the Currently Installed Programs list.

 If the Currently Installed Programs list isn't visible in the window, tap Change Or Remove Programs. That should bring the list into view.

Tap the program's icon to select it. One or more buttons should appear to the right of the icon. If there's a Remove button, tap that to remove the program. If there's a Change/Remove button, that will also work; you'll just need to select the Remove option when it is presented by the program. Figure 4-10 shows the Add Or Remove Programs window with a program that has a Change/Remove button.

If the program you want to uninstall doesn't appear in Add Or Remove Programs, or Add Or Remove Programs cannot remove the program for some reason, you can use the program's own uninstaller. Look for the program's folder in the Start menu. (Tap Start | All Programs, and then look for the name of the program or the name of the publisher of the program.) Look in the folder for a shortcut named Uninstall, or Remove, or something similar. Double-tap that program and follow the onscreen directions to uninstall the program.

There is one other way to remove a program from your Tablet PC, but don't use it if you don't have to. If you can't find any other way to delete a program, you can search your hard disk to find the program's folder (learn how to search your hard disk in the "Find Stuff with the Search Companion" section later in this chapter), and then delete that folder.

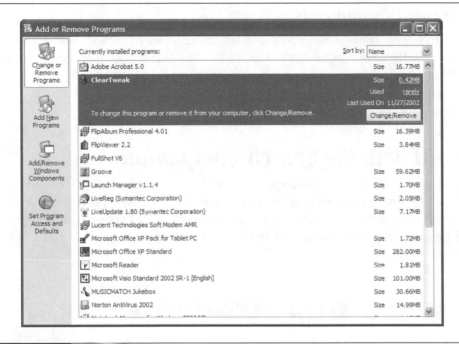

FIGURE 4-10   When it is time to remove a program from your Tablet PC, the Add Or
Remove Programs window gets the job done efficiently and cleanly.

Although this method will get rid of the program, it isn't a very neat solution.
Many programs have pieces of themselves scattered in various locations on your
hard disk. Deleting the main folder for a program will get rid of the majority of
the files, but probably not all of them. Worse, many programs make changes deep
inside Windows. Removing a program in one of the other ways will usually undo
those changes. Deleting the folder will not. So save this as a last resort.

When removing programs, be aware that even when you use their own uninstallers,
programs sometimes leave bits of themselves behind on your hard disk. This is
particularly true with pieces of programs called DLLs. What they are or why they're
there isn't relevant. What's important is that while you are removing a program from
your computer, Windows may ask you whether it should delete certain files. Unless
you are absolutely certain that deleting the files will not cause any problems, I
recommend telling Windows not to delete the files.

Files that are left behind but not used waste a tiny bit of disk space. Files that
are deleted when they shouldn't be can cause major problems for you. So play it
safe and tell Windows to leave them alone.

Remove Components

You remove Windows components in much the same way you add them, using the Add Or Remove Programs window. To start the Windows Components Wizard, tap Start | Control Panel | Add Or Remove Programs | Add/Remove Windows Components. Clear the check boxes of the components you want to remove, tap Next, and follow the instructions that appear.

Find Stuff with the Search Companion

For me, one of the keys to managing anything on your computer (or anywhere else in your life, for that matter) is being able to find it. That's why I love the *Search Companion.* The Search Companion panel (see Figure 4-11) is a general-purpose tool for searching out darn near anything on your computer. And I do mean darn near anything.

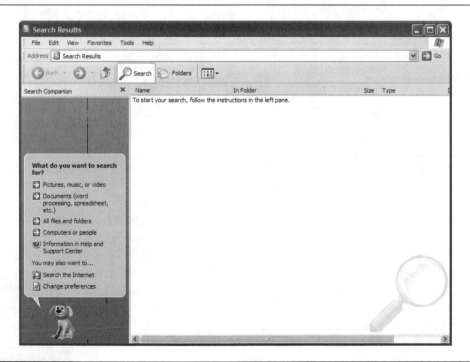

FIGURE 4-11   The Search Companion is a user-friendly way to find virtually anything stored on or connected to your Tablet PC.

The Search Companion can find the following:

- Files and folders

- People (users and groups in your Windows Address Book, on the computer, and across the network)

- Computers on the network

- Shared printers

- Information in the Windows help system

- Information on the Internet

The basics of using the Search Companion are the same for all types of searches, so we'll just look at one of them in more detail.

Search for Files and Folders

One of the most common uses for the Search Companion is finding files or folders. Tap Start | Search | All Files Or Folders to do this kind of search. This opens a new window. (See Figure 4-12.)

Here, you can enter search criteria specific to files and folders, such as the following:

- Full or partial filename

- Date created, modified, or last accessed

- File type or size

- A string of characters within the file

- Any combination of these criteria

The results of your search appear in the right-hand pane of the Search Results window.

When searching for filenames, the concept of wildcards comes into play. A *wildcard* is a character that can represent one or more other characters. In Windows, the asterisk (*) and the question mark (?) are wildcards when you use them in a filename. The question mark stands for any single character. If you use a question mark in a filename search, Windows can replace that question mark with any character.

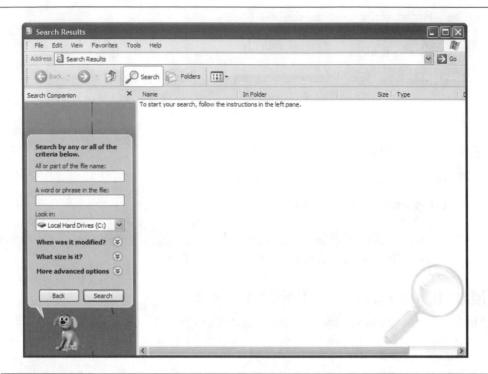

FIGURE 4-12   Fill in some or all of these fields to narrow your file or folder search.

Say, for example, you enter this text in the filename field: c?t.doc. When doing the search, Windows will find any filename that has the first letter *c,* followed by any valid character, followed by *t.doc.* So the search would find files with names like cat.doc, c1t.doc, cvt.doc, and so on. But the search wouldn't find filenames like cart.doc because the question mark represents only a single character.

The asterisk represents any number of characters. So if you did a search for c*t.doc, it would find files with names like cat.doc, c1t.doc, cvt.doc, and so on. And the search would find filenames like cart.doc because the asterisk can represent any number of characters. You can use wildcards in any search that includes a filename field.

Use More Advanced Search Techniques

Here are two more advanced search techniques you may wish to take advantage of.

Save and Reuse Searches

Someday you may find yourself doing the same search over and over again. You might, for example, be working on a book project and need to be able to find all the files containing the book's figures, wherever they may be on your computer. You can do this by entering all the search criteria every time you want to run the search. But you can also enter all the criteria and then run your search once. After the search returns its results, you can save the search (not the results of the search, but the search criteria) and reuse it another time.

To save a search, run the search as you would normally, and then tap File | Save Search. Windows opens a standard file search dialog box named Save Search, and allows you to save the search anywhere on your Tablet PC or the network. These saved searches are just a type of file that records the search criteria you used, and ends in .fnd. When saving a search, make sure the name Windows assigns to the search makes sense to you, or rename the search file to something that does make sense.

Because the saved searches are files, you have lots of flexibility. If the search is specific to a particular project, you can save the search in a folder reserved for that project. You can also copy the saved search into additional folders, even send a copy to other people. (This makes more sense when the search looks for things on the Internet or the corporate network.)

To reuse the saved search, you need to go to the folder you stored it in and double-tap it.

Use the Indexing Service

I often find myself searching for a file that has specific text within it. I do this by filling in the A Word Or Phrase In The File field. This kind of search can get you to the exact file or folder you need, but it is very time consuming. When performing this kind of search, Windows must examine the complete contents of every file it checks, instead of just looking at properties like the filename or date.

If you expect to do a lot of word or phrase searches, you might want to consider using the *Indexing Service.* This utility runs continuously, creating and maintaining an index of the contents and properties of files on your hard disk. As a result, you get much faster searches.

NOTE   *You can also set the Indexing Service to index shared disks on other computers on the network.*

The Indexing Service does its work when your machine is idle, so it shouldn't have too much of an effect on your day-to-day work. However, when your Tablet

PC is meant to use as little power as possible and go into standby when it is idle (at least when it is running on batteries), the benefits the Indexing Service will provide to you will vary.

> NOTE *The Indexing Service creates indexes on your hard disk that can take up considerable space. So if you're concerned about running out of disk space, you probably don't want to use the Indexing Service.*

Activating the Indexing Service is a little bit unusual. To do so, open the Search Companion window (tap Start | Search). Tap Change preferences. When the list of preferences appears in the Search Companion panel (it'll look like Figure 4-13), tap With Indexing Service or Without Indexing Service, whichever is available. When the Indexing Service panel appears, select the Indexing Service option you wish to use.

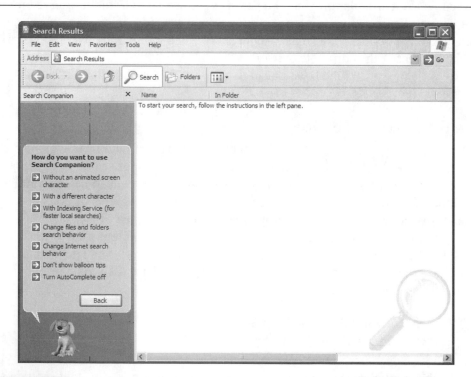

FIGURE 4-13   You turn the Indexing Service on or off from the Search Companion preferences list.

Work with the Recycle Bin

The *Recycle Bin* is a surprisingly useful part of Windows XP. This is the place where files, shortcuts, folders, programs, and anything else you delete ends up. If you're not familiar with the Recycle Bin, you may wonder why things don't just disappear from your computer when you delete them. The answer is simple. Sooner or later, everyone who uses a computer messes up and deletes something they wish they hadn't. Before the Recycle Bin, the only way to recover from this kind of mistake was to find a backup copy of whatever you accidentally deleted and install that.

CAUTION   *Items deleted from a floppy disk or network drive are not stored in the Recycle Bin when you delete them. They are instead immediately and permanently deleted from your computer.*

The Recycle Bin provides a temporary resting place for files on their way out. If you accidentally delete something (and you haven't yet emptied the Recycle Bin), you can easily retrieve it from the bin. This is much less hassle than finding a backup copy somewhere.

NOTE   *If a file doesn't fit in the Recycle Bin, Windows will ask you for permission to permanently delete it instead of storing it in the bin.*

As I mentioned previously, things you delete end up in the Recycle Bin automatically. To retrieve something from the Recycle Bin, open the bin. (Double-tap it just like any other icon.) This displays a pretty standard-looking

You May Have More Than One Recycle Bin?

If your Tablet PC has more than one hard disk, or your hard disk is partitioned (more on hard disks in Chapter 17), your computer has more than one Recycle Bin. In most cases, even if you do have more than one Recycle Bin, it will have no noticeable effect on your work. Although this situation shouldn't crop up too often on a Tablet PC, it is fairly common on desktop computers.

window like the one shown in Figure 4-14. In the right-hand pane of the window, you can see everything that's in the Recycle Bin.

Select the icon for the object you want to retrieve. Tap the Restore This Item link in the Recycle Bin Tasks pane to restore the object to its previous location. If you want to put the item somewhere else, just drag it to the new location.

Windows allocates a certain amount of disk space to the Recycle Bin, and it will eventually fill up. So you need to empty the Recycle Bin every so often. There are no official rules for emptying the Recycle Bin. Some people do so every day. Some do it once a week. Some (like me) tend to wait until the Recycle Bin is full before doing anything about it.

Some people go through the Recycle Bin before they empty it, making sure they will not need each item again before deleting it. Others (like me) assume that if something has been in the Recycle Bin for a while and they haven't missed it, they don't need it. We usually empty the Recycle Bin without examining what's inside.

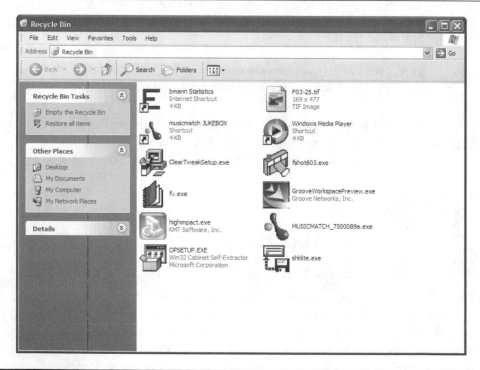

FIGURE 4-14   Open the Recycle Bin window to retrieve objects you don't want to delete quite yet.

How to ... Change the Size of the Recycle Bin

Although Windows allocates a certain amount of space to the Recycle Bin (typically 10 percent of each hard disk or partition), you can change this setting to suit the way you do things. You can also reduce the size of the Recycle Bin if you run low on disk space. To change the size of all the Recycle Bin or bins simultaneously, follow these steps:

1. Right-tap the Recycle Bin on the Windows desktop.

2. In the shortcut menu, tap Properties.

3. On the Global tab, select Use One Setting For All Drives.

4. Adjust the Maximum Size Of Recycle Bin slider to show the percentage of each disk or partition you want allocated to the Recycle Bin.

5. Do *not* set Do Not Move Files To The Recycle Bin unless you are prepared to permanently lose any objects that you delete by accident.

6. Tap OK to put the change into effect.

Whichever of the many strategies you choose for managing your Recycle Bin, you have three choices for how to empty it. The easy way is to right-tap the Recycle Bin icon on the desktop, and then tap Empty Recycle Bin. That permanently eliminates everything in the bin at once. The next approach is to open the Recycle Bin, and then tap Empty The Recycle Bin under Recycle Bin Tasks.

The third technique allows you to delete specific files without emptying the entire bin. Open the Recycle Bin, select the objects you want to get rid of, and then right-tap them and select Delete from the shortcut menu that appears.

Chapter 5

Manage Your Tablet PC Hardware

How to…

- Install and Remove Hardware
- Manage Hardware
- Set Up Hardware Profiles

You should find relatively little need to actively manage the hardware of your Tablet PC. Because they are high-end devices, most Tablet PCs come equipped with all the hardware they need, already configured and ready to run. And Windows XP Tablet PC edition is pretty smart about adding and removing hardware, handling most situations automatically. However, if you connect a camera, portable music player, or any other external gizmo to your Tablet PC, you may need to manage that hardware.

Did you know?

That Tablet PCs Are Designed to Be Legacy-Free?

One aspect of the design of Tablet PCs that's especially relevant to installing and managing hardware is the concept of *legacy-free* design. To reduce compatibility problems with older hardware, Microsoft has been moving computer makers toward legacy-free hardware design. What this means is that Tablet PCs don't have serial, parallel, or PS/2-compatible ports anymore. Old-style game and MIDI ports are also off limits.

Legacy-free machines like the Tablet PC can have any or all of the following kinds of ports and connectors: USB, IEEE 1394 (Firewire), Mini VGA (for an external monitor), PC Card, and CompactFlash, as well as the usual power, Ethernet and modem connectors, and microphone and headphone jacks. They can also have a docking connector.

While the legacy-free design concept increases the reliability of Tablet PCs, it means that some of your existing hardware may not work with your Tablet PC. If your printer only has a parallel port, you can't use it with your Tablet PC. Likewise, if you use an ergonomic keyboard that connects to your desktop computer through a PS/2 port (like me), it won't work with your Tablet PC.

Fortunately, if you depend on a piece of hardware that uses legacy ports, you may still be able to use it. Several manufacturers produce adapters that can connect legacy ports to USB ports. Say you need to connect a keyboard that uses a PS/2 port to your Tablet PC's USB port. You can go to a site like CNET Shopper.com (http://shopper.cnet.com) and search for the words USB PS/2 to get a list of USB to PS/2 adapters. You'll also get a list of devices that have USB or PS/2 ports, but it only takes a moment to track down a few adapters that should do the job.

5

This chapter gives you the information you're most likely to need to deal with any hardware-related situations that come up with your Tablet PC.

Install and Remove Hardware

Installing and removing hardware on computers running Windows XP is much simpler than it was with earlier versions of the operating system (OS). Most of the hardware you'll install or remove from your Tablet PC is external devices (sometimes called *peripherals*) like CD-ROM drives or digital cameras. And, today, most of those external devices are plug-and-play compatible, making your life even easier. *Plug-and-play* is a technology that allows Windows to automatically recognize and configure plug-and-play compatible hardware. In the next few sections, I show you how to install and remove plug-and-play hardware, as well as non-plug-and-play hardware.

The actual process of installing hardware includes physically connecting the hardware to the Tablet PC, as well as installing software that lets Windows interact with the hardware (this is known as *driver software*, or just a *driver*).

Install Plug-and-Play Hardware

Installing plug-and-play hardware is a joy. All you need to do is connect it to your Tablet PC, turn it on (if it even needs to be turned on), and wait. Within moments, Windows XP detects the new hardware and configures itself to work with that new hardware, including automatically installing the appropriate driver software. The external CD-ROM drive for my Acer is a plug-and-play device. The first time I wanted to use it, I connected the drive to my computer and turned on its power. Soon little bubble messages started appearing on my screen, telling me that Windows had found new hardware and was preparing to use it. A few seconds after that, the process was complete and my CD-ROM drive was ready to use.

The process was the same for my wife's Nikon Coolpix camera. I connected it to my Tablet PC and, within a minute, I was viewing the photos in the camera's memory. I didn't need to load software from a CD or anything. Windows recognized the camera, installed a copy of camera driver software, and integrated the camera into my computer system as if it had always been there.

It really is that simple—as long as you're working with plug-and-play hardware. Installing hardware that isn't plug-and-play is a little more work.

Install Non-Plug-and-Play Hardware

While most of the hardware you'll want to connect to your Tablet PC is plug-and-play-compatible, you may have occasion to use noncompatible hardware, perhaps your old scanner or printer. In situations like this, I strongly recommend you let the Add Hardware Wizard help you. First, though, turn off your computer, unplug it from the wall, and physically connect the hardware to the Tablet PC. Restart your computer and start the Add Hardware Wizard.

To start the wizard (shown in Figure 5-1), tap Start | Control Panel | Performance And Maintenance | System | Hardware | Add Hardware Wizard. As with all

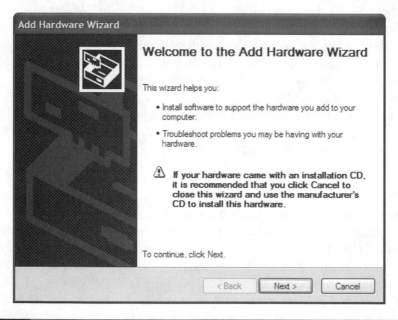

FIGURE 5-1   The Add Hardware Wizard can be invaluable when you want to install non-plug-and-play hardware on your Tablet PC.

Windows' wizards, you just need to follow the instructions that appear on the screen to accomplish the task at hand. In particular, heed the warning to use the manufacturer's installation CD if you have one. The wizard is good at his job, but the hardware manufacturer is the ultimate authority.

Remove Plug-and-Play Hardware

Removing plug-and-play hardware from your Tablet PC is easy. Unless you've added an internal device that must be extracted from your computer, you can remove the device without even turning off the machine. First, check in the notification area to see if the Safely Remove Hardware icon is visible. It looks like a PC card with a green arrow above it. Tap the icon, and then tap the names of the devices in the list that appears. This stops the devices and allows you to remove them without risk of data corruption.

Did you know?

There May Be Newer Installation Software on the Manufacturer's Web Site?

The Add Hardware Wizard recommends that you use the installation CD provided by the manufacturer when you're trying to install non-plug-and-play hardware. However, if the hardware you're trying to install is old, you should head to the Internet before using that installation CD.

Most computer hardware manufacturers post updates to their installation software on their web sites. These updates fix bugs in earlier versions of software and often include support for newer versions of Windows. The software on the installation CD might not explicitly support Windows XP Tablet PC edition (or even Windows XP Professional, the OS Windows XP Tablet PC edition is built on), while the version of the same software on the manufacturer's web site probably does. I recommend you check the manufacturer's web site before using any installation CD, just so you can be sure to use the latest version of the software.

Once you stop all the devices that appear in the Safely Remove Hardware list, physically disconnect the hardware. The Tablet PC will detect that the hardware has been removed and uninstall the driver software, which completes the removal.

Remove Non-Plug-and-Play Hardware

To remove non-plug-and-play hardware, use the uninstaller or removal utility on the manufacturer's CD (or included in the software you downloaded from the manufacturer's web site). If you don't have any software that uninstalls the hardware driver, you'll learn how to manually disable drivers in the section titled, "Use Device Manager" later in this chapter. Leave the hardware connected until then. Once you've disabled the drivers for the hardware, you can shut off your Tablet PC, unplug it from the wall and physically disconnect the hardware.

Manage Hardware

While you may not need to install or remove hardware, you do need to know how to manage the hardware that's connected to your Tablet PC. For example, you may need to specify which printer on the network your Tablet PC will use as its default printer or to adjust the settings for your Tablet PC's sound card.

Windows XP gives you a couple of areas where you can manage your hardware. Certain hardware, such as sound and audio devices, have their own categories in the Control Panel (see Figure 5-2), so Windows can help you manage them. Every bit of hardware built into or installed on your Tablet PC (including those devices that appear in the Control Panel) can be managed from the Device Manager. You're better off avoiding the Device Manager whenever possible, so we'll start by looking at the hardware devices with their own categories in the Control Panel.

Manage Sound, Speech, and Audio Devices

As Figure 5-3 shows, the Sounds, Speech, And Audio Devices window helps you with three common tasks related to sound and audio devices. It also lets you work directly with the relevant Control Panel icons and provides Troubleshooters for Sound devices and DVD players. Finally, this window links you to two additional spots in Windows that are related to sound, speech, and audio devices. If all you want to do is mute the sound or change the volume, see "How to Mute the Sound or Change the Volume" for instructions.

Tap one of the links under Pick a Task. Windows opens the relevant tab in the Sounds And Audio Devices Properties dialog box, so you can complete your task

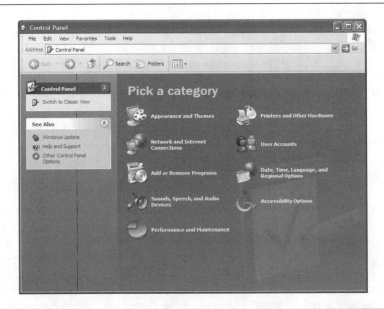

FIGURE 5-2   To make managing them quicker and easier, the Control Panel includes categories for hardware that commonly needs to be managed.

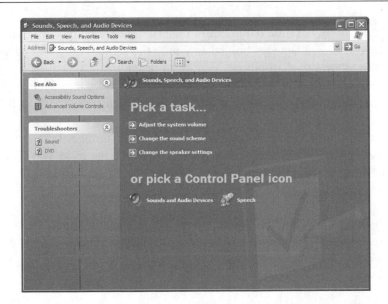

FIGURE 5-3   The Sounds, Speech, And Audio Devices window helps you manage related hardware without having to dig down into the Device Manager.

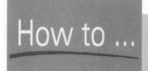 **Mute the Sound or Change the Volume**

If all you want to do is mute the sound or change the volume, you can do that with just a couple of taps. Tap the Volume icon in the notification area. This opens a small window with a Volume slide control and a Mute check box.

Drag the Volume slider up or down to increase or decrease the volume. When you release the slider, your computer beeps to give you an idea of the volume level that slider position corresponds to. Keep adjusting the slider until you get a volume you like.

To turn the sound on and off, set or clear the Mute check box. When the volume is muted, the Volume icon appears in the notification area with a slashed red circle to indicate no sound.

without spending lots of time navigating to the right tabbed page. As it turns out, the Sounds And Audio Devices link takes you to the same dialog box. If you tap the Hardware tab in this dialog box, Windows presents you with a list of every hardware device and software driver related to sounds and audio devices. You can select one of these items, and then tap Properties to learn virtually everything there is to know about that item.

You normally won't have to do anything with these items or their properties, unless something is wrong with your computer. If that's the case, you'll want to tap Troubleshoot and use the Sound Troubleshooter (Figure 5-4) to try to resolve the problem.

 If you can't resolve the problem with the help of the Sound Troubleshooter, I recommend you contact whoever is providing technical support for your Tablet PC. Unless you're a computer expert, you could well do more harm than good at this point.

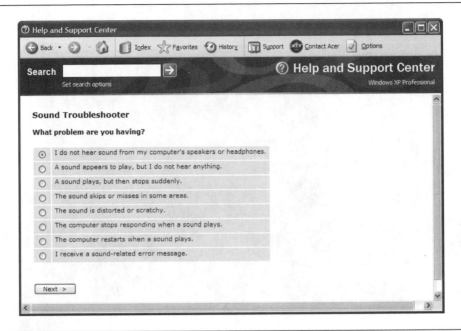

FIGURE 5-4   The Sound Troubleshooter will help you resolve a wide range of sound problems and, if it can't help you, it's time to call for professional help.

You can tap the Speech link to open the Speech Properties dialog box. This dialog box is covered in detail in Chapter 15.

Manage Printers and Other Hardware

The Printers And Other Hardware category contains the rest of the hardware you're likely to want to manage on your Tablet PC. As Figure 5-5 shows, the Printers And Other Hardware window helps with some printer-related tasks, but it also gives you quick access to the Properties dialog boxes for all sorts of hardware.

There's more specific information on managing the hardware for each of these devices in the relevant chapters. The following list contains the name of the hardware Control Panel icon and the number of the chapter you should refer to for more information:

■ Game Controllers (Chapter 6)

■ Keyboard (Chapter 3)

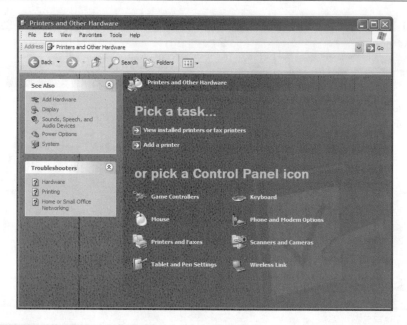

FIGURE 5-5 The Printers And Other Hardware Category brings most of the hardware devices you need to manage into a single location for easy access.

- Mouse (Chapter 3)

- Phone and Modem Options (Chapter 7)

- Printers and Faxes (Chapter 6)

- Scanners and Cameras (Chapter 6)

- Tablet and Pen Settings (Chapter 3)

- Wireless Link (Chapter 9)

Use Device Manager

The *Device Manager* window is your view into all the hardware installed on your Tablet PC. It lists every item of hardware, lets you view the properties of each item and the device drivers associated with them, and lets you reconfigure your system. The main uses of Device Manager are to check the status of your hardware and to update the device drivers.

Only people with Administrator accounts can make changes to your computer using Device Manager. Even Administrators can only make changes to the machine they're physically working on. They can't make changes across the network.

When you're working with non-plug-and-play hardware, you may need to configure your system by changing hardware configuration by hand.

5

CAUTION *You can damage your Tablet PC if you make the wrong changes when manually changing settings in the Device Manager. Please only make manual changes in Device Manager if you know what you're up to. Get help from technical support if you're unsure.*

To open the Device Manager window, tap Start | Control Panel | Performance And Maintenance | System | Hardware | Device Manager. The Device Manager window will open and look similar to Figure 5-6. The view in this figure is

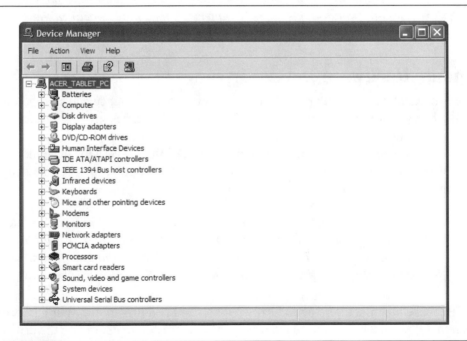

FIGURE 5-6   The Device Manager window gives you access to every piece of hardware installed on your Tablet PC.

Devices by type, which Windows uses by default and which is useful for spotting defective hardware. If a hardware device is defective, Windows displays this view, with the appropriate type expanded to make the defective device visible.

Check the Status of Your Hardware

To check the status of your hardware, open the Device Manager window. As I mentioned before, if anything is wrong with the hardware installed on the Tablet PC, Windows shows the defective devices. Usually, the problem device will be indicated by a yellow circle with a black exclamation point. If you right-tap a defective device, Windows displays that device's Properties dialog box. The contents of these dialog boxes will vary widely to reflect the wide variety of hardware devices. Whatever the contents look like, you should find useful information about the hardware here, as well as a Troubleshoot button you can tap to start diagnosing the problem. If all the hardware for a troublesome device appears to be working properly, the next step is to check the device drivers.

If you disable any devices (say, for example, you turn off the computer's wireless network adapter to save batteries), they may appear in the Device Manager with a red X over their icon. Don't worry about them.

Update Hardware Device Drivers

The best way to check and update a device driver is to open that device's Properties dialog box (right-tap the icon for the device and tap Properties in the shortcut menu) and view the Driver tab. Figure 5-7 shows the Properties dialog box for the 1394 (Firewire) network adapter on my Acer. All the Driver tabs have the same form, with basic driver information at the top and four buttons below. The descriptions next to each button nicely sum up what they do.

SHORTCUT   *You can avoid checking for updates like this if you use Windows Update. Windows Update can scan your computer and notify you of available updates. To get to Windows Update, go to http://www.microsoft.com, and then click the Windows Update link under the Resources heading.*

Because manufacturers periodically publish updated drivers for their hardware, there may be a new driver for the device you're interested in. Compare the driver version number shown in the Properties dialog box to that of the latest driver for your device on the manufacturer's web site. If a newer driver exists, download it to

FIGURE 5-7   This Driver tab has the same form as those for the rest of your Tablet PC's hardware devices.

your Tablet PC and follow any instructions provided by the manufacturer. Then tap Update Driver to start the Hardware Update Wizard. The opening screen of the wizard asks what you want it to do: you should tap Install from a list or specific location. On the next screen (Figure 5-8), select Include this location in the search, enter the path to the new driver file you downloaded, and then follow the wizard's instructions to complete the installation.

One nifty feature of Windows XP that I hope you'll never need to use is the capability to *roll back a driver* if the new device driver doesn't work properly. When you tap Roll Back Driver, Windows XP removes the current driver and replaces it with the previous version.

The Uninstall button is another button I hope you'll never have to tap. As you've already learned, when you remove a plug-and-play device from your Tablet PC, Windows automatically uninstalls the drivers for you. When you uninstall an non-plug-and-play device, and that device doesn't have an uninstall or remove utility, you can tap Uninstall and Windows will eliminate the driver for you.

FIGURE 5-8   Once you tell the Hardware Update Wizard where to find the latest driver for a hardware device, the wizard guides you through all the steps needed to update that driver.

Normally, this won't cause any problems, but the fewer manual operations you perform in Device Manager, the better.

Set Up Hardware Profiles

A *hardware profile* is a description of the hardware and other resources available to your computer. Hardware profiles are particularly useful for traditional notebook computers, which can have different resources available in different circumstances. For example, if a notebook computer has a dock, it likely has additional resources (a second monitor, a keyboard and mouse, additional disk drives, and perhaps a hardwired network connection are common) available to it when it's in the dock. In this case, you might want to have a hardware profile for when the notebook is docked and another for when it isn't. Windows would automatically give you an option of which hardware profile to use whenever you reboot your notebook.

But the situation isn't as clear for Tablet PCs. They're designed for *surprise hot docking*. In other words, you can grab your Tablet PC from its dock and walk off. You don't have to shut down the machine before removing it from the dock or inserting it into the dock. The computer has to figure out what's going on and reconfigure itself for the new situation. For example, if you use a separate monitor as your primary display when the Tablet PC is docked, the computer should automatically switch back to using its built-in display when you lift it out of the dock.

Similarly, when you put your Tablet PC into the dock, it should recognize that and reconfigure itself to take advantage of the available resources. There's no need to turn off the computer before docking or undocking and no opportunity to switch profiles. So, in my opinion, much of the need for hardware profiles disappears when you're using a Tablet PC.

However, everyone's circumstances are different, and multiple hardware profiles may be exactly what you need. Here's how you use them.

NOTE   *Before you begin creating a new hardware profile, you should configure your Tablet PC to use any hardware you want to be able to use.*

To reach the Hardware Profiles dialog box (see Figure 5-9), tap Start | Control Panel | Performance And Maintenance | System | Hardware | Hardware Profiles. Start by tapping the Copy button to make a copy of the current hardware profile. By working on the copy and leaving the original undisturbed, you guarantee that you can recover if you make a crippling mistake when creating your new hardware profile.

By default, the original hardware profile for your Tablet PC should include every bit of hardware installed and configured on your machine. So creating the new hardware profile involves disabling resources that aren't available to the new profile. But, first, you need to begin working in the new hardware profile, so reboot your Tablet PC. Now that you have more than one hardware profile, Windows will ask you which one it should use. Select the new profile.

To start with, the new hardware profile is identical to the original one. Using the Device Manager, disable the resources that won't be available to your Tablet PC when you select this profile in the future. That's all you need to do.

NOTE   *We'll talk about the hardware that connects your Tablet PC to a network in Chapters 8 and 9.*

FIGURE 5-9   The Hardware Profiles dialog box lets you create and manage hardware profiles that match the resources available to your Tablet PC in different environments.

Chapter 6

Connect to Peripheral Devices

How to...

- Choose Between Peripheral Formats and Connectors
- Connect to Printers and Faxes
- Connect to Scanners and Digital Cameras
- Connect to Other Peripherals

In Chapter 5, you learned the basics of managing the hardware that's installed on your Tablet PC. In this chapter, we'll go into some depth on connecting to certain popular types of peripherals (external hardware) that you can connect to your Tablet PC.

Because the Tablet PC is a legacy-free device, you may need to replace some of your existing peripherals with ones that are Tablet PC-compatible. Or, you may want to enhance your Tablet PC with add-ons appropriate to such a light-weight, mobile device. Whatever the reason, if you're looking for peripherals for your Tablet PC, you need some information to help you choose among the various forms (external, PC Card, CompactFlash) and connector types (USB, Firewire, wireless) your peripherals can have. The quick guide at the top of this chapter can help you choose.

Despite the Tablet PC's communication and storage capabilities, you'll likely still want to print or fax things every now and again to get information out of your computer.

Scanners and cameras are great ways to get certain kinds of information into your computer, and they can provide the raw material for the multimedia applications that came installed on your Tablet PC.

The experience you gain connecting peripherals in this chapter can serve you well if you ever need to connect to a peripheral that we don't discuss in this book.

NOTE *We talk more about the Windows XP multimedia applications themselves in Chapter 12.*

Choose Between Peripheral Formats and Connectors

If you ever added peripherals to a PC before, you probably puzzled over the options. Should you choose a serial or a parallel printer? What kind of connector do you need to get on your new ergonomic keyboard? Should you choose an internal or external modem?

If you want to add peripherals to your Tablet PC, you get a different set of things to puzzle over. Should you go with a printer that uses Firewire or USB? Should you add Bluetooth support? If you do, should you use a USB Bluetooth device or a PC Card device? Or, maybe a CompactFlash Bluetooth card will do the trick? For that matter, what's the difference between PC Card and CompactFlash anyway? This section of the chapter gives you a quick primer on these topics.

Choose Between Firewire and USB

Firewire (IEEE 1384) and USB are both high-speed connectors you can use to connect external peripherals to your Tablet PC. The key differences between them are

- Firewire is faster and often used to connect computers to digital video cameras

- USB is more widely supported

Another consideration is that Tablet PCs can support different versions of USB. You'll need to check the specifications of both your Tablet PC and the peripheral you're interested in to see if they can work together.

When considering Firewire peripherals, be sure to find out which type of Firewire connector your Tablet PC has. Firewire connectors can be either 6-pin connectors or 4-pin connectors. Consult your computer's documentation or look at the connector and count the number of holes in it. If your machine uses a different Firewire connector than the peripheral you plan to use, you should be able to find an adapter cable at the peripheral vendor's web site.

Choose Among External, PC Card, or CompactFlash Peripherals

Many kinds of peripherals, including wired and wireless network cards, additional memory, and even hard disks, come in multiple forms. For purposes of this discussion, we can consider three basic forms: external, PC Card, and CompactFlash.

An *external device* is one that connects to the Tablet PC through a USB or a Firewire connection and sits outside the case of the computer. PC Card and CompactFlash peripherals fit into slots in the body of your Tablet PC, without any external cables or (in most cases) anything at all protruding outside the computer's case.

PC Card or CompactFlash peripherals are preferable for a mobile device like a Tablet PC. They tend to be much smaller and lighter than external devices and because they fit within the Tablet PC, they're safer and more convenient, too.

When choosing between PC Card and CompactFlash peripherals, the most important consideration is whether your Tablet PC has a slot available for the peripheral. Some Tablet PCs include CompactFlash slots, while others, like my Acer, don't.

Once you know which kinds of slots your Tablet PC has, make sure that they're the right version to support the peripheral you want to use. PC Card slots can be Type I or Type II, as can CompactFlash slots.

Connect to Printers and Faxes

Printers are the most common peripherals people want to connect to their computers. Windows XP makes this easier than it has ever been, whether you're connecting directly to a printer, or connecting to one across a home or corporate network. Here we'll cover the direct connection.

While far fewer people send and receive faxes on their computers, fax machines and printers are a lot alike as far as Windows XP is concerned. This is why printers and faxes are grouped together. Because your Tablet PC likely came with a *fax modem* (a modem capable of sending and receiving faxes, as well as regular data) installed, we'll take a few minutes and learn the basics of how to use it.

The place to install and manage printers and faxes is the Printers And Faxes window, shown in Figure 6-1. The large pane on the right contains icons that represent the printers and faxes currently installed on your Tablet PC. Some of these icons represent real, physical devices, while others, like the Journal Note Writer shown in Figure 6-1, are virtual printers or fax machines. A *virtual printer* looks like a printer as far as your computer's applications can tell, but it's a piece of software that doesn't connect to a physical printer. The Journal Note Writer (covered in more detail in Chapter 13), for example, seems to be a printer, but it converts documents into a format that you can write on using Windows Journal.

Work with Printers

The options in the Printers Tasks pane on the left side of the window vary according to the device you select in the right pane. This makes it easy for you to complete the most common tasks for the selected item.

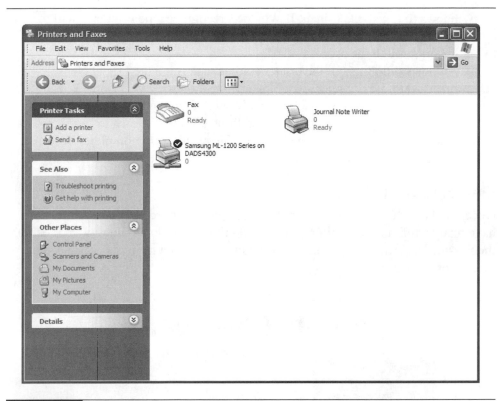

FIGURE 6-1   The Printers And Faxes window provides a central location for installing and managing printers and faxes.

Add a Printer

The Add Printer Wizard allows you to connect your Tablet PC to a printer or printers. But there's a good chance you won't need the wizard's help at all. If your printer is fairly new, there's a good chance that Windows XP will recognize it and install it automatically. So, let's look at that possibility first.

CAUTION   *Your printer needs a USB or Firewire connection (or an appropriate adapter) to connect to your Tablet PC.*

Following the instructions that came with your printer, connect it to your Tablet PC. Check your connections, then turn on the printer and wait a moment for Windows to detect the printer. If Windows recognizes the printer, it will automatically install the printer for you or start the Found New Hardware Wizard to guide you through the process.

If Windows didn't install the printer automatically and the Found New Hardware Wizard didn't appear, you'll need to call on the Add Printer Wizard to help you install the printer yourself. Start the wizard by tapping Add A Printer in the Printer Tasks pane. This opens the Add Printer Wizard shown in Figure 6-2. Follow the wizard's instructions and answer the questions to complete the installation.

Configure the Printer

Once you have the new printer installed, you can configure it. While printers can have many configuration options, you shouldn't need to do anything with most of them. One group of settings that's worth adjusting is on a printer's Advanced tab (see Figure 6-3).

FIGURE 6-2   The Add Printer Wizard helps you install printers that Windows can't install automatically.

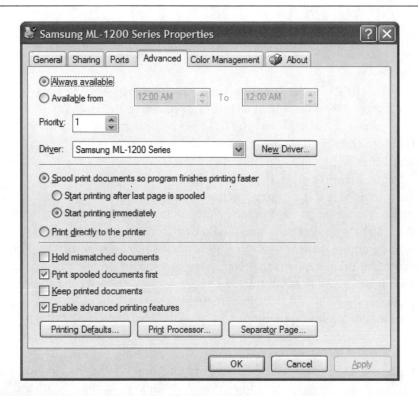

FIGURE 6-3   Some of the settings on a printer's Advanced tab are well-worth adjusting to improve your printing experience.

I strongly recommend that you turn on print spooling if it isn't already activated. *Print spooling* increases the usability of your computer by increasing the apparent speed of your printing. See the following "Did You Know How Printer Spooling Works?" box for an explanation of how this happens. Whether you're interested in the details or not, here's what you need to do to make sure print spooling is turned on.

Open the Advanced tab by tapping the printer you want to work with, and then Set Printer Properties in the Printer Tasks pane. When the Properties dialog box appears, tap Advanced. Make sure the Spool Print Documents So Program Finishes Printing Faster option is selected, instead of the Print Directly To The Printer option. You can also select Start Printing Immediately to ensure the greatest apparent speed.

Did you know?

How Printer Spooling Works?

You now know that printer spooling lets you get back to work faster when you're printing a long document or lots of documents. But did you know how spooling saves you time? When you tell your computer to print something, the computer converts the document you see on your screen into information and commands that the printer can understand. Your computer can generate this information quickly and blast it to the printer quickly, too.

The printer uses this information to control the print head and create the document you see on paper. But the printer, being a mechanical device, prints far slower than your computer can feed it new information. The printer may have some internal memory, so it can store some amount of information while it prints, but it often happens that your computer has to wait for the printer to be ready to accept more information. The application from which you're printing ends up waiting for the printer, and so do you.

A print spooler sits (metaphorically speaking) between the printer and your applications. When you send a print job to the printer, it goes to the spooler, which stores the information on the hard drive, and then feeds the stored information to the printer when it's ready to accept it. While this sounds like it could slow things down by creating extra work for your computer, instead, it speeds things up for you.

Spooling works for you because your computer can store information on the hard drive much, much faster than even the fastest laser printer can print the same information. And once your application sends all its information to the print spooler, it can go back to whatever it was doing. In other words, because the print spooler takes on the responsibility for feeding information to the printer when it needs it, you can get back to work sooner.

Manage Print Jobs

Now you're ready to print from your own applications. When you do print something, a printer icon will appear in the Notification Area of the toolbar. The icon represents the *print queue,* the list of print jobs that are in progress or waiting their turn.

Normally, you'll want to let your print jobs run without any interference. But, sometimes, you'll want to step in before all the print jobs in the queue are complete. I would rather not admit the number of times that I've accidentally started printing an entire document when all I really wanted was to print a page or two. Fortunately, you can manage your print jobs as long as they are still in the print queue.

To manage the print queue, you need to open the Print Control window for the printer (or for the relevant printer if you're printing to multiple printers simultaneously). To do this, tap Start | Control Panel | Printers And Other Hardware | Printers and Faxes. Tap the printer that has the queue you want to manage, and then tap See What's Printing in the Printer Tasks pane. This opens the Print Control window, which looks like Figure 6-4.

Once you have the Print Control window open, you can see the basic properties of all the print jobs in the queue and manage any of the print jobs.

NOTE *If your printer is shared on, or connected to, a network, your ability to view and manage print jobs is restricted. See Chapter 8 for more information.*

Normally, you'll want to manage a specific print job. Select the job you want to manage. The Document menu lets you Pause, Resume, Restart, or Cancel the selected job, as well as view its properties.

If you want to manage all the print jobs in the queue, you can use the Printer menu to pause or cancel all print jobs, along with some other less commonly used options.

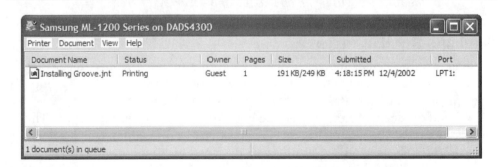

FIGURE 6-4   The Print Control window lets you manage print jobs that are underway or are awaiting their turn to print.

Work with Faxes

When people talk about connecting a fax to their computers, they're normally not talking about running a cable between the office fax machine and their Tablet PC. What they (and I) are talking about is a fax modem, not a stand-alone fax machine. A *fax modem* is a device that lets your computer send and receive faxes and other digital data through the phone system. You'll learn a lot more about using modems to do things like connect to the Internet in Chapter 7, so here we're just going to talk about using the fax capabilities of fax modems.

Most Tablet PCs come with modems. Most modems are fax modems. Most likely, your Tablet PC has a fax modem installed and ready to be put to use. We'll assume that's the situation for you and go from there.

NOTE   *If you need to physically install a fax modem for your Tablet PC, follow the manufacturer's instructions to get to the point where a fax icon shows up in the Printers and Faxes window. When you reach that point, you're ready to follow along again.*

Configure Your Fax

To begin configuring your fax modem, double-tap the Fax icon in the Printers and Faxes window. Assuming this is the first time you've tried to use the fax modem, Windows starts the Fax Configuration Wizard. This wizard primarily gathers the information necessary to fill in a fax cover page, as shown in Figure 6-5. Complete the wizard, and then your fax should be ready to send and receive.

NOTE   *Some of the details of configuring your particular fax modem may vary, but the process will be much like the one described here.*

Send and Receive Faxes

Sending faxes is pretty simple, and Windows even provides a wizard to help you get the job done. Receiving faxes is also simple, but using your Tablet PC for receiving anything more than the occasional fax has its drawbacks.

To send or receive faxes, you use the Fax Console, shown in Figure 6-6. This console is similar to Outlook Express in appearance and function, which shouldn't be a surprise because both applications are designed for sending and receiving messages. To open the Fax Console, double-tap the Fax icon in the Printers and Faxes window.

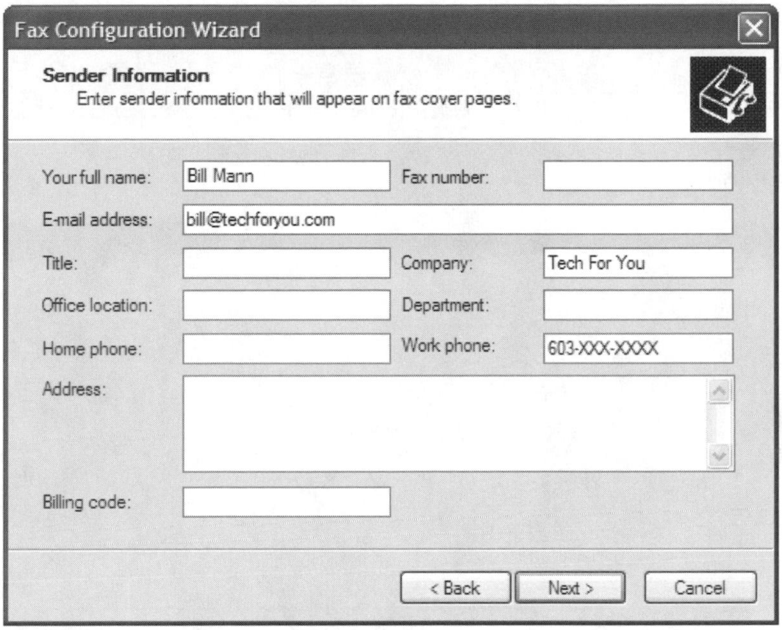

FIGURE 6-5 The Fax Configuration Wizard gathers some basic information the first time you use the fax.

The Send Fax Wizard appears whenever you want to send a fax and guides you through the process. The wizard makes everything go smoothly. You'll be ready to send your fax in less than two minutes.

To receive faxes with your Tablet PC, you can open the Fax Console and tap the Receive Now button. This launches the Fax Monitor, which waits for an incoming fax to arrive. This is where the usability snag comes up. To receive faxes, the fax modem must be connected to a phone line. But your Tablet PC is supposed to be with you most of the day, traveling to and from meetings, and generally being a poor choice for a full-time fax machine.

Manage Your Faxes

There isn't much to do to manage your faxes. However, if you look at the properties of your fax modem (in Printers and Faxes, tap the fax's icon, and then tap Set Printer Properties | Archives. The Fax Console archives every fax you send or receive, storing them in the folders specified on this page. You can turn off archiving or select a new folder for the archives from this page.

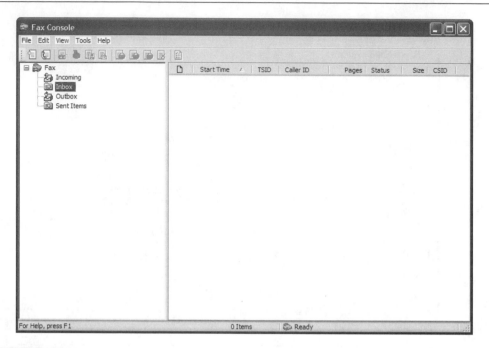

FIGURE 6-6   The Fax Console enables you to send and receive faxes on your Tablet PC.

Did you know?

You Can Receive Faxes by E-mail?

A few Internet services let you have a free phone number for receiving faxes. When you receive a fax at one of these numbers, a copy of it is automatically e-mailed to you. What's the benefit to you? With one of these services, there's always a fax machine connected to the phone line, so people can fax you whenever they want and the call will get through. EFax.com (www.efax.com) is probably the most popular such service. I use K7 (www.k7.net), which has always worked well for me.

Connect to Scanners and Digital Cameras

Scanners and digital cameras have become popular additions to home computer systems, and Windows XP includes extensive support for them. As a Tablet PC user, your needs may differ somewhat from those of typical home users. Even so, the capability to connect a scanner or digital camera to your Tablet PC can come in quite handy in many situations.

The place to install and manage scanners and digital cameras is the Scanners And Cameras window shown in Figure 6-7. As with the Printers And Faxes window, the large pane on the right contains icons that represent devices (scanners and digital cameras, in this case) currently installed on your Tablet PC. One thing that's a bit different here is that not every device installed on your computer has to appear here. For example, Windows sees my digital camera as a disk drive (more on that under

6

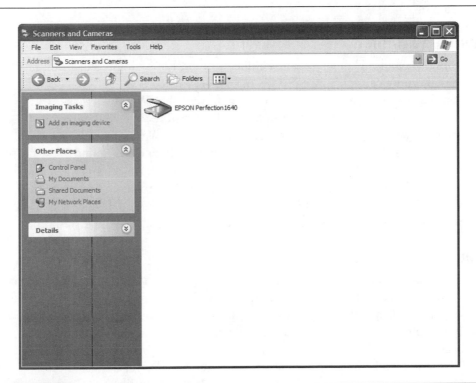

FIGURE 6-7   The Scanners And Cameras window is the closest thing to a single control point for scanners and cameras that your Tablet PC has.

"Work with Digital Cameras" later in this chapter) and doesn't ever show it in the Scanners and Cameras window. Also, a scanner or camera that's installed may not appear in the window if it's turned off or currently disconnected from the Tablet PC.

Because scanners do normally appear in the Scanners and Cameras window, let's talk about them first.

 *If a scanner or camera doesn't appear in this window, you may be able to find it in the Device Manager under the Imaging Devices heading.*

Work with Scanners

A lot of the details of working with a scanner depend on the specific scanner you have, the software it came with, and the applications you use it with. For that stuff, you'll have to rely on the documentation that came with the scanner and the applications you use with it. Here we'll concentrate on installing and configuring the scanner.

Install a Scanner

Installing a scanner is much like installing a printer. Following the instructions that came with your scanner, connect it to your Tablet PC. Check your connections, turn on the scanner, and then wait a moment to see what Windows makes of it. If the device is plug-and-play compatible, Windows will recognize the device and install it for you. Or, it may activate the New Hardware Wizard to lend a hand.

If Windows didn't install the scanner automatically and the Found New Hardware Wizard didn't appear, you'll want to activate the Scanner And Camera Installation Wizard (Figure 6-8) to guide you through the installation process. Start the wizard by tapping Add An Imaging Device in the Imaging Tasks pane. Follow the wizard's instructions and answer the questions to complete the installation.

Configure the Scanner

The process for configuring your scanner is similar to configuring a printer. Select the scanner in the right pane, and then tap View Device Properties in the Imaging Tasks pane. The specific properties that appear depend on the device, but you'll likely be able to do things like test the scanner and associate color profiles with the scanner.

You may also be able to configure your scanner to deliver images directly to a compatible application. Using the Events tab shown in Figure 6-9, you can select from a list of events and activate a program whenever this event takes place.

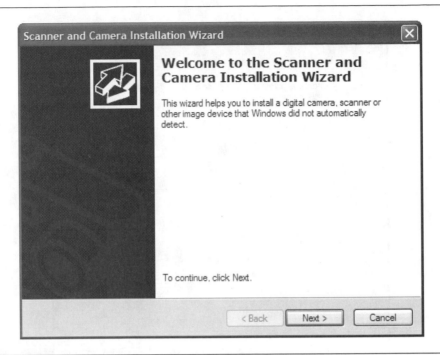

FIGURE 6-8   The Scanner And Camera Installation Wizard will help you install these devices when Windows doesn't do it automatically.

For example, you could configure your scanner to automatically activate your favorite graphics program whenever you press the Start button on the scanner.

Open the tab by tapping View Device Properties | Events. Select an event from the list, and then select one of the available actions to link to that event. If you choose to start a program when the event occurs, make sure you choose a program that knows what to do with a scanned image when it receives one. The program documentation will tell you if the program can handle the images your scanner will feed it. Again, the software that came with your scanner may handle tasks like this for you, eliminating the need to mess around with the scanner properties directly.

Work with Digital Cameras

You work with a digital camera much like you work with a scanner. The big difference is that the camera stores images instead of just capturing them and, thus, may be treated by your computer like a special type of folder.

Tell Windows how to respond to scanner button pushes and other events with the Events tab.

Install Your Camera

Following the camera's instructions, connect it to your Tablet PC. Check your connections, turn on the camera, and then wait a moment to see how Windows responds. If the camera is plug-and-play compatible, Windows will recognize and install it for you. Or, it may activate the New Hardware Wizard to lend a hand.

Many digital cameras appear to Windows as folders filled with image files. Windows needs to know what you want to do with those files, so it displays the dialog box shown in Figure 6-10.

FIGURE 6-10   Windows shows you this dialog box so you can specify how it treats the images in your camera.

TIP   *The fastest way to get photos out of a camera memory card and into your Tablet PC is this: remove the card from the camera and insert it directly into the computer, where Windows will detect it and give you direct access to it. If your Tablet PC doesn't have a CompactFlash slot you can use, several companies sell inexpensive adapters that let you plug a CompactFlash card into a PC Card slot.*

Select one of the options presented here. The default option is to let Windows start the Scanner and Camera Wizard to download images from your camera to a folder. I usually use the Open Folder To View Files option, which allows me to work with the images as if they were in a folder on my hard drive. The most important thing, though, is to choose the option that suits your needs at the moment.

If you want Windows always to do the same thing with the images from your camera, tap the Always Do The Selected Action check box. Tap OK and Windows takes the action you specified.

If Windows didn't install the camera automatically and the Found New Hardware Wizard didn't appear, use the Scanner And Camera Installation Wizard to complete the installation. Start the wizard by tapping Add An Imaging Device in the Imaging Tasks pane. Follow the wizard's instructions and answer the questions to complete the installation.

Manage Your Camera

There's usually not much managing you need to do with a digital camera. Using the software that came with the camera is the best way to do anything that does need to be done.

Connect to Other Peripherals

If you need to connect other kinds of peripherals to your Tablet PC, you can follow the same general approach used with printers, faxes, scanners, and digital cameras.

1. If the peripheral manufacturer provided complete instructions for installing the device under Windows XP, follow those instead of the instructions listed here.

2. Otherwise, follow the manufacturer's instructions to connect the device to the Tablet PC.

3. Turn on the device and wait a bit to see what Windows does with it.

4. If necessary, use the Add New Hardware Wizard to install the necessary drivers for the peripheral.

Chapter 7

Set Up an Internet Connection for Your Tablet PC

How to...

■ Install and Configure Dial-up Connections

■ Install and Configure Broadband Connections

■ Connect to the Internet

■ Use the Internet Applications Installed on your Tablet PC

One of the primary uses for computers these days is to connect to the vast supply of news, information, entertainment, and communication on the Internet. The goal of this chapter is to help you get your Tablet PC connected directly to the Internet. By that, I mean that your Tablet PC connects to the Internet without the aid of a network. Although Microsoft is kind enough to help you find an *Internet Service Provider,* or *ISP* (a company that provides the connection you use when you connect to the Internet), there are better ways to go about it. The "How to Find an ISP" box will help you do exactly that.

> **NOTE**   *If you want to connect your computer to the Internet through a network (either a small office/home office network, or a full-blown corporate network), the situation is a little different. For that, you'll need to read Chapter 8, where you'll learn how to connect your Tablet PC to a network, as well as through the network to the Internet.*

Once your Tablet PC is connected to the Internet through an ISP, you can try out the Internet applications that come with Windows XP Tablet PC edition. As a Tablet PC owner, you probably have at least a passing familiarity with web browsers and e-mail programs, so I've just given you a quick overview of the programs. Fewer people are familiar with instant messaging programs like the included Windows Messenger, so I've given you a little more depth on that one.

Last but not least, I've included some information on Remote Desktop, a feature of Windows XP Professional and Windows XP Tablet PC edition that allows you to control one computer from another. Because your Tablet PC is designed to be your primary computer (unlike a notebook computer, which is often used in addition to a desktop machine), Remote Desktop is likely of less importance to you. But it is a powerful feature to have when you need it, so I've given you the basics here.

Install and Configure Dial-Up Connections

A *dial-up connection* uses the standard phone lines that run into your home or office to connect your Tablet PC to an ISP, which provides a physical connection to the Internet. To establish a dial-up connection, you need a dial-up *modem* installed and configured to communicate with an ISP. A dial-up *modem* (short for modulator/ demodulator) is a device that converts the digital signals your computer uses into the analog signals the phone system uses, and vice versa. Most Tablet PCs come with a built-in modem, which eliminates the need to install it yourself.

CAUTION   *Some phone systems are digital instead of analog. Plugging your modem into a digital phone jack can damage it. If you're unsure whether a particular phone jack is analog or digital, ask first.*

TIP   *If your Tablet PC did not come with a dial-up modem, you can easily add one yourself. I strongly urge you to buy a plug-and-play modem that is compatible with Windows XP. You can find plug-and-play modems in PC Card, CompactFlash, and USB form factors. If you get one of these, all you'll need to do is connect it to your computer according to the instructions provided by the modem manufacturer, and Windows detects the modem and installs the required drivers for you.*

Configure Your Dial-Up Connection

Once the modem is installed, you may need to configure it. If the modem came installed in your Tablet PC or you're using a plug-and-play modem that's compatible with Windows XP, most of the work is done for you. You'll want to set up some dialing rules to simplify connecting your modem to the phone system from your location, and you'll need to configure your dial-up connection to work with your ISP. Because the process for configuring dial-up and broadband connections to an ISP is much the same, both are covered later in this chapter, in the section titled, "Connect to the Internet."

Create and Use Dialing Rules

When you use a modem with a mobile computer like a Tablet PC, chances are good that you'll want to dial in to your ISP or otherwise use your modem in different locations. But when you're in different locations, you likely need to configure your

7

How to ...   Find an ISP

As you'll learn in "Connect to the Internet" later in this chapter, the New Connection Wizard can help you find an ISP. However, it seems primarily geared toward getting you to sign up for MSN, Microsoft's ISP. You can use the New Connection Wizard to connect to any ISP, but you'll have to find that ISP and manually enter the relevant information through the wizard.

If you want an ISP for a dial-up connection and you don't travel much, you should consider a local ISP. Ask your friends and neighbors which one they use, and you'll likely find a local company that can handle your Internet access without costing you a lot of money.

If you plan on connecting frequently while on the road, you'll want to use one of the major ISPs, which have local dial-up numbers throughout much of North America. In this situation, you may well want to let the New Connection Wizard guide you to MSN.

If you want a broadband connection, you'll need to find out which broadband ISPs serve your area. To do that, you should visit the broadband provider search page at CableModemInfo.com (http://www.cablemodeminfo .com/SearchHighSpeed.html-ssi). This site lists the cable modem and DSL providers throughout the United States and in several other countries.

Once you find the ISP you want to use, sign up for an account; then get the information needed to connect to the ISP from your computer. Some ISPs provide automated tools that create a connection for you, whereas others provide you with all the information you need and let you enter it when the New Connection Wizard asks for it. Wait until you have your dial-up or broadband connection set up properly before running any automated connection tool, and don't forget to record any settings or other information the ISP tells you will be needed to establish a connection.

modem differently, to account for the local area code and other location-specific conditions. *Dialing rules* allow you to set up configurations that your Tablet PC and modem will use in each location. *Dialing locations* are a convenient way to quickly reconfigure Windows and your modem to function properly in that location.

View, Create, or Edit a Location

Anything you do with dialing rules, from viewing a list of the dialing locations defined in your Tablet PC, to creating new locations, to editing existing ones, you do from the Phone And Modem Options dialog box. To open this dialog box, tap Start | Control Panel | Printers And Other Hardware | Phone And Modem Options | Dialing Rules. You should see something very similar to Figure 7-1. You can view the list of dialing locations here, as well as create and edit them.

The Location list in Figure 7-1 shows that I have two dialing locations set up, with the one named My Location selected as the default the modem will use. This location shows up as the default whenever your modem or fax tries to dial a number. The first time you open the Phone And Modem Options dialog box, this list will likely include just the My Location dialing location, containing information gathered when you first set up your modem.

7

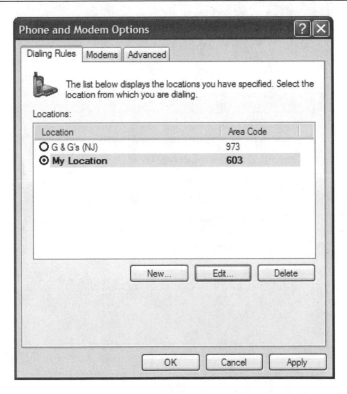

FIGURE 7-1 The Dialing Rules tab of the Phone And Modem Options dialog box allows you to quickly switch between the computer and modem configuration options for different locations.

If you want to create a new dialing location, tap New to open the New Location dialog box. Start on the General tab (shown in Figure 7-2). Enter the name you will use to identify this dialing location, along with the location from which you'll be dialing.

The rest of the information on this tab is specific to the telephone system your computer will be connecting to at this location. Use information from the local phone service to fill in the Dialing Rules fields, along with the To Disable Call Waiting, Dial, and Dial Using field. In particular, if the phone you'll be using has call waiting, you really want to disable that when the modem is in use. If you don't, every time someone attempts to call in on this line while you are using your modem, you'll lose your modem connection due to the call waiting beeps the phone system provides.

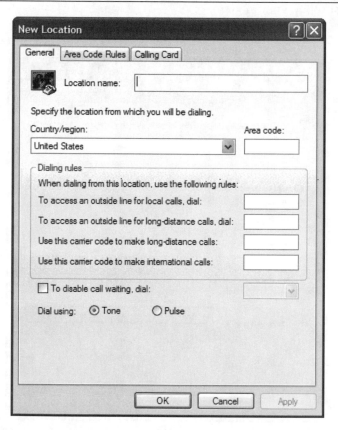

FIGURE 7-2   Start creating a new dialing location on the General tab of the New Location dialog box.

Next, you'll want to look at the Area Code Rules tab (Figure 7-3). With the increasing number of phone lines in the United States, the rules for dialing within and between area codes have become more complex. You may, for example, have to dial 1 and the area code of numbers even within your own area code. Or you may need to dial 9 to dial out from some hotel rooms. The Area Code Rules tab allows you to tell Windows how to handle situations like this.

This tab lists the rules that you've defined so far. From here, you can delete existing rules, edit the ones you have (convenient for the next time the system changes), and create new ones. To delete or edit a rule, select it in the Area Code Rules list and tap the appropriate button.

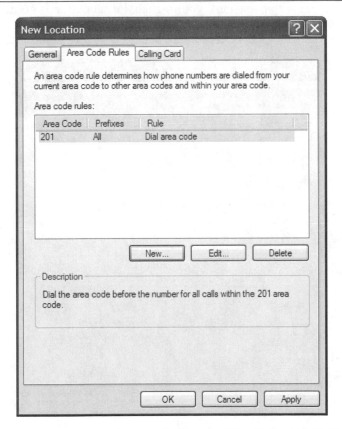

FIGURE 7-3   The Area Code Rules tab lists the rules you have defined for handling today's more complex phone dialing requirements.

You edit existing area code rules and create new ones using the same dialog box. (Just the name changes, appearing as Edit Area Code Rule when editing and New Area Code Rule when adding a new rule.) Figure 7-4 shows the New Area Code Rule dialog box.

To create the new rule, enter the area code for which the rule applies. (If you're dialing from the 603 area code, enter 603 here.) Then fill in the Prefixes and Rules sections of the dialog box as necessary and tap OK to save this new rule, which then appears in the Area Code Rules list.

If you use a calling card, tap the Calling Card tab. Here you can usually select your card from the extensive calling card list maintained by Windows. Then enter your account number, PIN, and access phone numbers. If your card doesn't appear in the list on this tab, tap New and fill in the relevant information.

Once you finish with these tabs, your new dialing location is complete.

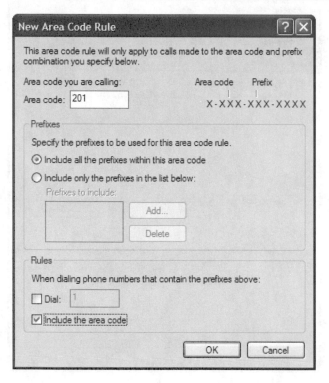

FIGURE 7-4   Use this dialog box to create the area code rules that appear in the Area Code Rules list of the Area Code Rules tab.

Use Dialing Rules

Your Tablet PC's dialing rules are embodied in the dialing locations you create. Setting up dialing rules for the areas where you frequently go online with your Tablet PC saves you time and headaches over the long run.

If you're working at one of your dialing locations, you don't need to manually configure all the dialing rules your computer needs. Simply go to the Phone And Modem Options dialog box and select it. That way, whenever your modem or fax tries to dial a number, it will use the right dialing location by default.

> **NOTE**   *Don't forget to restore the dialing location to normal when you return home.*

Install and Configure Broadband Connections

Installing and configuring broadband connections is conceptually similar to installing dial-up connections. You need to connect some sort of device to your computer (using the Ethernet connection on your Tablet PC) that translates information between the format the computer uses and the format the connection uses. This connection leads to an ISP, which provides the physical connection to the Internet. The biggest difference is in the details, with broadband connections going to something other than the standard phone line used by a dial-up connection.

Understand the Types of Broadband Connections

There are several ways to make a broadband connection to the Internet. The exact definition of a *broadband connection* varies with the person you're speaking to, but if you equate broadband to high speed, you're in pretty good shape. High speed here means much faster than a dial-up modem, which normally has a top speed of around 56 Kbps, and usually runs significantly slower than that. The next two sections cover the two most common types of broadband connections in the United States: cable modems and DSL.

Explore Cable Modems

A *cable modem* is a type of modem that connects your Tablet PC to your cable television system. Cable systems that support cable modems provide for two-way transmission: from the Internet through the cable system to your Tablet PC (downloading), and from your Tablet PC through the cable system to the Internet (uploading).

Did you know?

There Are Other Broadband Technologies Too?

Although cable modems and DSL are by far the most popular broadband Internet connections in the United States, a couple of other interesting technologies are out there. One is two-way satellite.

Two-way satellite systems are offered by companies like DIRECTV. These systems communicate to and from a fleet of satellites in earth orbit. They offer speeds that are greater than dial-up, but slower than DSL and cable modem. Two-way satellite is something to consider if you live in an area with no other broadband options.

Another broadband technology you can sometimes get is ISDN. This technology requires special equipment at your computer, and it must be supported by both your phone company and your ISP. Again, consider ISDN only when no other broadband options are available.

NOTE   *Some cable systems reportedly still use a hybrid system, where the cable system delivers information from the Internet to your Tablet PC by way of cable, but you have to send information to the cable system by way of a dial-up modem. If your cable system works this way, you'll have to weigh the costs of paying for cable but still having the inconveniences of dial-up access, against the clear benefit of receiving information from the Internet much faster than you would over the phone line.*

Cable modems offer three significant benefits over a dial-up connection:

- They're fast. Cable modems can download information at rates as high as 2 Mbps (millions of bits per second), although most systems run at 1 to 1.5 Mbps. Cable systems usually have much lower upload speeds, but you're still usually talking about speeds in excess of 200 Kbps (thousands of bits per second), which is still much faster than a dial-up connection. One point to note is that the cable to which your computer is connected is shared with other subscribers in your area. So if lots of people use cable modems nearby, you could see far slower speeds than those described here. Also, your cable company may provide only the Internet access and require you to sign up with an ISP such as AOL or Earthlink.

- They are always on. When your computer is connected to the cable modem, it has a live connection to the Internet. There's no need to wait while the computer dials in to your ISP. So not only does information move between your computer and the Internet much faster, but it takes far less time for the information to start moving.

- They don't tie up your phone line. Unless you are connected to one of the very early cable modem systems, all communication between your Tablet PC and the Internet goes through the cable, leaving your phone free for other uses.

Explore DSL

DSL stands for Digital Subscriber Line, and refers to a special type of phone line. DSL lines, as the name suggests, are digital phone lines. Most normal phone lines are analog lines, where sounds and information travel along the lines as continuously varying voltages. On a DSL line, everything is digital—a string of ones and zeros.

DSL offers the same three advantages over regular dial-up access that cable does, except it is usually somewhat slower than a cable modem. DSL services can require you to install a special networking protocol that can interfere with other networking services. DSL services may also require you to manually initiate a connection to the Internet instead of always being connected like a cable modem.

Install Your Broadband Connection

With the variety of available broadband connections, it's impossible to give you explicit instructions on how to install yours. The easiest approach is to have the cable company (for cable modems) or the phone company (for DSL) perform the installation for you. Of course, you'll probably have to pay an installation fee if you do it this way, but the installer should be knowledgeable and have you up and running with the minimum of pain.

If you're comfortable mucking around with the hardware side of your computer, you may be able to save some money by installing the connection yourself. In some cases, this is as simple as going to the local electronics store and picking up a complete installation kit. I've not taken this route myself, but I do know several technically inclined people who have found this to be an easy and practical way to get connected. Even so, I wouldn't recommend you do this unless you're confident of your technical abilities and prepared to deal with any snags that arise.

Configure Your Broadband Connection

As with installing your broadband connection, there are too many possibilities for me to provide detailed instructions on how to do this. If you had someone from the phone company or cable company install your hardware for you, that person should have completed all the necessary configuration work as well. If you bought some kind of kit and did it yourself, there should have been detailed instructions on how to do the configuration as well.

Connect to the Internet

The New Connection Wizard (Figure 7-5) is the fast and easy way to get connected to an ISP and thereby to the Internet. The wizard starts automatically if you try to run an Internet application (Internet Explorer, for example) without having at least one Internet connection configured. You can also start the wizard by tapping Start | All Programs | Accessories | Communications | New Connection Wizard.

On the Wizard's Network Connection Type screen, select Connect To The Internet and tap Next. On the Getting Ready screen, select Choose From A List Of Internet Service Providers (ISPs) if you want to use MSN or one of the other

FIGURE 7-5   The New Connection Wizard can help you connect your Tablet PC to the Internet.

ISPs Microsoft is promoting. If your ISP provided a list of settings for you to enter, select Set Up My Connection Manually, and if the ISP provided you with a CD-ROM for setting up a connection, select that option.

Continue through the wizard, entering your information and following the instructions provided to complete the connection. That's all there is to it. Your Tablet PC should now have a connection to the Internet through your ISP.

Use the Internet Applications Installed on Your Tablet PC

Windows XP Tablet PC edition comes with Microsoft's versions of the key Internet applications already installed. For many people, these three applications are all they'll need to do whatever they want to do on the Internet. The applications are as follows:

- **Internet Explorer**   Far and away the most widely used web browser in the world

- **Outlook Express**   A capable e-mail client, newsgroup reader, and contact manager all rolled in one

- **Windows Messenger**   One of the top instant messaging programs

Now that you have an Internet connection up and running, the rest of this chapter takes you on a tour of these three applications. As I mentioned at the beginning of the chapter, I'm figuring you've probably used a web browser before (quite likely an earlier version of Internet Explorer) and are familiar with e-mail programs like Outlook Express. So for these two applications, I'm giving a pretty quick overview. I've gone into greater depth for Windows Messenger because instant messaging applications like this are relatively new, and you're likely less familiar with them than you are with e-mail and web browsers.

NOTE   *You can find links to more detailed guides for either of these applications at the end of each section.*

Explore Internet Explorer

Internet Explorer is the number one web browser on earth. A *web browser* is a program that lets you view the information stored on a part of the Internet known as the *World Wide Web* (WWW). The World Wide Web (usually just called the *Web*) is what most people think of when they think of the Internet—Amazon.com, Yahoo!, eBay, those are all widely known web sites. To visit any of those places from your computer, you use a web browser, and more than 90 percent of the time, that web browser is Internet Explorer.

Use Internet Explorer

Figure 7-6 shows Internet Explorer viewing the Acer Worldwide web page. The Acer page is the home page for the copy of Internet Explorer that came installed on my Acer Tablet PC. The *home page* is the page that appears whenever I start Internet Explorer on this computer. You can change the home page for your browser. On my other computers I have other home pages set up, depending on what I use

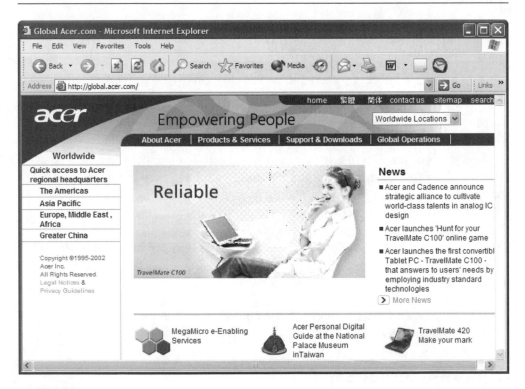

FIGURE 7-6   The Internet Explorer window displaying the Acer web page.

that computer for or depending on whatever I feel like looking at when I first start my web browser.

To start Internet Explorer, tap Start | Internet Explorer. Unless your Tablet PC manufacturer chose to use a different default web browser, Internet Explorer should appear under the Internet heading in the left-hand column of the Start menu. Internet Explorer (the big blue letter *e*) is selected in Figure 7-7.

NOTE   *The default web browser is the program that Windows runs whenever an application wants to connect to the Internet but hasn't specified a particular program to do it with.*

FIGURE 7-7   In this figure, Internet Explorer, with its big blue letter *e* icon, appears as the default web browser.

Did you know?

Your Tablet PC Has Two Web Browsers Installed?

Windows XP Tablet PC edition comes with two web browsers built in. You've already met Internet Explorer. The other is called MSN Explorer, which is very similar to Internet Explorer; however, you can use it only if you are an MSN (Microsoft's ISP) subscriber, or if you have a HotMail e-mail account. In other words, you must join one of Microsoft's Internet services to use MSN Explorer. Furthermore, when you use MSN Explorer, it forces you to work with much of your e-mail from within MSN Explorer, by preventing Outlook Express (the e-mail program that comes installed on your Tablet PC) from handling e-mail as it normally would.

What do you get in exchange for being forced to subscribe to a Microsoft Internet service and use the MSN e-mail interface? You get your web browser and some of your e-mail and MSN Messenger integrated into a single interface, along with some parental control features. For my money, using Internet Explorer is a better choice, but MSN Explorer is there if you want it.

You navigate the Internet by entering *URL*s (Uniform Resource Locators, the Internet equivalent of a street address) in the Address box, or tapping hyperlinks on a page. *Hyperlinks,* usually just called *links,* are connections to a URL somewhere on the current page or anywhere on the Internet. Links are usually blue text underlined in blue, but they can also be text of a different color, with or without the underline, or pictures. To tell if something is a link, hover the pen over it. If the cursor changes into a pointing hand, you've found a link.

To return to a web page you've already visited during this session, you can tap the Back arrow on the left side of the Standard Buttons toolbar. If you come across a web site that you want to be able to return to another day, you can memorize or write down the URL, or you can tap Favorites | Add To Favorites to open the Add Favorite dialog box shown in Figure 7-8.

NOTE *You want to tap the Favorites menu item, not the Favorites button.*

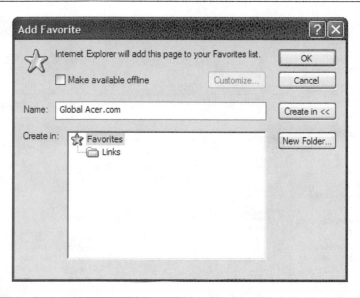

7

FIGURE 7-8   Use the Add Favorite dialog box to record the address of web pages you wish to visit again.

To return to a favorite web site, you tap the Favorites button on the Internet Explorer toolbar, instead of the one on the menu bar. This opens the *Explorer bar* (a pane that appears on the left side of the browser window), containing the contents of your Favorites list, as you can see in Figure 7-9. Although the Favorites list shown in Figure 7-9 isn't very large, the value of this feature really shines through when you've been using the same computer for a long time. On my old desktop machine, which is a little over a year old now, the Favorites list includes links to dozens of unrelated web pages, along with nine folders containing dozens more links related to specific topics. There's no way I would be able to remember and find my way back to so many web pages.

The Internet Explorer toolbar is the fastest way to take advantage of the application's capabilities. Here's what the major buttons on the toolbar do:

■ **Search**   Activates the search companion in the Explorer bar to search the Internet using MSN Search.

■ **Favorites**   Opens a list of your favorite web sites in the Explorer bar. This button is covered in detail in the paragraphs that precede this list.

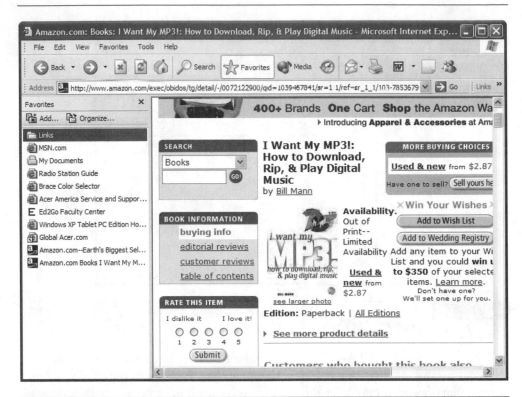

FIGURE 7-9   The Favorites Explorer bar gives you easy, one-click access to your favorite web sites.

- **Media**   Displays information from WindowsMedia.com in the Explorer bar. You can download audio and video content, then play the media using the controls at the bottom of the bar.

- **History**   Opens a list (in the Explorer bar) of the web pages you have visited recently. See "How to Find Web Pages with the History List" for more information on this button.

- **Mail**   Opens your default e-mail client or newsgroup reader. If no other applications have been specified for these tasks, Windows opens Outlook Express.

- **Edit**   Opens an editor so you can modify a copy of the web page visible in Internet Explorer. Internet Explorer gives you a list of editors to choose from, depending on which applications are installed on your Tablet PC. In Figure 7-9, the Microsoft Word icon appears on the Edit button, because Internet Explorer has selected Word as the default editor for my Tablet PC.

- **Discuss** Appears on the toolbar when you have Microsoft Office installed on your computer. If a network administrator sets up an appropriate web server, you can use the Discuss button (which looks like a yellow sticky note) to hold discussions of the visible page. Tapping the button toggles on or off a Discussions toolbar at the bottom of the main Internet Explorer window.

- **Messenger** Activates Windows Messenger so you can send or receive instant messages.

> NOTE
>
> *For more detailed information on how to use Internet Explorer, check out the Internet Explorer help system. Tap Help | Contents And Index | Getting Started With Internet Explorer. You can also take advantage of your new Internet connection and Internet Explorer to go to Microsoft's web site, "The Complete Internet Guide and Web Tutorial," and read the first half-dozen or so pages. To visit this site, enter **http://www.microsoft.com/insider/guide/intro.asp** in the Internet Explorer window's Address box and tap Go.*

7

How to ... Find Web Pages with the History List

The History list is automatically populated by Internet Explorer as you navigate the Internet. If you tap the History icon on the toolbar (it looks like a clock face with a green arrow pointing counterclockwise), a hierarchical list appears in a pane on the left side of the Internet Explorer window. If the Favorites pane is visible when you tap History, the History pane replaces the Favorites pane, and vice versa.

In the History pane, you'll find links to the pages you've recently visited. These pages are grouped according to when you visited them, and they are stored in top-level folders with names like Today, Last Week, 2 Weeks Ago, and so on. Within these folders, the links are further organized by domain, with all the links to a particular domain within that time period appearing together in one folder.

The History pane comes in particularly handy when you want to revisit a site that you saw recently but didn't include in the Favorites list. If you remember the day you last visited the site (even the week), you can look through the links for that time period until you find the one you need.

Explore Outlook Express

Outlook Express (Figure 7-10) is a free e-mail client and newsreader that Microsoft has included with Windows for several years now. It can manage multiple e-mail and newsgroup accounts for you under a single user identity, as well as supporting multiple identities. This means you can handle both your business and personal messages from the same program without mixing things up. It also means you can share your Tablet PC with other people without getting into each other's messages.

As you've already learned, Internet Explorer can call on Outlook Express to handle e-mail and newsgroups. Even if you have upgraded to Microsoft Outlook, the e-mail client and personal information manager used in many corporations, you'll find that both Outlook and Internet Explorer call on Outlook Express to handle newsgroups. If you use your Tablet PC as a communication tool, learning about Outlook Express is definitely worthwhile. We'll start by looking at the e-mail client side of Outlook Express.

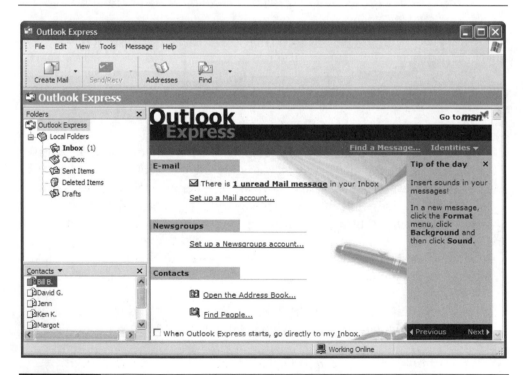

FIGURE 7-10   Outlook Express can handle all your basic e-mail, contact, and newsgroup needs in one simple program.

Use Outlook Express as an E-mail Client

If your Tablet PC came configured with the default Windows XP Tablet PC edition, Outlook Express should appear as the default e-mail program on the Start menu. The Outlook Express icon looks like an envelope with blue arrows around it. Tap the icon to open Outlook Express. The left side of the window contains two panes, one labeled Folders, the other Contacts. Tap the Inbox folder to put Outlook Express into its e-mail handling configuration, as shown in Figure 7-11.

In Figure 7-11, the contents of the selected folder (in this case, the Inbox) appear in the View pane. A preview of the selected message appears in the Preview pane beneath the View pane. You can see that I've been using Outlook Express on my Tablet PC, because there are additional folders in the Folders list, contacts in the Contacts list, and several e-mail messages in the Inbox.

When you open Outlook Express for the first time, you just have a few folders. If you want to use Outlook Express as an e-mail client, the first step is to configure

7

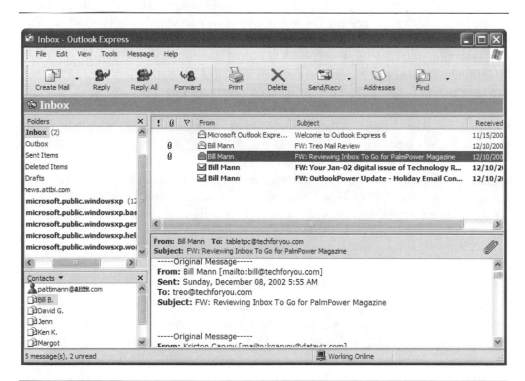

FIGURE 7-11   As an e-mail client, Outlook Express can exchange messages with almost any kind of e-mail service.

one or more e-mail accounts. Assuming you have an existing e-mail account somewhere that you want to access with Outlook Express, tap Tools | Accounts, and then select the Mail tab in the Internet Accounts dialog box. You can use this dialog box to add or remove e-mail and newsgroup accounts, as well as to import and export existing accounts from other e-mail clients and newsreaders. To add your account information, tap Add | Mail, and then follow the directions in the Internet Connection Wizard, which guides you through the process.

NOTE   *We're not going to cover importing and exporting existing accounts or the use of Directory Services in this quick tour. The Outlook Express help system or your network administrator can assist you with these activities.*

To create a new e-mail message, tap Create Mail; then compose your message as you would with any other e-mail client. You can type the addresses of the recipients into the appropriate text boxes, or you can use the Outlook Express Address Book, which is represented by a picture of an open book. This opens the Select Recipients dialog box, which displays any Outlook Express contacts you have entered. When you're ready to send your message, tap Send.

By default, Outlook Express checks its e-mail accounts for new messages every 30 minutes. If you have any new messages, they appear in the View pane. You can read the message in the Preview pane by selecting it in the View pane, or you can read it in a separate window by double-tapping it. To respond to the current message, tap Reply, Reply All, or Forward in the message window's toolbar or the Outlook Express toolbar.

To add contacts to the Contacts list (which is itself just a view into the Outlook Express Address Book), tap the Contacts heading, and then tap New Contact on the menu that appears. Tap New Online Contact instead if you are adding a contact for a person who uses Windows Messenger. That will allow you to send instant messages to the contact (using Windows Messenger) as well as sending e-mail. In Figure 7-11, the first contact is an online contact and the rest are normal contacts.

Use Outlook Express as a Newsreader

When you use Outlook Express as a newsreader, you're using it to post and view newsgroup messages. Outlook Express can work with one or more news servers to provide coverage of public newsgroups as well as private corporate ones. And if the preceding sentences didn't make any sense to you, read "Did You Know How Newsgroups Work?" for more information.

Just as you needed to configure Outlook Express for an e-mail account before you could use it as an e-mail client, you need to configure it to work with a news

Did you know?

How Newsgroups Work?

A *newsgroup* is the Internet equivalent of a bulletin board. People who are subscribed to a newsgroup can post messages to the group. These messages can be viewed by any other subscriber of the newsgroup. People can respond to messages they see posted, and others can respond to their response and so on, creating what are known as *discussion threads*.

Newsgroups have been around a long time. Usenet, a network of *news servers* (computers that host newsgroups), is more than 20 years old. Google, the Internet search site, maintains an archive containing the last 20 years' worth of Usenet newsgroup messages. This archive contains over 700 million messages. You can visit it by going to the Google web site (http://www.google.com) and then tapping the Groups tab.

In addition to the vast array of public newsgroups, an unknown number of private newsgroups are available on corporate news servers. These newsgroups usually have restricted memberships and deal, not surprisingly, with issues of importance to the company or organization that hosts them.

server before you can use Outlook Express as a newsreader. The news server is provided by your ISP, and you'll need to get the appropriate information from the ISP before configuring Outlook Express.

The process is much the same as setting up an e-mail account. If you have access to a news server, you can tap Tools | Accounts, and then select the News tab in the Internet Accounts dialog box. To add the newsreader account information, tap Add | News. Then follow the directions in the Internet Connection Wizard, which guides you through the process.

Once you have the new server account set up, Outlook Express gives you the option to download a list of the newsgroups available on that news server. This process can take a while because there will probably be quite a list to download. For example, the news server I use supports something north of 36,000 newsgroups.

Once you have the list of available newsgroups, you can start looking for some to join. To do this, tap the Newsgroups button in the View pane. This opens the Newsgroup Subscriptions dialog box shown in Figure 7-12. The box titled "How to Find Newsgroups to Join" shows you how to find and join newsgroups in the vast sea of possibilities.

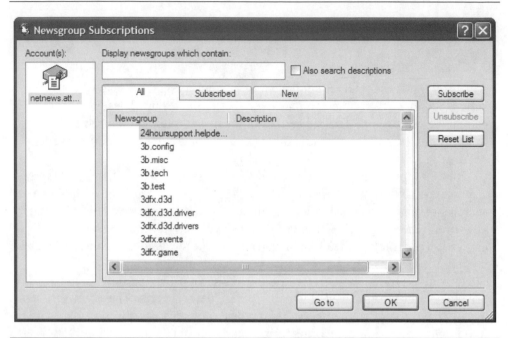

FIGURE 7-12 Use the Newsgroup Subscriptions dialog box to search for, and subscribe to, interesting and useful newsgroups.

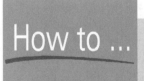 **Find Newsgroups to Join**

With so many newsgroups to choose from, how can you figure out which ones to subscribe to? One answer is to already know the name of the newsgroup you're interested in when you start. Sometimes people, web sites, or other newsgroups refer you to a particular newsgroup you want to explore. In this case, subscribing is easy. Enter the name of the newsgroup in the Display Newsgroups Which Contain box of the Newsgroup Subscriptions dialog box. If your news server carries that newsgroup, it appears in the list. Select the newsgroup, and then tap Subscribe.

What if you don't know the name of a particular newsgroup? Then the Display Newsgroups Which Contain box becomes very helpful. Enter the name of the subject you're interested in, and Outlook Express displays a list of all the newsgroups that contain it in their name. Enter **poker**, for example, and Outlook Express lists every newsgroup that has the word "poker" in its name. To increase your chances of finding a newsgroup on your subject, set the Also Search Descriptions check box. Some (but not all or even most) newsgroups provide a description that explains the purpose of the newsgroup in some detail. This description may list the subject you're interested in, even if the newsgroup's name doesn't.

Once you've subscribed to some newsgroups, you're ready to start reading messages. In the View pane, tap the Synchronize Account button. Outlook Express downloads the headers of all the available messages (that you haven't downloaded before) on all the newsgroups to which you've subscribed. Like downloading the list of available newsgroups, downloading the headers of all the messages can take a while. Between them, the five newsgroups shown in Figure 7-13 contain around 13,000 messages that I haven't read yet.

> **TIP**
> *The best strategy for using newsgroups without wasting vast quantities of time is to skim the subjects of the messages you haven't read yet, and select only ones that really interest you. It's easy to spend hours viewing messages that are totally unrelated to whatever it is you're supposed to be doing. One helpful thing is that Outlook Express shows entire message threads as a single entry that you can expand.*

> **CAUTION**
> *Because most newsgroups are completely unmoderated, people can post anything they want. Some newsgroups contain material that is illegal in most of the world. Just as randomly exploring links on the World Wide Web can expose you to material you don't want to see, dipping into newsgroups with suspicious-sounding names can lead you to stuff that's just as bad.*

Tap a message in the View pane to make its contents appear in the Preview pane. Double-tap it in the View pane to make the message appear in a separate window.

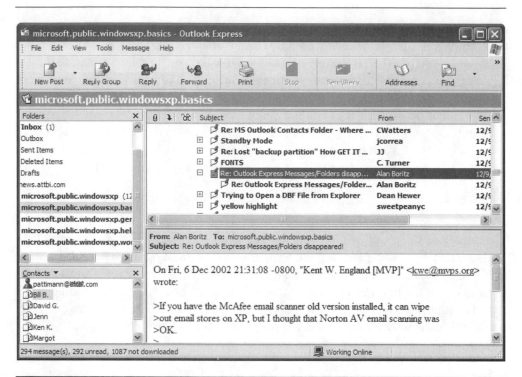

FIGURE 7-13 Outlook Express makes it easy to participate in newsgroups; worldwide public discussions containing thousands of messages on any of literally tens of thousands of subjects.

Responding to a newsgroup message is similar to responding to an e-mail message. The difference is that instead of a Reply All button, you have a Reply Group button. Reply Group posts your response to the entire newsgroup, whereas Reply posts your response to the person who posted the message to the newsgroup.

Work with Windows Messenger

The latest addition to the world of personal computer communication tools is *instant messaging*. Windows Messenger, shown in Figure 7-14, is the instant messaging program included with Windows XP. It allows instant text chatting between any two Windows Messenger users who are online at the same time. In addition, Windows Messenger is enhanced to support file transfers and group chats, and it allows you to make voice calls to other computers or even telephone calls from your Tablet PC. The rest of this chapter is dedicated to helping you start using this powerful communication tool.

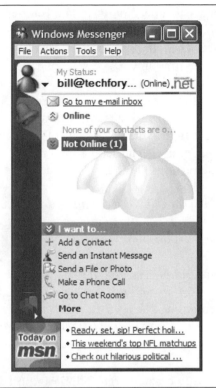

FIGURE 7-14   Windows Messenger provides a superset of instant messaging services such as the ability to send files and photos, visit chat rooms, and even make telephone calls!

CAUTION   *There is one drawback to using Windows Messenger as your instant messaging program. Unlike e-mail and newsgroups, where you can use whatever reader or client you want and still communicate, Windows Messenger users can exchange instant messages only with other Windows Messenger users. Until the companies making the various instant messaging applications agree to some standards (or have them forced down their throats by the United States government) the world of instant messaging will remain fragmented and far less useful than it could be.*

Set Up Windows Messenger

Setting up Windows Messenger is simple. Your Tablet PC almost certainly came with Windows Messenger configured to start whenever Windows starts. The little head and shoulders icon in the notification area is the Windows Messenger icon.

To use Windows Messenger you need only sign in. But before you can sign in, you must have an account with *.NET Passport*, the latest version of Microsoft's Passport user identification service. The .NET Passport Wizard appears when you start Windows Messenger for the first time.

If you use Microsoft's HotMail e-mail service, you already have a .NET Passport you can use with the wizard. If you don't use HotMail, you can create a .NET Passport by giving the wizard the name of one of your existing e-mail accounts. The best choice is to give the wizard one of your primary e-mail addresses, because Windows Messenger users can send e-mail to that address if they want to get a message to you but you aren't online.

CAUTION   *You must give the wizard a valid e-mail address because the address you enter will receive a confirmation message you must reply to before you can use the .NET Passport account.*

TIP   *Some people have trouble creating a .NET Passport account that isn't attached to a HotMail account. If you have trouble with this, create the HotMail account, and then go to .NET Passport Member Services (http://memberservices.passport.net/memberservice.asp) and change your .NET Passport profile to use the e-mail address you want.*

Once you've successfully created your .NET Passport account, you'll see a dialog box (Figure 7-15) where you can sign in to the *.NET Messenger Service*, the instant messaging service Windows Messenger uses. Consider setting the Sign Me In Automatically check box so you don't have to log in to the .NET Messenger Service every time you start Windows Messenger.

Use Windows Messenger

Contacts are the key to using Windows Messenger. The program keeps track of which of your contacts are online and lets you communicate with them easily. So how do you add contacts to Windows Messenger?

You can add contacts manually by tapping Add A Contact in the I Want To list at the bottom of the Windows Messenger window. This starts the Add A Contact Wizard, which walks you through the process. Using this wizard, you can enter the person's e-mail address or sign-in name directly, or search for that person in the .NET Messenger Service's database.

You can also use Outlook Express contacts. Windows Messenger and Outlook Express share the Outlook Express Address Book, so any of your Outlook Express contacts who are also Windows Messenger users automatically appear as contacts in Windows Messenger.

FIGURE 7-15   You'll have to face this dialog box every time you start Windows
Messenger unless you set the Sign Me In Automatically check box.

To actually reach a contact, select the contact in the main Windows Messenger
window, and then tap the option you want to use in the I Want To list at the bottom
of the window. If the person is online, you can send an instant message. If the person
is offline, you'll be given the option to contact another person. You can send an
e-mail message to a person who is offline by double-clicking his or her icon. This
opens a new message window in your default e-mail program.

If someone sends you an instant message, Windows Messenger pops up a small
box in the corner of your screen, which persists for a few seconds and then disappears.
Tap the box to open a Conversation window. If you don't tap the little box in time,
you don't lose the conversation—it's still available on the taskbar.

When people add you to their Contacts list, Windows Messenger displays a
dialog box that lets you control how you interact with them. You can allow them
to see when you are online and send you messages, or you can block them from
seeing when you are online and prevent them from sending you messages. This

feature protects your privacy, because people need your active permission to send you messages or even to know when you are connected to the .NET Messenger Service.

Learn What You Can Do in a Conversation

Once you have a Conversation window like the one in Figure 7-16 open, you can do more than just type messages back and forth.

Here are your options, any of which you can select by tapping the appropriate option from the list on the right side of the Conversation window.

- **Start Camera**   If your computer has a video camera connected to it, you can send video to the person with whom you're having a conversation. Your pictures will appear in the upper-right corner of that person's Conversation window.

- **Start Talking**   If your computer is equipped with a microphone and speakers (and what Tablet PC isn't?), tapping this option allows you to add voice to your conversation. Of course the computer on the other end must also have speakers and a microphone for a full voice conversation.

- **Invite Someone To This Conversation**   You can expand a conversation to include more than one other person simply by inviting others to join.

- **Send A File Or Photo**   A dialog box opens that you can use to select the file or photo you wish to send. The recipient must accept the file or photo before Windows Messenger will transmit it. Windows Messenger normally stores the files you receive in the My Received Files folder, which is in your My Documents folder.

- **Send E-mail**   Your default e-mail client opens so you can send e-mail to the person or persons in the conversation.

- **Ask For Remote Assistance**   If you're having trouble with your Tablet PC or some application running on it, you can ask the person you're conversing with to help you use Remote Assistance. Remote Assistance allows the other person to view your screen while chatting with you. With your permission, the other person can also take control of your computer, controlling it from their machine to show you how to resolve the problem.

CAUTION   *When someone else is controlling your computer, you should avoid using the keyboard or mouse (or pen) yourself. It gets very confusing when two people try to control one computer at the same time.*

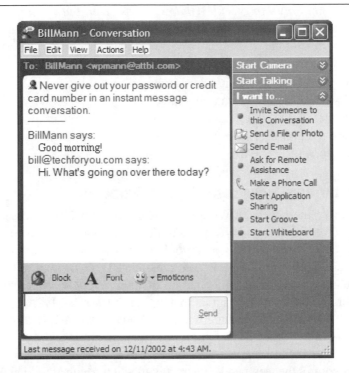

FIGURE 7-16   Windows Messenger gives you many communication options once you have a conversation going with another person.

- **Make A Phone Call**   If you sign up with a Voice Service Provider (Windows Messenger helps you do this), you can make calls from your computer to a regular telephone. You will have to pay to use any of these providers.

- **Start Application Sharing**   Everyone in the conversation can work on one application at the same time. You run the application on your computer, then share it with others in the conversation. You can allow others to control the application, or they can just watch what you do.

- **Start Groove**   Windows Messenger can interact with programs that are designed to work with it. *Groove* is an Internet application that makes direct connections between people for communication or collaboration, and is one such program. Various applications and games are designed to work with Windows Messenger in this way and appear in this list if you have them installed on your Tablet PC.

NOTE *Groove not only works with Windows Messenger, but the latest version has some interesting Tablet PC–specific features. You can learn more about Groove in Chapter 13.*

- **Start Whiteboard**   Whiteboard is an online equivalent to the white, dry-erase marker board you may have in your office at work. When you run Whiteboard with others in the conversation, you can all simultaneously draw on the board, with each person's drawings appearing simultaneously on everyone else's board.

Set Your Windows Messenger Status Properly

One last point to remember with Windows Messenger: The .NET Messenger Service knows when you are online and when you're not, and passes this information along to other users. If people see that you are online, they will usually assume that you are available and willing to accept instant messages. But this may not actually be the case. You can provide more information to other Windows Messenger users by setting your status. You set your status by tapping the words My Status that appear at the top of the Windows Messenger window. You can use a half-dozen status settings, as shown in Figure 7-17: Online, Busy, Be Right Back, Away, On The Phone, Out To Lunch, and Appear Offline. By setting the right status at all times, you can better control the way people interact with you through Windows Messenger.

Use Remote Desktop to Control Another Computer

Remote Desktop is a tool that allows you to take control of another computer from elsewhere on the corporate network or even across the Internet. It differs from Remote Assistance in that when you are connected to a computer through Remote Desktop, that computer is locked and cannot be used by someone else.

Remote Desktop can be very useful when you have a desktop computer as your primary machine, and use a notebook (or perhaps borrow a spare desktop) when traveling. Then you can use Remote Desktop to work with your key files and applications back at the office. But the Tablet PC is designed to be your primary computer and to go with you wherever you go. Therefore, much of the need for Remote Desktop disappears when you're using a Tablet PC.

If you do ever need to use Remote Desktop, you'll want to consult the Windows help system for detailed instructions. At a minimum, you'll need to meet the following requirements:

■ The computer that will be remotely controlled must be running either Windows NT, Windows 2000, Windows XP Professional, or Windows XP Tablet PC edition.

■ The computer that will be controlling the remote system must have Remote Desktop Connection (formerly called the Terminal Services client) installed.

■ The two computers must be connected by a LAN or across the Internet. If the connection is across the Internet, the computer being controlled must also have the Remote Desktop Web Connection installed and running on it.

■ The machine that will be controlled remotely must have this capability enabled. You must have Administrator rights to enable Remote Desktop.

FIGURE 7-17   Use Windows Messenger status to let your contacts know when you're available and when you're not.

Chapter 8

Use Your Tablet PC on a Network

How to...

- ■ Use Your Tablet PC on a Corporate Network
- ■ Use Your Tablet PC on Your Home Network
- ■ Build a Simple Home Network

While Tablet PCs are powerful and useful machines by themselves, they become even more useful when connected to a network. At work, most desktop computer users have a wired connection to the corporate network and rely on it for access to key information and tools, as well as e-mail and the Internet. For you as a Tablet PC user, the ability to connect to the corporate network is no less important. In this chapter, we'll talk about the Tablet PC features and tools you need to be able to connect to corporate networks.

NOTE   *This chapter does not tell you how to design, build, or administer a corporate network. The focus is strictly on connecting your Tablet PC to an existing wired network.*

If you have a home computer or a home computer network, you've probably thought about connecting your Tablet PC into a home network. Although a wireless home network (see Chapter 9) is a better choice in most situations, this chapter tells you what you need to know to connect your Tablet PC to an existing wired home network. Finally, if you don't have a home network, but you do have a computer with an Internet connection you would like to share with your Tablet PC, this chapter tells you how to build a simple, two-computer wired network for sharing an Internet connection.

NOTE   *This chapter assumes that the corporate network you are connecting your Tablet PC to is a Windows network (one running on Microsoft Windows servers). If your corporate network does not run on Windows, some of the instructions in this chapter may be incorrect for your environment. I urge you to get instructions from your network administrator before attempting to connect your Tablet PC to a non-Windows network.*

TIP   *This chapter provides limited coverage of the complex topic of networking. If you want more information on the subject, my favorite resource is the PracticallyNetworked web site at: http://www.practicallynetworked.com.*

Use Your Tablet PC on a Corporate Network

In most respects, using your Tablet PC on a corporate network is no different than using any Windows XP computer on that same network. Once you have a physical connection to the network, and your system is configured to communicate with the network, your Tablet PC looks (to the network) the same as any other computer.

There is, however, one big difference between Tablet PCs and normal desktop machines. Your Tablet PC (like a notebook computer, but more so) is likely to connect to, and disconnect from, the network frequently. This means information on your Tablet PC, even if stored in a shared folder, will be available only intermittently. If you want to share information with others, you should consider storing it somewhere on the network, then using the Synchronize utility to get up to date when your machine is next connected to the network.

NOTE *See the Synchronize section in Chapter 11 for more information on the Synchronize utility.*

8

Most network administrators will handle all aspects of connecting your Tablet PC to the network themselves, leaving you with nothing to do beyond entering your username and password when asked. For those situations where you need to do some of this work, I've included basic information that will help you get your Tablet PC connected to the corporate network.

Make the Physical Connection

Most corporate networks run on Ethernet, and most Tablet PCs come with Ethernet connections built in, making the physical connection between Tablet PC and network trivial. Connect the Ethernet cable from the network to the Ethernet port on your Tablet PC and you're done.

TIP *If you do plan on using your Tablet PC away from the desk a lot, it would be worth investigating a docking station at your main work location that could stay permanently connected to the network and save you from constantly having to connect and disconnect that Ethernet cable.*

Make the Logical Connection

Again, your network administrator is likely to configure the logical connection of your Tablet PC to the network for you. However, sometimes a network administrator will provide you with the information and leave it up to you to configure your computer to talk to the network properly. In this case, you can configure your Tablet PC's network card through the Network Connections folder. Here's what you need to do:

1. Open the Network Connections folder by tapping Start | Control Panel | Network And Internet Connections | Network Connections. Your available network connections (one for each network adapter) appear in this folder, as shown in Figure 8-1.

NOTE   *Some Tablet PCs will not show an Ethernet connection in the Network Connections folder if the Tablet PC's wireless network adapter is active. If this happens to you, consult your Tablet PC's documentation for instructions on disabling the wireless adapter.*

2. Examine the icon for your Local Area Connection. If it is active, it will look like the first icon in the following illustration, which is taken from the "Local Area Connections Overview" in the Windows XP help system. If the icon indicates that the connection is disconnected, make sure the network cable is plugged in properly. If it still shows disconnected, contact your network administrator for help. If the driver is disabled, right-tap the icon and then

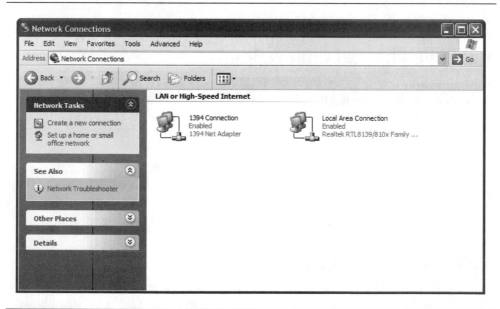

FIGURE 8-1   The Network Connections folder contains network connections that are enabled on your Tablet PC.

tap Enable in the shortcut menu. If the driver remains disabled, contact your network administrator for help.

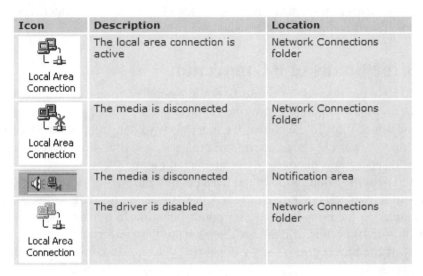

Icon	Description	Location
Local Area Connection	The local area connection is active	Network Connections folder
Local Area Connection	The media is disconnected	Network Connections folder
	The media is disconnected	Notification area
Local Area Connection	The driver is disabled	Network Connections folder

3. Once you have an active connection, right-tap the icon for that connection. In the shortcut menu that appears, tap Properties to open the connection's Properties dialog box as shown here:

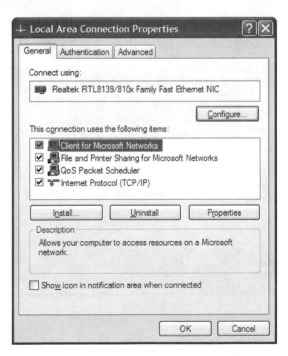

4. Configure the connection by entering the information provided to you by the network administrator. To configure the Internet Protocol (TCP/IP) or other items in the This Connection Uses The Following Items list, select the item then tap the Properties button below the list.

Check the Status of a Connection

Once you have configured the connection to the network, you can easily check its status. To do this, tap Start | Control Panel | Network And Internet Connections | Network Connections. In the Network Connections folder, right-tap the icon of the connection you want to check, then tap Status in the shortcut menu that appears. You should see a status dialog box like the one in Figure 8-2.

First look at the information in the Connection section of the dialog box. The duration should match the length of time since you set up this connection, and the speed should match the speed of the corporate network. In practice, Speed should be 10 Mbps or 100 Mbps. If it is less, there's a problem and you should get help. Similarly, if the Status doesn't say Connected, you should contact your network administrator for help.

Next check the Activity section of the dialog box. If the connection is set up properly and the Tablet PC is talking to the network, both the Sent and Received Packets should be greater than zero. If these values are zero, this is a sign to seek help.

FIGURE 8-2   This dialog box allows you to check the status of a network connection.

If the dialog box shows Status as Connected, Speed at 10 Mbps or 100 Mbps, and Packets Sent and Received are both greater than zero, your connection is set and you're ready to use the network.

 *Once your network connection is set up properly, you may still need to configure applications like Microsoft Outlook or Internet Explorer to work on this network. Your network administrator can provide more information.*

Connect to the Internet Across the Network

Once your Tablet PC has an active connection to a corporate network, you can probably use that network to connect to the Internet. Most corporate networks provide high-speed Internet access, often through dedicated lines that are even faster than DSL and cable modem connections. You may already be able to connect to the Internet. To find out, start Internet Explorer and see if it can display its home page. If so, you're all set.

If you can't connect to the Internet immediately, you can configure Internet access across the corporate network with only a few moments work. To do so, tap Start | Control Panel | Network And Internet Connections. In the Network And Internet Connections folder that appears, tap Set Up Or Change Your Internet Connection. This opens the Internet Properties dialog box shown in Figure 8-3.

Since you're going to connect to the Internet through the corporate network (also known as a local area network, or LAN), tap LAN Settings to open the Local Area Network (LAN) Settings dialog box. Unless your network administrator has provided you with information about an automatic configuration script or has informed you that the network uses a Proxy server, make sure that the Automatically Detect Settings check box is set, and tap OK then tap OK again. You should now be able to connect to the Web and the rest of the Internet across the network using Internet Explorer and other applications.

Use Your Tablet PC on a Home Network

Connecting your Tablet PC to your home network is very much like connecting it to your corporate network, except that there's no network administrator to turn to except yourself. Exactly what you need to do to connect your Tablet PC to your network is determined by the way you built the network in the first place. That said, the following section walks you through an approach that should work for many people.

FIGURE 8-3   Create a new Internet connection from the Internet Properties dialog box.

Make Network Connections

Networking is a complex subject, and it is beyond the scope of this book to address all the ways you can connect your Tablet PC to a network. This section describes one approach that will work in many cases, but the final decision as to the best approach for connecting your Tablet PC to your network must come from you. In particular, this approach assumes that your network uses DHCP to provide IP addresses automatically, and not manual IP addresses.

The Network Setup Wizard can connect your Tablet PC to your existing network. Start by physically connecting your Tablet PC to the network, using an Ethernet cable from the Ethernet connector on your Tablet PC to the network hub or router. Once your Tablet PC is connected, it's time to start the Network Setup Wizard.

NOTE   *The account you use when you connect the Tablet PC to the network must have Administrator rights.*

To start the wizard, tap Start | Control Panel | Network And Internet Connections | Set Up Or Change Your Home Or Small Office Network. Carefully read the instructions the wizard displays, and follow its directions until you come to the Select A Connection Method screen shown in Figure 8-4.

Since you are connecting your Tablet PC to the existing network, you do not want to connect directly to the Internet. Select This Computer Connects To The Internet Through Another Computer On My Network Or Through a Residential Gateway. Tap OK to continue.

Most Tablet PCs have multiple network connections. The wizard will offer to bridge those connections for you in order to connect separate network segments together. Unless you're sure you know what you're doing, don't do this. You aren't trying to bridge multiple networks, so select the Let Me Choose The Connections To My Network option.

The next screen asks you to select the connections to bridge, and displays all the available network connections on your system as shown in Figure 8-5. Avoid the whole bridging scene by clearing the check boxes next to all the network connections except

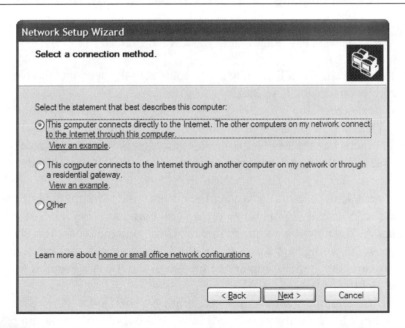

FIGURE 8-4   Make sure you choose the proper connection method here if you want your Tablet PC to connect to the Internet through your existing network.

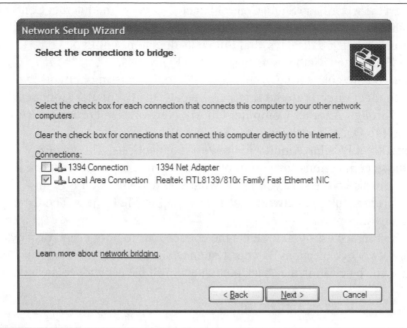

FIGURE 8-5   Make sure that only the Ethernet connection you'll use to connect to your network is selected before you leave this screen.

the Ethernet connection you'll actually use to connect to the network. Tap Next when only the correct connection is selected.

On the next screen, the wizard asks you to enter a name and description for this computer. This name and description will be used to identify your Tablet PC on the network in places like the My Network Places folder. If you already have a name and description set up for this computer, don't change it. Doing so may disrupt your Internet access.

On the next screen, you need to enter the name of the workgroup your computer will belong to. Normally for a home network, all computers belong to a single workgroup. As the network administrator for your home network, you should already know the workgroup name. If you don't remember it, you can find out what it is by looking at the Computer Name tab of the System Properties dialog box in the Control Panel.

The wizard should now be ready to configure your Tablet PC to work on the network. Check all the settings on the Ready To Apply Network Settings screen, and if all is well, tap Next. Configuring the system will likely take a few minutes.

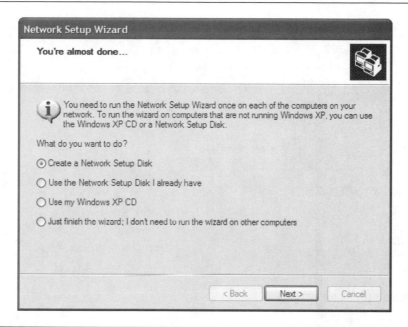

FIGURE 8-6   You're almost done connecting your Tablet PC to the network when you see this screen.

When the wizard is done setting up your system, it displays the You're Almost Done screen shown in Figure 8-6. Since you're connecting your Tablet PC to an existing network, the right option is to select Just Finish The Wizard; I Don't Need To Run The Wizard On Other Computers.

Tap Next to see the Completing The Network Setup Wizard screen, then Finish to be done. You should now be able to see the rest of the computers on the network (actually the computers in your workgroup). To find out, open the My Network Places folder (tap Start | My Network Places). Under Network Tasks, tap View Workgroup Computers. Your Tablet PC and the other computers on the network should appear in this folder, as the computers on my home network do in Figure 8-7.

Assuming that your home network already has provisions for sharing an Internet connection, the wizard should have automatically set up your Tablet PC to share that connection. If you don't have a form of Internet connection sharing set up on your network, you may be able to use Windows XP Internet Connection Sharing (ICS) to add that capability. The article "Windows XP Internet Connection Sharing" at PracticallyNetworked.com (http://www.practicallynetworked.com/sharing/xp_ics/) is one good source for more information on this issue.

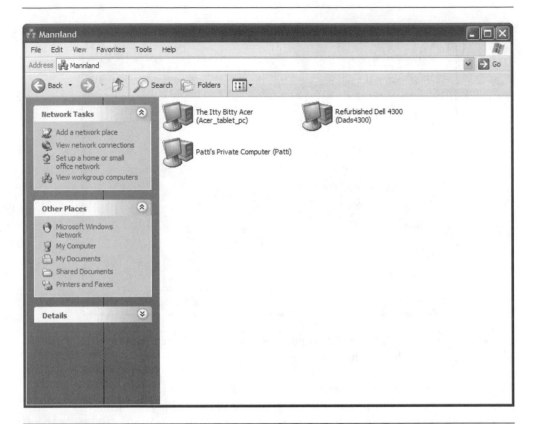

Tap View Workgroup Computers in My Network Places to see all the computers connected to your home network.

Build a Simple Home Network

If you already have a computer at home that's connected to the Internet, you can let your Tablet PC share that access by creating a very simple home network. As I mentioned earlier, networking can be complex, and there's more than one way to do anything. However, if you have a Windows XP computer at home with a broadband Internet connection (this is probably a fairly common situation for anyone reading this book), the rest of this chapter shows you one way to create the network and share that high-speed Internet access with a minimum of fuss and bother. The network will look like the one in the following illustration. In this illustration, the modem represents whichever means of high-speed Internet access you use: cable modem, DSL, satellite. It's a simple, clean solution that won't cost you very much to build.

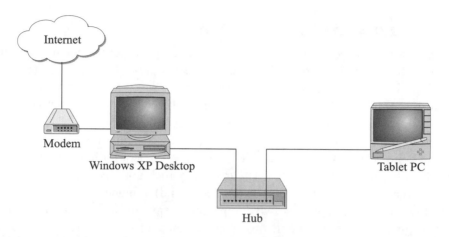

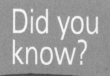 *I did this diagram with Microsoft Visio. Like Paint, Visio is a program that becomes much easier and more natural to use on a Tablet PC, even without any Tablet PC–specific enhancements. You can find out more about Visio at: http://www.microsoft.com/office/visio/.*

Building a simple network like this one is a four-step process. Here are the four steps you need to follow:

1. Figure out what hardware you need.

2. Buy and install the hardware.

3. Connect the computers.

4. Run the Network Setup Wizard on each computer.

Did you know?

Home Networks Are Hot?

Although the U.S. economy may be slow and sales of home computers are stagnant, home networks are high on people's shopping list. According to a recent report by Parks Associates, almost one-third of U.S. households with a broadband Internet connection plan to purchase home networking equipment in 2003.

Figure Out What Hardware You Need

To create this network, each computer must have an Ethernet connection to a hub. A *hub* is little more than a box with several Ethernet ports. It interconnects all the computers in the network so that they can send messages back and forth. There are more sophisticated ways of interconnecting the computers in a network, but for one like this, with only two computers, a hub is fine.

Before going further, we need to talk a bit about the speed of the network you're about to build. The commonly available Ethernet equipment for home users runs at either 10 Mbps or 100 Mbps, with many units supporting both speeds. Most corporate networks run at 100 Mbps (100 million bits per second) or higher.

But we're talking about just two computers sharing an Internet connection. Considering that the fastest home broadband connections seldom reach speeds of even 3 Mbps, even 10 Mbps is more than fast enough for our purposes. So you can let cost, availability, and your plans for the future of your network guide you. If cost is the primary consideration, feel free to buy 10 Mbps parts. If you're considering adding additional computers to your network someday or are thinking about using your network for more than just sharing Internet access (multiplayer games and streaming video across the network are two possibilities), you should strongly consider spending a few extra dollars to get 100 Mbps parts.

Each computer in your network needs an Ethernet port of some sort to connect to the hub. Your Tablet PC should have an available Ethernet port, but your desktop probably doesn't. The Ethernet port on your desktop computer is almost certainly connected to the broadband modem that gives you your high-speed Internet access. So you'll likely need to add a Network Interface Card (NIC) to your desktop computer.

NICs are normally installed in one of the open PCI slots inside your computer. If you're uncomfortable with the idea of working inside the machine, you can either buy the NIC from a store that will install it for you, or use an external USB-to-Ethernet adapter. In either case, the equipment isn't expensive—you can get 10/100 Mbps NICs for under $20, and USB-to-Ethernet adapters for not much more.

Besides the NIC, you'll need a hub to connect the computers. Unless you're planning on adding several computers to your network later, a basic four-port hub should serve your needs and cost you around $30.

NOTE   *If you do plan on adding computers to the network, you should consider spending a little more money and using a switch instead of a hub. A switch allows any two computers on the network to connect to each other directly, without slowing down any other network communications.*

The last bit of equipment you need to consider is the Ethernet cables to connect everything together. You'll need two cables, one from each computer to the hub. Many stores sell Ethernet cable in standard lengths, with prices on the order of $1 per foot.

So your shopping list will probably look like this:

- 1 Ethernet NIC, or 1 USB-to-Ethernet adapter

- 1 Ethernet Hub, speed compatible with the NIC or adapter

- 2 Ethernet cables, of sufficient length to connect your computers to the hub from the locations where you'll use them.

Buy and Install the Hardware

Buying the hardware calls for a trip to your local computer store or an online computer store like CompUSA (www.compusa.com). If you shop at your local computer store, you can explain what you're up to and confirm your selections with their staff before buying everything.

Installing the hardware is really just a matter of carefully following the instructions that come with the NIC or USB-to-Ethernet adapter you bought. If you are installing the NIC, make sure the computer is turned off and unplugged before opening the case.

Connect the Computers

Connecting the computers is also pretty straightforward. Connect the NIC or adapter on the desktop computer to the hub, and connect the hub to the Ethernet port on your Tablet PC. Make sure everything is plugged in and turned on.

Before going any further, confirm that the Internet connection on your desktop computer still functions properly.

Next, confirm that you have active connections between the computers and the hub. To do this, you'll use the Network Connections folder. On the desktop PC, tap Start | Control Panel | Network And Internet Connections | Network Connections. This opens the Network Connections folder. Your available network connections (one for each network adapter on the computer) appear in this folder. Confirm that the network connection between the computer and the hub is active by examining the icon for that connection.

 *Some Tablet PCs will not show an Ethernet connection in the Network Connections folder if the Tablet PC's wireless network adapter is active. If this happens to you, consult your Tablet PC's documentation for instructions on disabling the wireless adapter.*

If it is active, it will look like the first icon in the following illustration, which is taken from the "Local Area Connections Overview" in the Windows XP help system. If it is disconnected, make sure the network cable is plugged in properly. If it still shows disconnected, or if it indicates that the driver is disabled, it's time to fire up the Drives and Network Adapters Troubleshooter. See "Troubleshoot Network Adapter Problems" later in this chapter for more on this troubleshooter.

Icon	Description	Location
Local Area Connection	The local area connection is active	Network Connections folder
Local Area Connection	The media is disconnected	Network Connections folder
	The media is disconnected	Notification area
Local Area Connection	The driver is disabled	Network Connections folder

Once the network connections on both the desktop PC and the Tablet PC are active, you're ready to run the Network Setup Wizard and get the machines talking to each other.

Run the Network Setup Wizard on Each Computer

Among its many talents, the Network Setup Wizard can connect all the computers in your new network. You want to start by running the wizard on your desktop computer. To start the wizard, tap Start | Control Panel | Network And Internet Connections | Set Up Or Change Your Home Or Small Office Network. Carefully read the instructions the wizard displays and follow its directions until you come to the Select A Connection Method screen.

Run the Network Setup Wizard on Your Desktop Computer

Your desktop computer is the one that will provide the Internet connection for your network, but you still need to figure out which of the options in Figure 8-8 to select. In most cases, you have a dial-up modem, cable modem, or DSL equipment plugged directly into your desktop computer, so you should choose This Computer Connects Directly To The Internet. If you have some other kind of connection to the Internet set up, I'll leave it to you to decide which option to select.

Your desktop PC may now have more than one network connection (the NIC that connects to your broadband Internet access and the one that will connect to your network), so in the next screen, the wizard will offer to bridge those connections for you in order to connect separate network segments together. You aren't trying to bridge multiple networks, so select the Let Me Choose The Connections To My Network option.

The next screen asks you to select the connections to bridge, and displays all the available network connections on your system. Clear the check boxes next to all the network connections except the Ethernet connection you'll actually use to connect to the rest of the network. Tap Next when only the correct connection is selected.

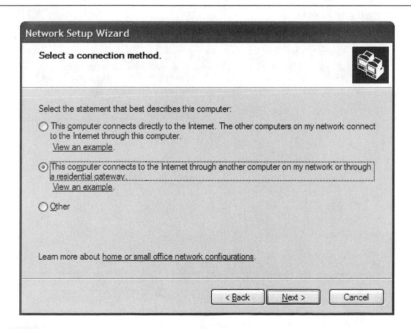

FIGURE 8-8   You use this dialog box to specify how your desktop computer connects to the Internet.

On the next screen, the wizard asks you to enter a name and description for this computer. This name and description will be used to identify your Tablet PC on the network in places like the My Network Places folder. If you already have a name and description set up for this computer, don't change it. Doing so may disrupt your Internet access.

On the next screen, you need to enter the name of the workgroup your computer will belong to. Normally for a home network, all computers belong to a single workgroup. Assign a name you can easily remember. You'll need to know it in a little while, when you connect the Tablet PC into the network.

The wizard should now be ready to configure your desktop computer as part of a network. Check all the settings on the Ready To Apply Network Settings screen, and if all is well, tap Next. Configuring the system will likely take a few minutes.

When the wizard is done setting up your system, it displays the You're Almost Done screen shown in Figure 8-9. Since you will be connecting your Tablet PC to this network, and that Tablet PC probably doesn't have a floppy disk drive, the right option to select is Use My Windows XP CD.

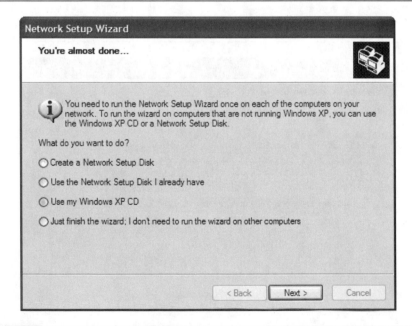

FIGURE 8-9   Use the Windows XP CD to add your Tablet PC to the network.

Tap Next to see the Completing The Network Setup Wizard screen, then Finish to end the wizard. The next step is to use the Windows XP CD from your Tablet PC to configure it for the network.

Run the Network Setup Wizard on Your Tablet PC

Now, you can connect your Tablet PC to the network. Insert your Windows XP CD (the one that came with your Tablet PC) into the Tablet PC's CD-ROM drive. When the Windows XP menu appears, tap Perform Additional Tasks | Set Up Home Or Small Office Networking.

> **NOTE** *The account you use when you connect the Tablet PC to the network must have Administrator rights.*

The procedure you follow is basically the same as the one you just went through with your desktop computer. However, this time around, when you get to the Select A Connection Method screen, select This Computer Connects To The Internet Through Another Computer On My Network Or Through a Residential Gateway. Tap OK to continue. The rest of the process is the same as you used for your desktop computer.

Once you finish running the wizard, you should be able to see the rest of the computers on the network. To find out if you really can, open the My Network Places folder (tap Start | My Network Places). Under Network Tasks, tap View Workgroup Computers. Your Tablet PC and the other computers on the network should appear in this folder.

Your simple home network is now complete.

Troubleshoot Network Adapter Problems

If you're having problems with the connections in your network, the Drives and Network Adapters Troubleshooter may be able to help resolve them. To run this troubleshooter, tap Start | Help And Support to open the Windows XP Help and Support Center. Somewhere near the top of the Help and Support Center, you'll find a Search box, like the one below the left side of the toolbar in Figure 8-10. The exact location and appearance of the box can change, as the page can be customized by the computer manufacturers.

Once you find the Search box, search for "network adapters troubleshooter." A link to the Drives and Network Adapters Troubleshooter appears in the Suggested Topics list. Tap that to activate the troubleshooter, which appears in Figure 8-11.

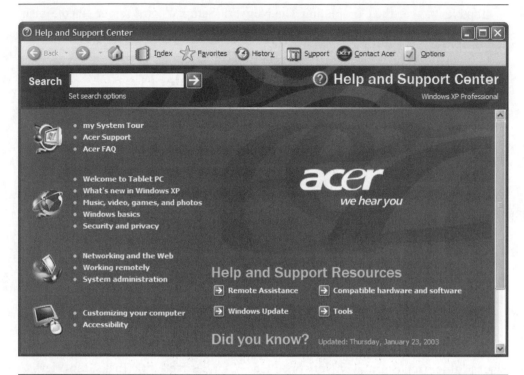

FIGURE 8-10 The Search box can move around in the Help and Support Center window, but it should always be there somewhere.

The Drives and Network Adapters Troubleshooter asks you a series of questions and asks you to perform certain tasks, with the goal of helping you narrow down or completely resolve a network adapter problem. If you still can't resolve the problem with the help of the troubleshooter, you need to call in some help. The staff at the store where you buy your computer equipment or a knowledgeable technician at work may be able to help you.

Fortunately, in most cases you don't ever need to deal with the Drives and Network Adapters Troubleshooter, and if you do, the chances are pretty good that it'll help you resolve the problem.

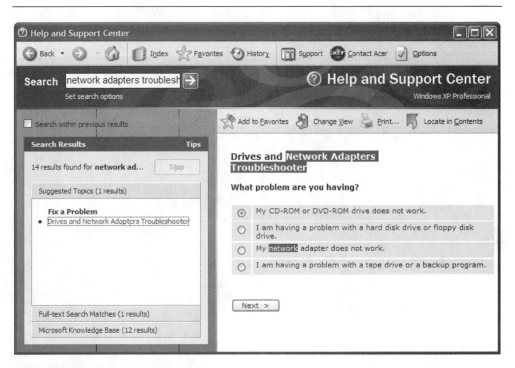

FIGURE 8-11   The Drives and Network Adapters Troubleshooter can help resolve
problems with your network adapters.

Chapter 9

Go Wireless

How to...

- Understand Wireless Networking Basics
- Connect Your Tablet PC to an Existing Wireless Network
- Build a Simple Wireless Network

In Chapter 8, you learned how to connect your Tablet PC to a regular wired Ethernet network. But if you think like I do, you may have felt there was something, if not quite wrong, then not quite right either, about tying your Tablet PC down with a network cable. One of the points of a Tablet PC is to be able to do your work wherever you happen to be. And you can, as long as you don't need access to the corporate network or the Internet.

This is why I think wireless networking is such an important part of the Tablet PC concept. With the wireless network card that's built into most Tablet PCs, and a wireless access point attached to your network, you get the full capabilities of your Tablet PC wherever you are (as long as you are within wireless range).

In this chapter, you'll learn a bit about wireless networking, as well as learning how to connect your Tablet PC to an existing wireless network. We'll also go one step further. In Chapter 8, I showed you how to build a simple wired network for your home, one that would allow you to share the broadband Internet access already enjoyed by your desktop PC. In this chapter, I'll show you how to build what I think is an even better solution, a simple home wireless network. Building this will cost you more than building a wired network, but you'll gain some real advantages, like freedom from the need to run Ethernet cable all over your house, and the freedom to use your network and Internet access from wherever in the house you and your Tablet PC happen to be.

 *If you want more in-depth information on wireless networking, or networking in general, my favorite resource is the PracticallyNetworked web site at: http://www.practicallynetworked.com.*

Understand Wireless Networking Basics

In the next few pages, we'll take a look at the basics of wireless networking, with an eye toward covering only what you need to know to get your Tablet PC connected to a wireless network (or build a basic network for sharing Internet access).

What's the Big Deal about Wireless?

Wireless networking is a hot topic these days, even though wireless networks are slower than wired ones, have significant security issues, and are susceptible to interference. So what is the big deal about wireless? Three factors make wireless networking a big deal:

- Convenience

- Cost

- Coolness

Let's take a quick look at each of these factors.

Convenience

With a wireless network, you don't need to run Ethernet cables to each computer. When you're dealing with desktop machines that generally stay put, running cables is bad enough. But when you're dealing with a mobile computer like the Tablet PC, running cables becomes a real headache.

Do you run the cables to certain spots, then go work in one of those spots when you need to connect your Tablet PC to the network or the Internet? If you can't use your Tablet PC where you want to, it defeats the whole purpose of the machine. You could always snake some network cable across the floor to the spot where you want to work, but that's a major disaster waiting to happen. A wireless network makes this kind of problem disappear along with the cables you no longer need.

Cost

The cost factor is a little less obvious than the convenience factor. Wireless network interface cards (NICs) are generally more expensive than wired NICs. A wireless access point (which you'll learn more about later in the chapter) costs somewhat more than a hub or switch does. So where are the cost savings?

The cost savings in wireless networks come from eliminating the cost of the cables, eliminating the cost of laying the cables, and eliminating the cost of redoing everything the first time you move equipment around.

The cost of network cables is a small part of the overall cost, but laying them can be very expensive. Running cable usually involves punching holes in walls and snaking it through the structure of the building, which is time-consuming, and therefore expensive, work. Even worse, unless you initially run cable to every location that might require it, you'll need to run additional cables when you move things around. Then you'll need to reconnect and test everything again in its new location. All the costs related to cables go away with a wireless network. If the wireless NIC in the computer gets a good signal, you're set.

Coolness

While this factor is somewhat less overwhelming than it used to be, wireless networks are just cooler than wired ones. The freedom of movement afforded by a wireless network makes cool things possible, like the mobile meeting capabilities of WebEx Meeting Center (see the "Did You Know WebEx Mobilizes Meetings on the Tablet PC?" box for more information).

Now that we've talked about why wireless networking is a good thing, it's time to dig into the alphabet soup of wireless networking standards. But don't worry. We'll only go far enough for you to understand what you need to know to get your Tablet PC connected to a wireless network.

Get the Terminology Straight

Unfortunately, the world of wireless networking is chock full of geeky terms like 802.11b and Wi-Fi. Fortunately, these two are the two main terms you need to know. First off, 802.11b is the name of a specification that defines how wireless networks communicate. Any machines in the initial crop of Tablet PCs that

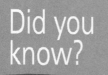

WebEx Mobilizes Meeting on the Tablet PC?

WebEx is a system that makes possible online meetings and conferences. The WebEx Meeting Center works with a web browser and a telephone to let you make presentations, share documents and applications, poll participants, even share control of desktop applications and deliver voice over IP (voice over the Internet) communications. WebEx Meeting Center is fully Tablet PC compatible, which means you can conduct interactive, online meetings anywhere your Tablet PC can make a wireless (or wired) connection to the Internet. It's just another example of the way that the power and flexibility of the Tablet PC can change the way you work.

included wireless NICs use the 802.11b specification for wireless communication. Wi-Fi is a marketing name for devices that work on the 802.11b and 802.11a standards and are certified to be compatible with other Wi-Fi devices. You can get more information on Wi-Fi at the Wi-Fi Alliance web site (Figure 9-1).

These 802.11b devices are by far the most commonly used wireless networking equipment today. They can communicate at speeds of 11 Mbps, although a significant amount of that capacity is used by the network itself. While this is nowhere near the 100 Mbps or faster that many corporate networks can provide, it is plenty fast for most uses. This is particularly true for home use, where the main purpose of a network is usually to share broadband Internet access. Since few home broadband systems can connect to the Internet at even 3 Mbps, the 11 Mbps of 802.11b is just fine.

FIGURE 9-1   The Wi-Fi Alliance certifies interoperability of wireless devices like your Tablet PC that use the 802.11b specification.

What about Security?

You may have heard some of the ruckus about Wi-Fi security, or the lack of it. The encryption standard that Wi-Fi devices originally shipped with is called WEP, or Wired Equivalent Privacy, and it has turned out to be anything but private. New approaches to cracking WEP showed it to be very vulnerable to a determined hacker. Even so, WEP still provides a basic level of protection for a wireless network. It can stop the casual snoop, as well as people looking to use your network for some free, unauthorized Internet access.

The biggest security risk for wireless networks is that most of them don't even have WEP turned on. On a network without WEP activated, anyone with the right software (which is freely available on the Internet) can connect to that network in seconds. Vast numbers of the wireless networks in use today, even at major corporations, are running without WEP activated.

If you are connecting your Tablet PC to a corporate wireless network, you must, of course, do so in the manner prescribed by the network administrator. But if you are building your own wireless network, I advise you to activate WEP during the setup. The documentation that comes with your wireless networking equipment will tell you how.

Other Things to Know about Wireless Networking

We've almost covered all the basics now. Here are a few other things to be aware of when it comes to wireless networking:

- **You probably won't get the range that's advertised.** As you might expect, all wireless networking equipment has a limited range. That range is limited by the power of the wireless transmitter and the efficiency (called gain) of the antennas on the transmitter and receiver. The ranges advertised by manufacturers, which are often hundreds of feet, tend to be best-case results, under ideal conditions. In my experience, you're likely to see significantly less range than advertised under real-world conditions.

- **The further you are from the access point, the slower the connection becomes.** The further a Wi-Fi signal travels, the lower the signal strength at the receiving end. To compensate for this, Wi-Fi devices reduce the speed at which they transmit data when the signal strength declines. So you have a trade-off of distance for speed. Exactly how far your Tablet PC can be from an access point before the network speed declines depends on everything from the design of the specific equipment you use, to the orientation of the

Tablet PC relative to the access point, to the properties of the materials between the access point and your computer. Figure 9-2 gives you some idea of what you might expect.

■ The signal from your access point or gateway travels out from the device in a more or less spherical pattern. That means you can usually get a connection on different floors than the one containing the device.

■ The radio frequency used by 802.11b devices (2.4 GHz) is also used by microwave ovens, Bluetooth wireless headphones, and some cell phones. Your wireless network may experience some interference from these devices.

■ Public wireless access points (called wireless hot spots) are appearing around the world. There are thousands of them in the United States alone. Some are provided as a public service by individuals, some are run as money-making operations by businesses—and some are inadvertent gifts from people who don't use WEP or other security measures on their networks. If you want to investigate the availability of intentional hot spots in your area, see the "How to Find Wireless Hot Spots" box. You can also spot the signs of nearby hot spots (intentional and unintentional ones) if you

9

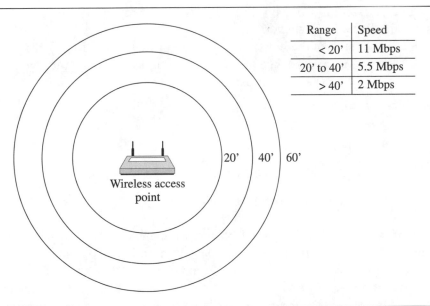

Range	Speed
< 20'	11 Mbps
20' to 40'	5.5 Mbps
> 40'	2 Mbps

FIGURE 9-2   This figure gives you a somewhat conservative idea of the range and speed you might get from a wireless access point.

know what to look for. See "How to Find Wireless Hot Spots, Part II" for more information on the practice of warchalking and what it can tell you about nearby wireless networks.

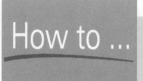 **Find Wireless Hot Spots**

Perhaps the biggest issue with using wireless hot spots is finding them. There are thousands of hot spots active in the United States already, and the number is growing rapidly. But with a coverage radius of at most a few hundred feet per hot spot, that still leaves the vast majority of the country without hot spot coverage.

Further complicating the situation is the fact that the hot spots that are in place belong to several different networks. So you not only have to find a hot spot, it has to be a hot spot that belongs to a network you belong to. One way to find out if a free wireless hot spot is available in an area is to visit the FreeNetworks.org web site (http://www.freenetworks.org). This site provides a ton of general information on the free network movement, as well as links to several affiliated free networks.

One bright spot in the hot spot scene (if you're willing to pay for your wireless access) is the existence of several companies trying to knit together national hot spot networks. Four that you might want to investigate are:

- Boingo Wireless (http://www.boingo.com)

- Joltage (http://www.joltage.com)

- T-Mobile HotSpot (http://locations.hotspot.t-mobile.com)

- Wayport (http://www.wayport.com)

As of January 2003, T-Mobile HotSpot was clearly the leading provider, with over 2,000 hot spots, in about two dozen states, including the ones in Starbucks coffee shops, as you can see from this map. The web sites for each of these four networks provide the ability to search for a hot spot in a particular location, so it should only take a few minutes to determine if one of them provides the coverage you need. And don't forget that these networks are all growing rapidly, so it's worth checking back every so often.

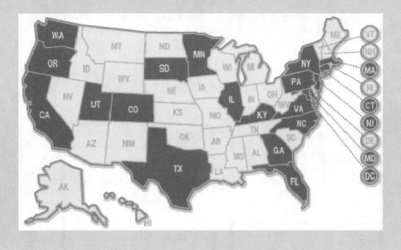

9

CAUTION   *If you use public hot spots, it's possible that someone will try to gain wireless access to your Tablet PC. A good basic precaution is to disable any shared drives or folders. You may also want to activate the Internet Connection Firewall on your Tablet PC. You can find complete information on using the Internet Connection Firewall in the Windows XP help system.*

How to ...   Find Wireless Hot Spots, Part II

There is one other way to find wireless access that's a little bit unusual, and perhaps even a bit naughty. That way is to look for warchalk marks. Warchalking, the practice of using chalk marks to indicate nearby wireless access points, was inspired by the Depression-era practices of hobos, who would reportedly use chalk marks to indicate friendly homes. The morality and legality of warchalking are something we won't cover here, but if you go to http://notabug.com/warchalking/card300.png, you can see what the basic warchalking symbols look like.

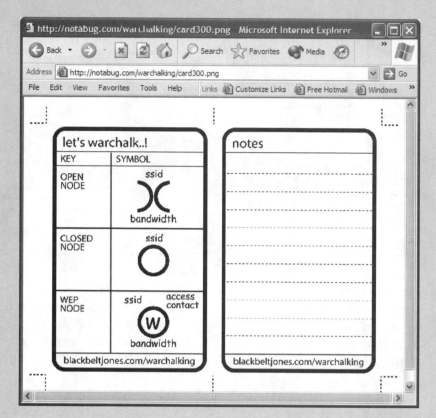

If you find warchalk marks on a surface somewhere, you can be sure that there's a wireless access point nearby. For the details on warchalking, including how to make and interpret the symbols, go to the Warchalking.org web site, http://www.warchalking.org.

Connect Your Tablet PC to an Existing Wireless Network

Now that you know the basics of wireless networking, it's time to learn how to connect your Tablet PC to an existing wireless network. As usual, if you're connecting to the company network, your network administrator should provide you with complete instructions on how to get connected. If you're responsible for setting up the connection yourself, follow these instructions.

Connecting your Tablet PC to a wireless network is pretty simple, since Windows XP provides native Wi-Fi support. First you need to know if the network you're connecting to uses WEP for security. If so, you need to know the network key before starting this process:

1. Ensure that the wireless network card in your Tablet PC is active. Check the documentation that came with your computer for details on how to turn it on.

2. With the Tablet PC near a wireless access point, right-tap the Network Connection icon in the notification area, then tap View Available Wireless Networks. This opens a dialog box (Figure 9-3) that shows all the wireless networks your Tablet PC can detect right now.

3. If necessary, tap the name of the network you want your Tablet PC connected to in the Available Wireless Networks box. If the network

FIGURE 9-3   This dialog box tells you which wireless networks your Tablet PC can detect, and warns you if they aren't using WEP security.

you wish to connect to is not using WEP for security, you will see the warning shown in the figure. In that case, you'll need to set the Allow Me To Connect To The Selected Wireless Network, Even Though It Is Not Secure check box, then tap Connect to connect to the network.

> **TIP** *If you regularly run into situations where you have access to multiple wireless networks simultaneously, consider setting up a list of Preferred Networks. To do this, tap the Advanced button in the View Available Wireless Networks dialog box, then tap the Setting Up Wireless Network Configuration link on the Wireless Network Properties tab for more information on preferred networks. Finally, fill in the Preferred Networks list on the Wireless Network Properties tab.*

4. If the network you are connecting to does use WEP, the dialog box will look like the one in Figure 9-4. In this case, you'll need to enter the network key in the appropriate text boxes, then tap Connect to connect to the network.

Once you connect to the network, Windows should display a bubble message near the notification area, telling you the status of the connection. If you didn't see

FIGURE 9-4 If WEP is active on the network you're connecting to, you'll need to enter a network key to connect.

this message, hover the pen over the Network Connections icon in the notification area. After a moment, the current status of your network connection will appear.

Your Tablet PC should now be connected to the network, and if Internet Connection Sharing is set up, it should be able to browse the Internet. For any additional network services, such as access to shared folders or membership in a workgroup, consult your network administrator.

Build a Simple Wireless Network

In the last part of this chapter, we're going to design a simple wireless network. As in Chapter 8, the goal here is to create a network that allows your Tablet PC to share broadband Internet access with your desktop PC. But this time, the network will be wireless, and it will use a wireless access point, a hub, and a router to connect the computers to the broadband modem and to each other. The network will look like the SOHO (small office, home office) network design at the Wi-Fi Alliance web site (www.weca.net) shown in Figure 9-5.

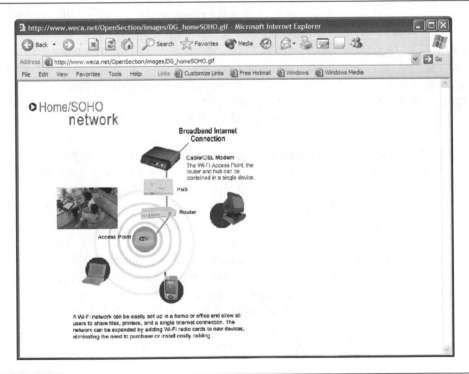

FIGURE 9-5   The simple wireless network we're designing in this section is built around a wireless access point.

Although you'll have to spend more money on equipment for this kind of setup than you would for the simple wired network in Chapter 8, you get some real benefits. For one thing, you won't need to run network cables all over the place. For another, the wireless access point, hub, and router handle all the switching and interconnecting of computers and broadband access, so your desktop computer doesn't have to be running for you to connect to the Internet.

Decide How You Will Handle Security

Deciding how you will handle security is really pretty simple. If you don't mind letting anyone who wanders by with the right equipment get onto your network (which gives them access to all the computers on the network), run with WEP turned off. If you want a reasonable amount of protection without a lot of headaches, enable WEP. If you want the best possible security, you should reconsider building a wireless network.

Figure Out What Hardware You Need

As we design this network, I'll assume that your desktop PC is physically connected to your broadband connection (cable modem, satellite hookup, DSL connection, whatever) through an Ethernet cable. In other words, I'll assume that your desktop computer has an Ethernet network interface card (NIC) installed and that this NIC is connected to your cable modem or other broadband device. I'll also assume that your Tablet PC does have 802.11b equipment built in.

One thing you need to think about is the access point, hub, and router. While you can buy those three pieces separately, then connect them together as shown in Figure 9-5, you can also get all three components together in a single package known as a gateway or base station. These combined units are generally more practical than having separate pieces of equipment strung together. Most of the major Wi-Fi vendors offer units like this, and you should strongly consider buying one.

Another thing to think about: In its pure form, this network features wireless connections to each computer. But your desktop computer already has an Ethernet NIC, and your new hub or gateway should have one or more open Ethernet ports. You can save a bit of money by making a direct wired connection between your desktop computer and the hub or gateway, instead of a wireless one. By doing this, you can save the expense of one wireless NIC, at the cost of a little more complexity when setting up the network. If this approach appeals to you, read "Build a Simple Home Network" in Chapter 8 for guidance on how to connect the wired part of your network.

NOTE

Many of the available gateways or base stations have a built-in switch instead of a hub. This provides performance benefits for all but the smallest networks and is worth looking for if you're going to connect more computers to your network.

One last thing to ponder before coming up with a hardware shopping list: Can you get the coverage you need with a single wireless access point, gateway, or base station? In general, any of these devices, when placed more or less in the center of your house, should provide coverage throughout the house. If you need to cover an area that's too large for a single access point or gateway, you can set up a network with more than one such device, but doing so is beyond the scope of this chapter. We're going to stick to a design with a single access point.

After thinking about all the issues I've just touched on, here's what your typical simple wireless network shopping list might look like:

■ One wireless gateway or base station with router and hub (or preferably a switch) built in. Or a wireless access point, a router, and a hub or switch.

■ One wireless NIC for your desktop computer (if you want to connect this machine to the network wirelessly). This can be either an internally mounted device or an external interface that connects to one of your desktop PC's USB ports. USB devices, as well as some internally mounted devices, allow you to place the antenna a short distance away from the computer. This can reduce the interference caused by the metal chassis of your desktop machine and is worth considering if you plan to place the desktop machine far from the access point or gateway.

■ Additional cables to connect everything if you don't buy an integrated gateway or base station.

Buy and Install the Hardware

Buying the hardware calls for a trip to your local computer store or an online computer store like CompUSA (www.compusa.com). If you shop at your local computer store, you can explain what you're up to and confirm your selections with their staff before buying everything.

When it comes to the brand of equipment, you have lots of options. LinkSys has been around for a relatively long time and sells a ton of equipment. The only problem is that their equipment seems more geared to techie types than to someone who just wants to get their wireless network up and running with the minimum of fuss. I have a degree in Electrical Engineering and found myself confused a few times when I set up my network with LinkSys equipment.

Microsoft recently began selling broadband networking gear like base stations and wireless adapters. While I haven't used their equipment myself, I've heard good things about it. And I have looked at the documentation that comes with the Microsoft hardware. The documentation is well done and guides you through the whole procedure step-by-step. You should certainly consider their equipment.

TIP *Both LinkSys and Microsoft provide 24-hour support for people setting up their networking equipment. You probably won't need it, but it's nice to know there's someone to call if you do get stuck.*

Installing the hardware is really just a matter of carefully following the instructions that come with the equipment. These instructions will guide you all the way through the process, from hooking up the hardware, to getting the network talking wirelessly, to configuring the access point or gateway to use WEP.

CAUTION *Make sure the desktop computer is turned off and unplugged before opening the case if you decide to go with an internal wireless NIC.*

The general process is to connect the access point or gateway, followed by a single computer. You then use these two pieces to get the basic network up and running. Then you add the other computer to the network.

NOTE *You may need to make a wired connection to the access point or gateway to do the initial configuration, so don't be surprised if the installation instructions require you to make that connection even though you're planning a totally wireless network. Once the configuration is complete, you'll be able to disconnect that cable.*

Part III

Put Your Tablet PC to Work

Chapter 10

Understand Handwritten Input on the Tablet PC

How to...

■ Understand Handwritten Input Basics

■ Understand Tablet PC Digital Ink

■ Understand Tablet PC Handwriting Recognition

Handwritten input is the key feature of Tablet PCs. Although Tablet PCs running Windows XP Tablet PC edition aren't the first computers to use handwritten input, they surely offer the best implementation of handwritten input to date.

You've already used the pen to work with your Tablet PC, and you've probably already done some handwritten input using Windows Journal and the Tablet PC Input Panel. This chapter looks at handwritten input in some detail. Starting with the basic handwritten input concepts, you'll learn how this technology works and how to get the maximum benefit from it. Along the way, you'll learn about the digital ink that seems to flow from your pen when you write on the screen, and represents a powerful new way to treat handwritten input. We'll wrap up the chapter with an overview of the vexing problem of handwriting recognition, and you'll learn some tips on how you can get the best recognition results.

Understand Handwritten Input Basics

Handwritten input is a form of *natural interface*. Natural interfaces are meant to allow users to interact with computers in ways that are natural to people, instead of in ways that are easy for the machine. Typed input is easy for a computer to understand, but relatively hard, or at least unnatural, for a human to use. Handwritten input is tough for the computer to understand, but relatively easy, or at least natural, for a human to use.

NOTE   *Speech recognition, another type of natural interface that you can use with your Tablet PC, is covered in Chapter 15.*

Many companies, including Microsoft, have been pursuing the concept of handwritten input for years. Due to the wide variety of human handwriting styles, and the surprising difficulty computers have with tasks like character recognition, success has been pretty limited, and people have resorted to various compromise measures to come up with any kind of useful handwritten input. To give you a feel for the way handwritten input has evolved over the years, this timeline shows some of the steps along the path to the Tablet PC of today:

- **1990**   Apple Computer approves the design concept for the Newton. Handwriting recognition and digital ink are two key features of the design.

- **1992**   Word gets out that Microsoft is working on the WinPad, a device with a pen interface that is to compete against the Newton.

- **1993**   Apple Computer releases the Newton. The handwriting recognition doesn't work well enough for most people.

- **1994**   Microsoft launches the WinPad, which uses Windows for Pen, Microsoft's first handwriting recognition engine. It fails in the marketplace.

- **1994**   Palm Computing announces Graffiti, a character recognition system that requires users to learn a new version of the alphabet.

- **1996**   Microsoft releases Windows CE 1.0. This operating system for handheld computers uses character recognition.

- **1996**   Palm ships first Pilot devices. These handhelds use Graffiti for character recognition, as well as an onscreen keyboard option. Despite its limitations, Graffiti is very successful with handheld users.

- **1998**   Apple Computer halts all production and support for the Newton.

- **2000**   Microsoft launches the Pocket PC. These new handheld computers also successfully use a character recognition system. A version of this system is included as an option in the Tablet PC Input Panel.

- **2001**   IBM launches the TransNote, a notebook computer that accepts handwritten input but doesn't really do much with it except record it.

- **2002**   Microsoft launches the Tablet PC, which treats ink as a data type and features full handwriting recognition.

As you can see from the timeline, the handwritten input successes to date have been *character recognition* systems. In a character recognition system, the user enters one character at a time, allowing the system to process that character before entering the next. Although this is a slow way to enter information, it has advantages. One is that the user can ensure that each character is recognized correctly before

10

entering the next. Another advantage is that character recognition systems have tricks they use to get your help in improving their recognition.

The Graffiti system used by Palm OS devices has two main tricks. First, it uses its own version of the alphabet. Creating a special version of the alphabet allows the developers to reduce the chance of confusion between characters by changing the way they are written on the screen. Figure 10-1 shows a page (http://www.palm.com/products/input/) at the Palm, Inc. web site where you can take a look at the Graffiti alphabet, and even try writing with it.

The second trick it uses is to have you enter different types of characters in different areas of the screen. Graffiti uses two areas. One is for alphabetic characters, and the other is for numeric characters and symbols. This strategy can greatly improves recognition accuracy, because it eliminates problems like

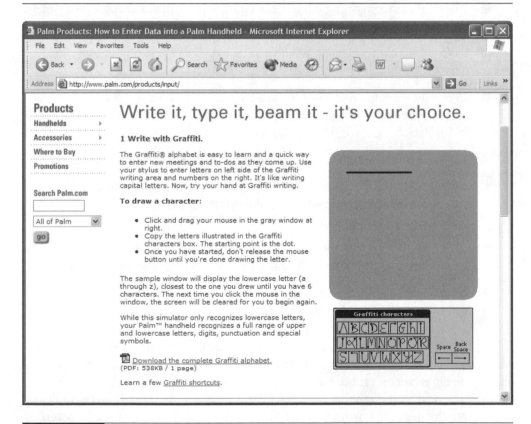

FIGURE 10-1   Making you write with a custom version of the alphabet is one way the Graffiti character recognition system from Palm, Inc. improves its accuracy.

distinguishing between the numeral 1 and the letter *l*, or between the numeral 0 and the letter *O*.

The character recognizer on your Tablet PC also uses the trick of having separate areas for different types of characters. You can see this for yourself. Give character input a try by opening the Tablet PC Input Panel and then tapping Tools | Options | Writing Tools | Show Character Recognizer On Writing Pad. This opens the Options dialog box shown in Figure 10-2 and enables the character recognizer.

You now have a choice of any of the three versions of the character recognizer (called the Pocket PC letter recognizer here) the Table PC Input Panel supports. We'll look at each of these modes in Chapter 13, so for now, just make sure the Use Pocket PC Letter Recognizer option is selected. Tap Apply, and then tap the Writing Pad tab on the Table PC Input Panel.

The Tablet PC Input Panel's Writing Pad now includes an area for entering individual characters instead of words and sentences. (See Figure 10-3.) This area

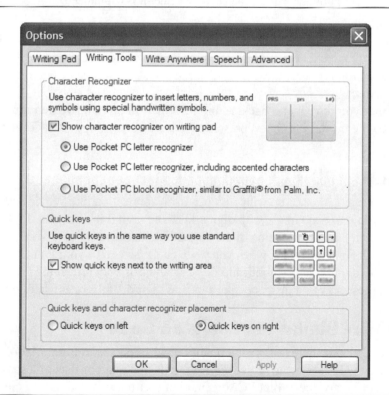

FIGURE 10-2   You can set the Tablet PC Input Panel to use a character recognizer instead of full handwriting recognition.

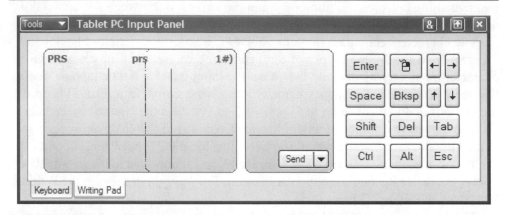

FIGURE 10-3   This Pocket PC–style character recognizer mode increases its accuracy by requiring you to enter characters into three different areas, depending on the type of character and whether it is capitalized.

is subdivided into three sections. The leftmost section (containing the text PRS) is for entering letters that should be capitalized. The center section is for entering letters that should be made lowercase. The rightmost section is for entering numerals and punctuation.

Now that you have some background information on handwritten input, let's move on to the digital ink that represents the handwritten input on a Tablet PC.

Understand Tablet PC Digital Ink

When you write on the screen with your pen in an application like Windows Journal, the marks you make are made with digital ink. The digital ink on your Tablet PC screen is a pretty good simulation of the kind of ink that comes out of your ballpoint pen. Unlike the marks you get when you write on the screen of your Palm or Pocket PC handheld, digital ink is smooth and flowing, and can even reflect the pressure with which you press down on the pen. Take a look at Figure 10-4 to see what I mean.

Learn Why Digital Ink Looks So Good

Several factors contribute to the high quality results you see in Figure 10-4. Tablet PCs use what is known as an *active digitizer*: a device that consists of a sensor array under the surface of the Tablet PC screen, along with a pen containing electronic

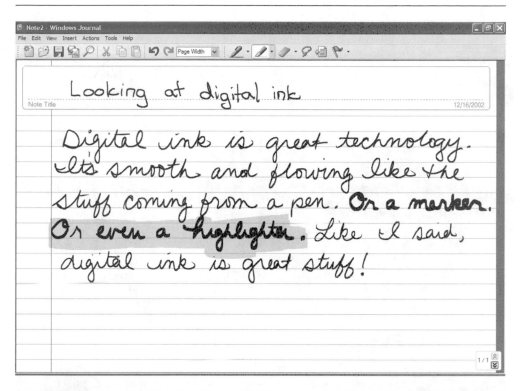

FIGURE 10-4 The experience of writing with digital ink on a Tablet PC is much closer to that of writing with pen and paper than with previous handwritten input systems.

circuitry. Figure 10-5 shows the innards of a Tablet PC using Wacom active digitizer technology (an Acer from the looks of it) with the various components broken out.

Electromagnetic signals travel between the pen and the sensor array. These signals are analyzed by the system to determine the position of the pen relative to the sensor array, including whether the pen is touching the surface of the screen. In some cases (with an appropriate pen and the right driver software), the pressure being applied to the tip of the pen is also transferred and analyzed.

NOTE *All the Tablet PCs available at this writing use active digitizers from either Wacom Technology Corp. or FinePoint Innovations Inc.*

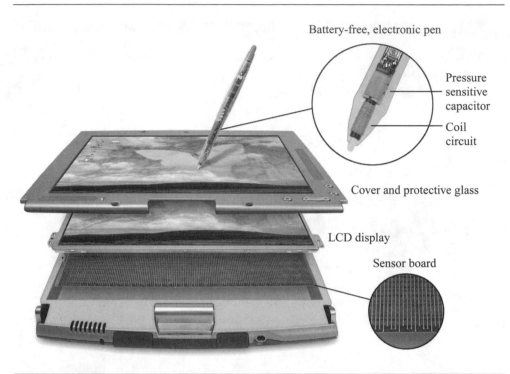

Battery-free, electronic pen

Pressure sensitive capacitor

Coil circuit

Cover and protective glass

LCD display

Sensor board

FIGURE 10-5   This figure illustrates the components of a Wacom active digitizer system for a Tablet PC. (Source: Wacom Technology Corp.)

The active digitizer systems in Tablet PCs measure the position of the pen approximately 133 times a second, with accuracies of a fraction of a millimeter and high positional resolution. The high speed and accuracy of the position and pressure sensing make for an accurate reproduction of the path of the pen across the screen.

Understand Characteristics of Digital Ink

Digital ink on the Tablet PC is treated very differently than ink is treated on most computers that accept handwritten input. Typically on other machines, what you write on the screen is stored as a bitmap, in a literal reproduction of the pattern the pen traced across the screen. When stored this way, ink takes up lots of space and is a static pattern that you can't do much with.

On the Tablet PC, ink isn't represented as a bitmap. Instead, it is treated by the Tablet PC as a data type, just as the information you type into a word processor is a data type within your computer. The information you type into your word processor

Did you know?

How Windows Represents Ink?

When you write on the Tablet PC screen, the strokes you make with the pen are called ink. But did you ever wonder how Windows sees ink? To Windows, ink is a set of equations. These equations describe the position, pressure, and other characteristics of each of your ink strokes.

consists of the characters you typed, along with various attributes related to what you typed.

For example, when I typed this chapter into Microsoft Word, the program stored not only the characters I typed, but also information about the font I used, the date and time I saved the file, where it is stored on my hard disk, and so on. Because the information I typed into Word is stored as a data type, I can manipulate it.

Similarly, whatever you ink (write on the screen) on your Tablet PC is treated as a type of data instead of a static pattern. Whatever you ink is broken down into *strokes,* where each stroke represents a single stroke of the pen across the screen. For each stroke, Windows stores information like the position, color, and pressure. Because the information for the strokes you inked is stored as a data type, your computer can manipulate it.

What does it mean to manipulate digital ink? Tablet PC applications can do all sorts of interesting things with digital ink, as shown in Figure 10-6 and described in the list that follows.

- Reformat a section of ink, changing the color and width of groups of strokes.

- Bold or italicize strokes.

- Change the size and shape of groups of strokes by stretching or shrinking them as necessary.

- Cut and paste groups of strokes.

- Undo or redo strokes.

- Erase entire words or phrases using the *Scratch-out gesture* (see "Understand Gestures" later in this chapter) instead of dragging the eraser across every bit of the word or phrase.

- Convert words or phrases to text using handwriting recognition.

10

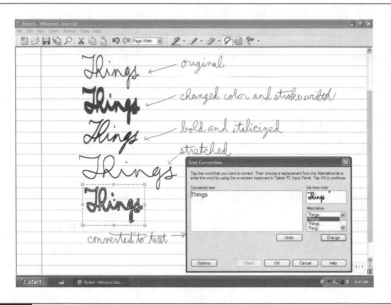

FIGURE 10-6   Treating ink as a data type offers many benefits.

As the preceding list and Figure 10-6 show, there are clear benefits to treating ink as a data type instead of as a static bitmap. And although Microsoft is emphasizing the benefits of using ink as ink, converting handwritten input to text is one of the key concerns for many people. So it's time to talk about handwriting recognition.

Some Tablet PC Pens Have Erasers?

Some Tablet PC pens include erasers. When you use one of these pens, the back end of the pen is a button that looks a little like a pencil eraser. When you press this eraser against the screen in applications that have an erase capability, it is as if you were using a pencil eraser on a piece of paper. It's quite a natural thing to do.

Not all Wacom pens have erasers. My Acer, for example, came with two pens. The main one is full-sized and has a functional eraser. The spare pen, which fits into a slot on the machine when not in use, is small and has no eraser on the end of the pen.

Understand Tablet PC Handwriting Recognition

The quality of the handwriting recognition software on the Tablet PC has been the subject of debate from the very beginning. Some commentators find it to work pretty well. Others think it stinks. Microsoft says it is the best handwriting recognition available today. I think all three are correct.

For some people (me included), the handwriting recognition software works about as well as you have a right to expect. I find that the system is over 90 percent accurate, which means that less than one word in ten is incorrectly recognized. Other people find that the system is only about 60 percent accurate, incorrectly recognizing four out of every ten words, which is pretty miserable.

I can't really tell you why there's such a discrepancy in recognition rates. It's difficult to see why the recognizer works for my handwriting and doesn't work for someone else's.

Some past handwriting recognition systems attacked this problem by making the recognition system trainable. You could write words and let the recognizer try to figure out what they were. When it got the wrong answer, you could tell it the right one, and the system would try to learn from its mistakes.

The handwriting recognition system in the Tablet PC is not trainable. It cannot learn from its mistakes and gradually become better at recognizing your handwriting. Reports that I've seen suggest this is the subject of debate within Microsoft, but at least for now, the Tablet PC handwriting recognition system is not trainable. Apparently there's some risk that attempting to train the system can reduce its recognition accuracy instead of increasing it. There are some things you can do to improve the accuracy of handwriting recognition on a Tablet PC, but training it to recognize your writing style isn't one of them.

10

> **TIP**   *See "Learn How to Get Better Handwriting Recognition" later in this chapter for some specific steps you can take.*

Now back to Microsoft's claim of providing the best handwriting recognition available. With the wide variation in recognition rates that people experience, it's hard to quantify the accuracy of Microsoft's handwriting recognition software. Clearly, Microsoft has invested a lot of time and money in developing the best handwriting recognition system they could. The Microsoft system is built on software developed by Microsoft over the last decade, combined with software licensed from outside the company.

Some people claim that a handwriting recognition system isn't usable unless it can recognize 99 percent or 99.9 percent of the words entered. Whether such high

Did you know?

It Takes a Lot of Samples to Make a Good Handwriting Recognizer?

Coming up with a good handwriting recognizer takes a lot of work. Because human handwriting varies so much, you need to analyze a lot of writing samples when you design your recognizer. Did you know that Microsoft has gathered millions of handwriting samples over the last ten years to help with their handwriting recognition? Numbers like these make it clear that handwriting recognition is hard to do.

recognition accuracy is necessary for a usable system is one question. Whether such high recognition accuracy is possible is another.

The required accuracy is probably a function of what the output of the recognizer is being used for. If the task is to recognize handwritten notes from an emergency room doctor, extremely high accuracy is a must. If the task is to recognize the handwritten text of an e-mail message to some friends, high accuracy isn't a necessity.

Also, the benefits of handwriting recognition are much greater in some parts of the world than in others. Many computer users in Asia must press several keys on the keyboard to enter a single character. People in such situations are likely to be more accepting of the quirks of handwriting recognition, and they will likely be willing to put more effort into writing neatly to gain those benefits.

Then there's the question of how accurately any system can recognize handwriting. Even humans, with our incredibly capable brains and visual systems, can't always recognize other people's handwriting. If we're honest, most of us would have to admit that we can't always recognize our own handwriting.

Humans also have an advantage over Tablet PCs in that we can use context to help us recognize handwriting. Here's an example. Look at Figure 10-7 and tell me whether the word in the center of the figure is moon or noon. There's really no way to tell, and you would have only a 50-50 chance of correctly recognizing this word.

Now imagine the word in Figure 10-7 is part of a letter written by a friend of yours. He is describing his first night using a new telescope to study the stars, and that word appears in this sentence, "The viewing was great, except that the ?oon was quite bright and drowned out the stars near it." You would have no trouble deciding whether that word was moon or noon now. We'll have to develop artificially intelligent computers and feed them with a wide range of knowledge about the world at large before they can hope to use context like this to improve their handwriting recognition accuracy.

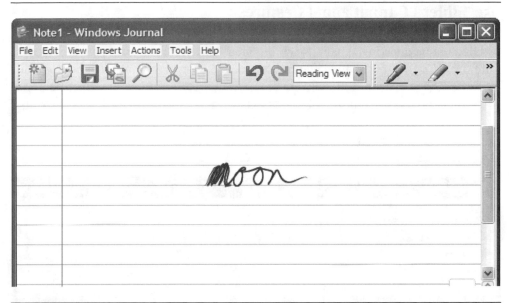

FIGURE 10-7 Recognizing handwriting is hard, and we humans take advantage of context to help us.

NOTE *The handwriting recognizer on the Tablet PC can take advantage of a form of context. Applications can be designed so they provide the recognizer with a list of acceptable words for particular situations. With that information, the recognizer can rule out words that are similar but not on the list, greatly increasing its accuracy.*

What all this boils down to is that the handwriting recognition on the Tablet PC is probably at or at least near the state of the art for the year 2002. Whether that is good enough for you depends on your personal tolerance for incorrect recognition and on what you are doing with your Tablet PC.

Understand Gestures

Gestures can be understood as handwritten shortcuts for performing certain tasks. When a gesture exists for a particular action or keystroke, it is usually faster and more convenient to use the gesture than to enter the corresponding keystroke or complete the corresponding action.

The Tablet PC Input Panel uses several gestures to speed things up during handwritten input, whereas Windows Journal and Windows itself each have a gesture representing certain activities.

Use Tablet PC Input Panel Gestures

The Tablet PC Input Panel supports the five gestures shown in Figure 10-8, all of which must be done in the panel's writing area. The first four, Backspace, Space, Enter, and Tab, represent those commonly used keystrokes, and must be done when no text is visible in the writing area. The Scratch-out gesture must be done while the text you want to scratch out is visible in the writing area. In other words,

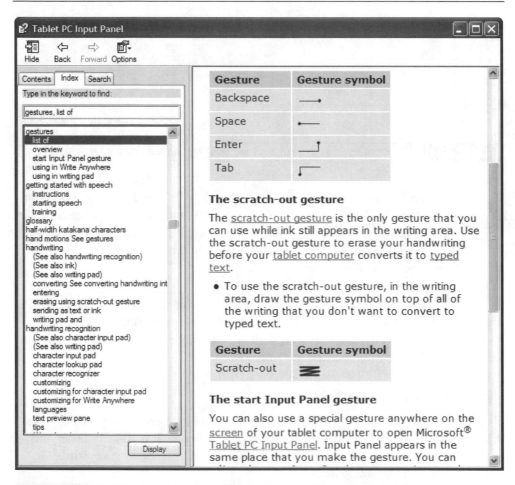

FIGURE 10-8   Help on the five gestures supported by the Tablet PC Input Panel is readily available in the application.

if you're going to scratch out some text, you need to do it quickly, before Windows converts it to text and clears the writing area.

Use Gestures in Windows Journal and Windows Itself

Windows Journal also uses the Scratch-out gesture supported by the Tablet PC Input Panel, but it works slightly differently. Because you write anywhere on the screen in Windows Journal, and whatever you write stays put (unless you move it yourself), using the Scratch-out gesture isn't a race against the handwriting recognition engine in your computer.

The Start Tablet PC Input Panel gesture is supported by Windows XP Tablet PC edition, so you can use it whenever you want, regardless of the application that's running. This gesture is useful even when the panel is already open because the panel moves to the location of the gesture, allowing you to quickly move it if the panel is covering something you want to see.

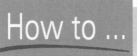 **Make the Scratch-out Gesture**

Like most tasks related to handwritten input on the Tablet PC, the Scratch-out gesture is easy to use and feels quite natural, once you have the hang of it. Here's how you do it:

1. Quickly draw a horizontal line from left to right, then back again. This line should cross the ink strokes you want to scratch out.

2. Repeat this motion at least three times until you cover the entire group of ink strokes you want to scratch out.

3. Lift the pen from the screen.

If you are working in Windows Journal and the Scratch-out gesture doesn't work, you can try again by tapping Edit | Undo Ink Stroke, and repeating it until all the scratch-out marks are gone. Then give it another shot. Make sure to cover the entire selection of strokes you want to remove, and make sure to lift the pen from the screen. With a few minutes practice, you'll be all set.

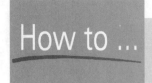 **Do the Start Tablet PC Input Panel Gesture**

Given the importance of the Tablet PC Input Panel, you should surely learn how to do this gesture. It isn't hard at all. Just follow these steps:

1. Decide where you want the Tablet PC Input Panel to appear on the screen.

2. Hold the pen in this location, with the tip near the screen (close enough to move the cursor around with it) but not touching the surface.

3. Quickly move the pen back and forth several times. A horizontal or diagonal motion seems to work best.

Customize the Start Tablet PC Input Panel Gesture

If the Start Tablet PC Input Panel gesture gives you trouble, you can customize it. You might find that the panel appears when you move your pen over the screen in the course of regular activities. Or you might find that the motions needed to make the panel appear require uncomfortably long movements of the pen. In either case, you can customize the gesture to help.

Start by tapping Start | Control Panel | Printers And Other Hardware | Tablet And Pen Settings | Pen Options. On the Pen Options tab, tap Start Input Panel Gesture in the Pen Actions list, and then tap Settings to open the Start Input Panel Gesture Settings dialog box shown in Figure 10-9.

If you are inadvertently activating the panel, drag the Gesture Setting slider toward Large to decrease the chance of accidental activation. If you find the gesture hard to perform or dislike the size of the strokes required, drag the Gesture Setting slider toward Small to decrease the amount of pen movement required.

If you really dislike the Start Tablet PC Input Panel gesture, you can clear the check box at the top of the dialog box to disable the gesture.

The Tablet PC Input Panel and Windows Journal aren't the only Tablet PC applications that support some form of gestures. Alias SketchBook, for example, uses its own form of gestures to control what it calls marking menus. Likewise, Corel Grafigo uses a combination of standard and custom gestures to do everything from scratching out text to zooming and navigating its layers of onionskins. Gestures on

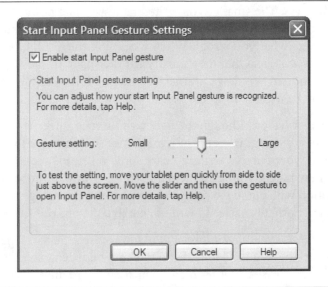

FIGURE 10-9   Adjust the size of the Start Tablet PC Input Panel gesture in this dialog box.

Tablet PC applications are likely to become as widespread and as useful as keyboard shortcuts are on regular applications.

NOTE   *You can find out more about Alias SketchBook, Corel Grafigo, marking menus, and onionskins in Chapter 12.*

Learn How to Get Better Handwriting Recognition

Although you can't train the Tablet PC handwriting recognition system to work better with your handwriting, you can change your handwriting to make the job of the recognizer easier. I'm not talking about a wholesale relearning of the way your write, like is required to use Graffiti on Palm devices. I'm talking about some simple steps you can take that will pay off in better recognition without causing you a lot of grief.

To get the best possible handwriting recognition without abandoning your own writing style, keep these tips in mind:

■ *Write neater.*   The simple act of writing neatly can greatly increase the recognition rate. If what you write on the screen is only a vague approximation of the common shapes and proportions that handwritten letters normally have, the recognizer doesn't stand much of a chance. Write neatly to be recognized.

10

- *Write larger.*   The smaller you write, the fewer data points the recognizer has available to define your strokes and the harder it is for the recognizer to recognize what you wrote. When writing in the Tablet PC Input Panel, write your words so that they mostly fill the space in the writing area. When writing in Windows Journal, let the ruled lines of the "paper" you're writing on be a guide as to the size of your writing.

- *Write in cursive.*   Although the handwriting recognizer works with printed and cursive writing, it seems to work better with cursive (script) writing. Assuming your cursive writing bears some resemblance to the proper shapes they taught you in elementary school, you will probably get better recognition with cursive writing than with printed writing. As an added bonus, it's normally faster to write in cursive than to print.

- *Make capital letters much larger than lowercase letters.*   The handwriting recognizer does a good job at distinguishing between capital and lowercase letters in most cases. But problems can arise with letters like *C*. The shape of the capital *C* is the same as that of the lowercase *c*. So when you write the word "cat," for example, there's little to help the system distinguish between a capital *C* and a lowercase *c* other than the size of the letters. So if you make it a habit to make your capital letters much larger than your lowercase letters, you should experience higher recognition accuracy, at least when it comes to capitalization.

- *Add words to the text correction dictionary.*   When you enter some handwriting in the Tablet PC Input Panel and it doesn't get recognized properly, you can correct the mistake. At the same time, you can also add the correct word to the correction dictionary. Because the recognizer is much more effective at recognizing words it knows than words it doesn't, adding the words you frequently use to the dictionary is an easy way to increase recognition accuracy. To see how you add words to the dictionary, see Chapter 11.

NOTE   *Other applications like Corel Grafigo have the same ability to add words to the dictionary for increased recognition accuracy.*

- *Practice your handwriting with the Writing Recognition Game.*   The Writing Recognition Game is designed to help you make your handwriting more legible to the character recognizer by means of a game.

Play the Writing Recognition Game

Some time after launching the Tablet PC, Microsoft released a set of Tablet PC
PowerToys: utilities that Microsoft doesn't provide support for, but that will quite
likely work for you without problems. One Power Toy worth noting in the context
of handwriting recognition is the Writing Recognition Game. This game calls for
the user to stop rain from striking the ground by writing letters that the handwriting
recognizer sees as matching those within the falling drops. Figure 10-10 shows the
Writing Recognition Game in progress.

FIGURE 10-10   Improve your computer's handwriting recognition (by improving your
writing) with the Writing Recognition Game.

The idea here is that the game, by forcing you to write letters the recognizer understands, will train you to work better with the recognizer, instead of training the recognizer to work better with you. This isn't exactly a mind-stimulating game, but if you're trying to increase handwriting recognition accuracy, spending some time playing with it can't hurt.

The biggest drawback to the Writing Recognition Game right now is that it supports only printed letters. Perhaps by the time you read this, Microsoft will have enhanced the game to include cursive characters, as well as common printed and cursive words. Even better, perhaps Microsoft will iron out the problems with training the handwriting recognition engine and come out with a trainable version.

TIP

If you decide you don't like handwriting recognition, it doesn't work for you, or you find that you just don't use it, you could consider disabling or even removing it altogether. Why? Because the handwriting recognition engine uses memory and processing power, and it occupies space on the hard disk. To do this, search for the Remove Handwriting Recognition topic in the Windows Help system (tap Start | Help And Support) and follow the directions there.

Chapter 11

Take Advantage of Accessories

How to...

- Explore the Accessories Folder
- Try the Snipping Tool

Microsoft Windows has traditionally come with a set of accessory programs—smaller utilities and tools that handle specific tasks. Windows XP Tablet PC edition is no exception. This chapter looks at those accessories, as well as the Snipping Tool, a very cool tool that fits the accessory description, even though you need to download it from the Microsoft web site.

Many of the items in the Accessories folder or its subfolders are covered elsewhere in this book. For each of the folders within the Accessories folder, I've included a small table that lists such items and where they are covered.

Explore the Accessories Folder

The Accessories folder contains utilities and other programs that are included with Windows XP and perform assorted functions. The Accessories folder itself contains some subfolders, as well as a number of stand-alone programs. The rest of this section explores those items in the Accessories folder and its subfolders that aren't already covered in detail elsewhere in the book.

The Accessibility Folder

We touched on the Accessibility folder a bit in Chapter 3, where I suggested you use the Accessibility Wizard (see the "Configure Accessibility Options" section in Chapter 3) to configure your Tablet PC for your needs. The Accessibility Wizard serves as a single interface to the individual accessibility programs contained in this folder.

> **TIP**
> *According to Microsoft, the accessories in the Accessibility folder are only meant to provide a minimum level of functionality for users needing assistive technologies. Microsoft provides links to more powerful assistive technologies on their web site at http://www.microsoft.com/enable/.*

The Accessibility accessories covered in this section are:

- Magnifier

- Narrator

- On-Screen Keyboard

- Utility Manager

Magnifier

Magnifier is a basic screen magnification utility. It zooms in on the section of the screen near the cursor and displays a magnified image of that section at the top of the screen. A small Magnifier dialog box controls the magnification level and other characteristics. Figure 11-1 shows Magnifier in action, providing 2 times magnification of a section of its own dialog box.

Narrator

Narrator is a screen reader. Narrator can read menu commands, dialog box options, and more. Like Magnifier, Narrator has a small dialog box that controls its function.

11

FIGURE 11-1   Magnifier provides basic screen magnification help for people with slight visual impairments.

On-Screen Keyboard

The On-Screen Keyboard (see Figure 11-2) is distinct from the on-screen keyboard in the Tablet PC Input Panel. The on-screen keyboard that's part of the Input Panel is the best choice for most users, since that's the one designed explicitly for the Tablet PC. The On-Screen Keyboard in the Accessibility folder is designed to provide minimal capabilities for people who are slightly mobility-impaired. Users can enter data on this keyboard using a pointing device or a joystick.

The On-Screen Keyboard provides three typing modes to support various user input abilities:

- In clicking mode, you can tap the key you want to type, or click it with a mouse.

- In scanning mode, the keyboard constantly scans across all the keys, highlighting one key after another. You can select the keys you want to type by pressing a hot key or using a switch input device.

- In hovering mode, you use the pen, mouse, or joystick to point at the key you want to type. After you hover over the key for a specified length of time, the keyboard types that key.

FIGURE 11-2   The On-Screen Keyboard in the Accessibility folder is designed to work with various assistive technologies.

Utility Manager

The Utility Manager allows you to turn the accessibility accessories (Magnifier, Narrator, and On-Screen Keyboard) on or off without having to run the Accessibility Wizard. You can also use the Utility Manager to configure each utility to start automatically under certain conditions.

 *You can start the Utility Manager by typing* WINDOWS+U *on the keyboard, or by tapping the same on the Tablet PC Input Panel keyboard.*

Figure 11-3 shows the Utility Manager dialog box. The list at the top of the dialog box shows the current state of each accessibility accessory. The Start and Stop buttons, as well as the three check boxes below them, apply to whichever of the accessories is selected in the list, meaning each accessory can be controlled independently.

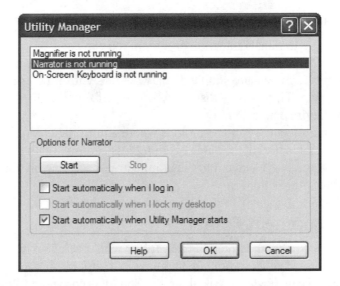

FIGURE 11-3   The Utility Manager gives you complete control over when each of the accessibility accessories runs.

The Communications Folder

The Communications folder contains accessories that are related to establishing communications between your computer and other computers. Most of the accessories in this folder are therefore discussed in Chapters 7 and 8 (as shown in the following table), where you learn to connect your Tablet PC to the Internet and to a network.

Accessory	Covered In
Network Connections	Chapter 8, Making Network Connections
Network Setup Wizard	Chapter 8, Making Network Connections
New Connection Wizard	Chapter 7, Connect to an ISP
Remote Desktop Connection	Chapter 7, Use Remote Desktop to Control Another Computer

The one program you'll find in this folder that isn't covered elsewhere in the book is HyperTerminal.

HyperTerminal

HyperTerminal is a terminal emulation program. You can use it to make your Tablet PC act like the old *dumb terminals* that were commonly connected to large computers years ago. Dumb terminals are simple display devices with little or no processing power of their own. They simply display whatever information they receive from the computer they're connected to.

Although there are still some situations where a terminal emulation program like HyperTerminal is useful, they are becoming less common with each day. If you are in such a situation, I'll leave it to the administrator responsible for your plight to provide more information.

The Entertainment Folder

While it would seem that the Entertainment folder would be chock full of cool stuff like MovieMaker and other multimedia applications, it isn't. In fact, it's normally mostly empty. We can, however, talk about the Sound Recorder and Windows Media Player.

Accessory	Covered In
Volume Control	Chapter 5, How to Mute the Sound or Change the Volume
Windows Media Player	Chapter 12, Introduction to Windows Media Player

Did you know?

The MP3 Format Is Controversial?

The MP3 digital music format has been the center of controversy for the last couple of years. Using MP3, it is possible to greatly reduce the storage space required for a copy of a song (or any sound) as compared to the way they are stored on an audio CD. In fact, by storing a song in MP3 format, you can make it small enough to make it practical to transfer over the Internet without seriously reducing the sound quality.

This has led to things like portable MP3 players as well as the ability to put your entire music collection on your Tablet PC's hard drive. It has also led to massive piracy of music, with virtually any song you might want to listen to available somewhere on the Internet in MP3 format.

And that has led the music industry into a massive legal assault on pirate music web sites. Unfortunately, the industry is also going after colleges, businesses, and any other institution where people might be sharing music in MP3 format. The industry is also pushing for tougher antipiracy laws and legally mandated changes to digital equipment to prevent users from doing things with content that the music and movie industries don't want them to. Consumer groups and the computer industry have generally lined up against these proposals, ensuring the controversy will endure for the foreseeable future.

11

Sound Recorder

The Sound Recorder is a utility that lets you record, mix, play, and edit sounds. Sound Recorder works with WAV files, a simple, uncompressed sound format understood by Windows. Most of the sounds that Windows makes are recorded as WAV files. Figure 11-4 shows the Sound Recorder in the process of playing a WAV file. Notice how the central portion of the Sound Recorder window shows the actual waveform of the sound being played.

One of the interesting things about the Sound Recorder is that you can use it to convert WAV files into many formats, including MPEG Layer 3 (more commonly known as MP3). There is a lot of controversy around the MP3 format, specifically around the way it can be used to distribute illegal copies of music. See the "Did You Know the MP3 Format Is Controversial?" box for a quick introduction to the subject.

The controls on the Sound Recorder work very much like the controls on a tape recorder: Skip to the beginning, Skip to the end, Play, Stop, and Record. The Effects

FIGURE 11-4 Use the Sound Recorder when you want to record, mix, or manipulate WAV sound files.

menu lets you do basic manipulations of the sound, like increasing and decreasing the volume or speed of playback. It's actually a fun little accessory to play with, and it should take you only a little while to master.

The System Tools Folder

This folder contains a collection of tools used primarily to maintain your Tablet PC. Almost all of them are covered elsewhere in the book, with the exception of the Character Map.

Accessory	Covered In
Disk Cleanup	Chapter 16, Free Disk Space with Disk Cleanup
Disk Defragmenter	Chapter 16, Defragment Your Hard Disk
Files and Settings Transfer Wizard	Chapter 3, Import Your Old Files and Settings
Scheduled Tasks	Chapter 16, Schedule Maintenance Tasks
System Information	Chapter 18, Investigate Problems with System Information
System Restore	Chapter 17, Use System Restore to Quickly Recover from Problems

Character Map

The Character Map is an accessory you use when creating documents. Most character sets (fonts) contain far more characters than you can enter by just tapping keys on the keyboard or by writing them in the Tablet PC Input Panel. If you need special characters that aren't part of the standard set on the keyboard (perhaps Æ, È, or ù), the Character Map can help you enter them.

When you start the Character Map, you see a window similar to the one in Figure 11-5. At the top of the window is a Font list. Open the list and select either the font that corresponds to the one you're using in your document or a font that contains the character you need. Once you select the font you will use, look for the character you need in the large list of characters that occupies most of the Character Map window.

Tap a character to see a magnified view of it. Double-tap a character to add it to the Characters To Copy text box. When you've added all the characters you want to this text box, tap Copy to save a copy of those characters for insertion into your document. Switch to your document window and paste the characters into the document.

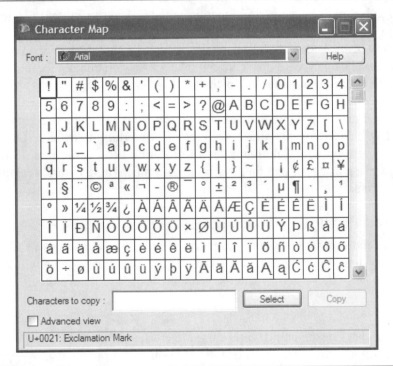

FIGURE 11-5   The Character Map helps you use the many additional characters found in most fonts.

Other Common Accessories

These programs are included in the Accessories folder but are not part of any of the subfolders. You'll find a little bit of everything here.

Accessory	Covered In
Address Book	Chapter 7, Using Outlook Express as an E-mail Client
Paint	Chapter 2, Draw Pictures on the Screen
Program Compatibility Wizard	Chapter 18, Use the Program Compatibility Wizard

Calculator

For as long as I can remember, Windows has come with a Calculator. The Windows XP version has both Standard and Scientific modes. But the Tablet PC adds a new twist to using the Calculator. You'll surely find that it's much quicker and easier to use Windows Calculator with the pen on the screen of your Tablet PC than it is to use with a mouse and a keyboard on a conventional PC. So stop hunting for that handheld calculator and use your Tablet PC instead.

To switch between Standard and Scientific, just tap View and select the mode you want. Or tap Help if you need assistance with some of the more complicated features like performing statistical calculations or working in extended precision mode. Play around with Calculator for a few minutes to get the feel of it. I think you'll agree that using the pen on the screen has a much more natural feel than using the keyboard and mouse.

Command Prompt

The Command Prompt lets you go back to the bad old days before the Windows operating system. When you run the Command Prompt, you open a window where you can run MS-DOS-based programs. With any luck, you'll never need to go here.

Notepad

Notepad is a basic text editor. It can be used to create, view, and edit text documents (documents with a .txt file extension). In addition, some people use Notepad as a simple tool for creating web pages. Notepad can actually be better for this purpose than more powerful editors such as Word or TextPad because Notepad doesn't support any special formatting characters that can cause problems in web pages.

As Figure 11-6 shows, Notepad is about as basic as you can get. About the only formatting you can do is changing the font style and size, and even that change applies

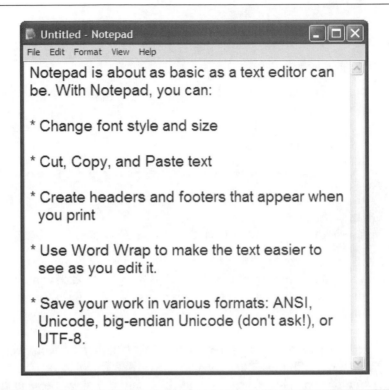

FIGURE 11-6   Consider using Notepad when all you want is a basic text document without any special formatting embedded in it.

to all the text in your document. If you decide to use Notepad to edit web pages, you'll have to format those pages the old-fashioned way: by manually entering the HTML tags.

When it comes time to save your documents, you can choose the format that's most appropriate for your project—the default choice is ANSI, the format normally used for text files in Windows.

Synchronize

One potential problem with a mobile computer like a Tablet PC is the possibility of files on the computer getting out of synchronization with files on the network. Windows has the ability to automatically synchronize *offline files* (copies of files that you can work with while disconnected from the network) with their counterparts

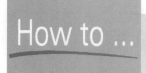 **Prepare to Use a File Offline**

First you must make sure that your computer is set up to use offline files. Here's how you do it:

1. Tap Start | My Computer.

2. In the My Computer window, tap Tools | Folder Options to open the Folder Options dialog box.

3. On the Offline Files tab, set the Enable Offline Files check box. This option isn't available if you have Fast User Switching enabled.

4. Set Synchronize All Offline Files Before Logging Off to ensure that you have the most current version of all the files you're working with offline. This option isn't available if you have Fast User Switching enabled.

See "How to Turn On Fast User Switching" in Chapter 4 if you need to disable fast user switching so that you can use offline files.

To make a file available offline, you need to share it. Follow these instructions to share a file:

1. Tap Start | My Computer (if you don't already have My Computer open).

2. Navigate to the network drive containing the file you want to be available offline. Find and select the file.

3. Tap File | Make Available Offline.

on the network. When Windows synchronizes a file, it compares the version on your computer with the version on the network and puts the most up-to-date version of the file in both places. You can synchronize individual files (including offline web pages) and entire folders.

CAUTION *You don't want to synchronize a file that could be modified by someone else while you're not connected to the network. That can lead to data loss. Imagine this situation: You make a document available offline and head out of the office for the day. While you're out, you modify your offline copy of the document. Sometime during the day, a coworker modifies the version of the file that's on the network. When you connect to the network again and synchronize the files, the copy of the file that was updated most recently gets stored in both places, and the copy that was modified first is lost, along with the changes that were made to it.*

To use a file offline, you must first set up your computer to use offline files, then make the specific files available. See the "How to Prepare to Use a File Offline" box for instructions on how to do this.

Once you have files set up to be used offline, tap Synchronize in the Accessories folder to activate the Items To Synchronize window shown in Figure 11-7. Items that are available for synchronization appear in the window's list. Set the check box next to the name of any items you want to synchronize, and clear it for items you don't want to synchronize.

Once you have selected all the items you want to synchronize, tap Setup to define when each item will be synchronized. The Synchronization Settings dialog box that appears has three tabs, allowing you to specify that a particular file will be synchronized

11

- When you log on or log off
- When your Tablet PC has been idle for a certain amount of time
- On a schedule you specify

Tour Windows XP

The name of this item gives it all away. Tour Windows XP is a guided tour to the Windows XP Professional operating system. When you select this accessory, you'll see that the tour is available in animated and nonanimated forms. The tour itself is a decent introduction to Windows XP Professional, but it doesn't address any of the Tablet PC–specific features.

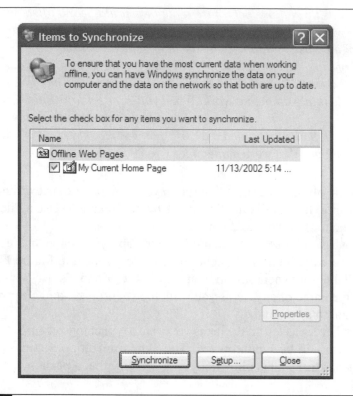

FIGURE 11-7 Use this window to determine which items your computer will synchronize for offline use.

Windows Explorer

Windows Explorer is a window that shows you the hierarchical organization of all the files and folders on all the hard drives on your computer. It also shows any network drives that appear as additional drive letters on your computer. Figure 11-8 shows a Windows Explorer view of the My Documents folder on my Tablet PC.

While you can customize the view Windows Explorer provides, the basic layout includes a hierarchical list of the information on your computer in the Folders pane, while showing the contents of the selected folder in the View pane on the right. You can view or hide what's inside folders by tapping the plus or minus sign to the left of their icons in the Folders list.

Windows Explorer works like any other Windows XP window. You have the same menu options and can use the same views as with any other folder. In fact, if you tap

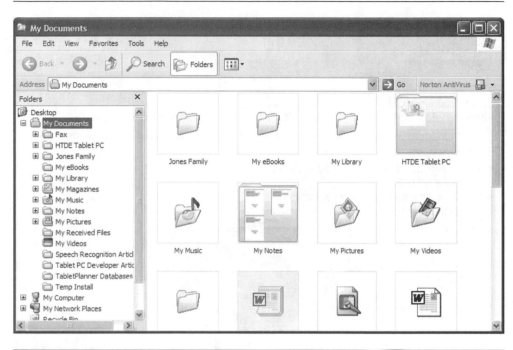

FIGURE 11-8   Windows Explorer provides a single window for viewing and manipulating the information on your computer.

Start | My Documents, you open the Windows Explorer window, just as if you tapped Windows Explorer in the Accessories folder.

WordPad

WordPad is an editor that has some additional capabilities beyond those in Notepad. While it is no replacement for Microsoft Word or any other full-blown word processor (you can't create tables, for example), WordPad can generate much more attractive and functional documents than Notepad, as you can see from Figure 11-9.

You apply many of the WordPad formatting options by selecting the text you want to format, then selecting the formatting option from the format bar. For even more formatting possibilities, tap Insert or Format on the menu bar. If you've ever used a real word processor, it should take you only a few minutes to get up to speed with WordPad. Even if you haven't, with a little experimentation (and maybe even some time delving into the help system) you'll soon be ready to create nicely formatted documents with WordPad.

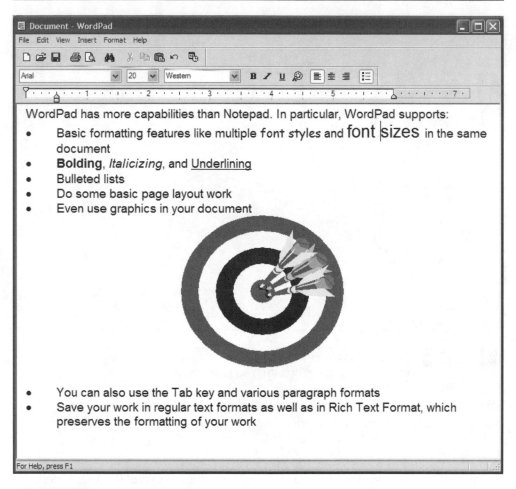

FIGURE 11-9   Use WordPad when you need to be able to format your document or
include graphics in it.

Try the Snipping Tool

The Snipping Tool is a program that should be part of the Accessories folder, but
isn't. Sometimes the easiest way to get your point across is with a picture. With your
Tablet PC, you can draw pictures and use them in documents or even e-mail them.
But what if the picture you want to use is already on your screen, perhaps on a web
page? You could use a link to the page, then describe what's relevant on that page.

Or you could use the Snipping Tool (see Figure 11-10), a free utility for any Tablet PC. The Snipping Tool lets you use your pen to capture anything on the screen, simply by circling it. In addition, the Snipping Tool lets you annotate these clips, then save them, print them, or e-mail them to someone.

Microsoft Snipping Tool for Tablet PC Preview Release (the Snipping Tool) is one of the PowerToys for the Tablet PC. PowerToys are utilities or other programs designed for a particular operating system that aren't part of the official release. Normally, PowerToys work great, but their unofficial status means that Microsoft Technical Support doesn't support them if you have problems.

Download and Install the Snipping Tool

As of the beginning of 2003, the Snipping Tool is available only as a free download from the Microsoft PowerToys for Windows XP Tablet PC Edition web page at http://www.microsoft.com/windowsxp/tabletpc/downloads/powertoys.asp. To download it, look for the file setup.exe under the heading Snipping Tool for Tablet PC. Figure 11-11 shows this page.

FIGURE 11-10   Use the Snipping Tool to grab images from the screen, annotate them, then save 'em, print 'em, or e-mail 'em.

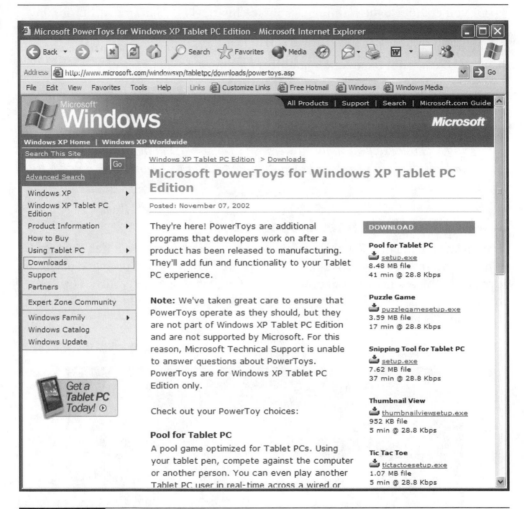

FIGURE 11-11   Download the Snipping Tool from the Microsoft PowerToys for Windows XP Tablet PC Edition web page.

Tap the filename (visible on the right side of Figure 11-11) to start the download. As usual, your best bet is to save the file to the hard disk first, then install it. Tap Save in the File Download dialog box that appears, and save the file. Tap Open when the download is complete and follow the onscreen instructions from the InstallShield Wizard that installs the Snipping Tool.

Use the Snipping Tool

To start the Snipping Tool, tap Start | All Programs | PowerToys For Tablet PC | Microsoft Snipping Tool For Tablet PC Preview Release | Microsoft Snipping Tool.

When running, the Snipping Tool appears as an icon (a pair of scissors in a circle) in the notification area.

To snip a *clip* (a section of a screen image) you tap the Snipping Tool icon in the notification area. This causes the screen to dim, and the Snipping Tools floating toolbar to appear, as shown in Figure 11-12. At this point, nothing that is dimmed can change—it all remains frozen until you snip a clip or tap the Exit icon on the Snipping Tools floating toolbar.

This is where things get cool. Say I think my buddy Joe should buy a Tablet PC, and the Get a Tablet PC Today! image in Figure 11-12 expresses my sentiments exactly. To create a clip of that image, all I need to do is circle it. When I do, the Snipping Tool figures out which part of the screen I'm interested in, and restores that part of the screen to full brightness. Figure 11-13 shows what this looks like.

If I don't like my clip (I circled too much or too little of the screen, perhaps) I can tap the New Capture button (it's a box with a check mark in it) on the toolbar. This deselects the clip I had circled and gives me another shot at it.

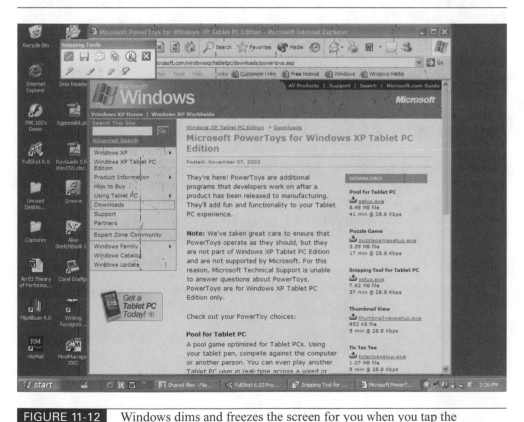

11

| **FIGURE 11-12** | Windows dims and freezes the screen for you when you tap the Snipping Tool icon in the notification area. |

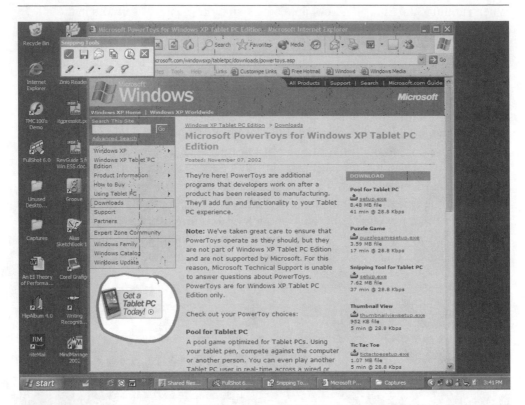

FIGURE 11-13   Circle the area of the screen you want to capture as a clip, and the Snipping Tool captures it for you.

When I do get a clip I like, I can annotate it. That is, I can write on the screen and my writing will be included in the clip. Once you circle a section of the screen, the four writing tools in the Snipping Tools menu become active so that you can annotate the clip. The tools are the Pen, Highlighter, Eraser, and Lasso. They work as follows:

- **Pen and Highlighter**   These two tools work as you would expect, allowing you to write or highlight anywhere on the screen.

- **Eraser**   This tool erases only your ink strokes, so you don't have to worry about accidentally erasing part of the clipped image if you want to erase something you wrote.

■ **Lasso**   This tool selects only your ink strokes. When you lasso some of your strokes on the screen, they're surrounded by a selection box that allows you to drag and resize what you wrote.

Once you're done annotating the clip, you have four options. You can save it as a Snip file (a file ending with a .snip file extension), e-mail it to someone, or copy it to the Windows Clipboard so that you can paste it into a document.

E-mail Clips   If you elect to e-mail a clip, the format of that clip depends on the applications installed on your computer. Assuming you have Microsoft Outlook and Word installed, the Snipping Tool opens a Word e-mail window and includes the clip as an inline image like the one shown in Figure 11-14.

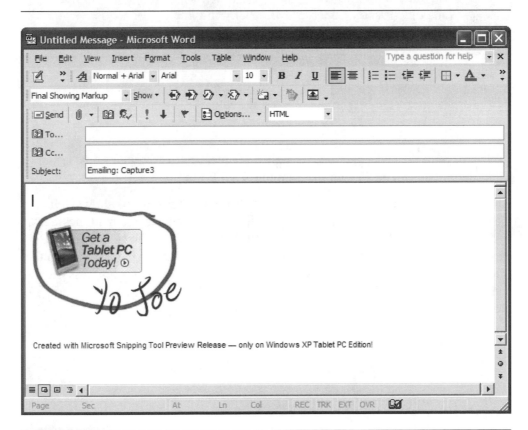

FIGURE 11-14   The Snipping Tool defaults to e-mailing clips as inline images if you have the applications to support that.

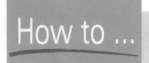

How to ... Use the Snipping Tool Tutorial

The Snipping Tool Tutorial provides helpful information on how to use both the Snipping Tool and the Snipping Tool Editor. However, this isn't the same kind of tutorial as we've seen for using the Tablet PC Input Panel or Windows Journal. This tutorial takes the form of a large topic in the Snipping Tool help system. Here are the three steps you need to take to get to the tutorial:

1. Start the Snipping Tool if it is not already running (tap Start | All Programs | PowerToys For Tablet PC | Microsoft Snipping Tool For Tablet PC Preview Release | Microsoft Snipping Tool).

2. Tap Start | All Programs | PowerToys For Tablet PC | Microsoft Snipping Tool For Tablet PC Preview Release | Microsoft Snipping Tool Help.

3. In the help Contents pane, tap Tutorial and work your way through the procedures in the Microsoft Snipping Tool Tutorial help topic.

If you want to send a clip as an e-mail attachment or to edit your clips before using them, you can do so with the Snipping Tool Editor.

Edit Clips with the Snipping Tool Editor   The Snipping Tool Editor allows you to view clips you've already captured, include clips as attachments to e-mail messages, easily make a series of clips, as well as print and save clips. We're not going to explore the capabilities of the Snipping Tool Editor here. Instead, I refer you to the Microsoft Snipping Tool tutorial, which is part of the Snipping Tool help system and covers both the Snipping Tool and the Snipping Tool Editor. See "How to Use the Snipping Tool Tutorial" for more information.

Chapter 12

Get the Most from Those Multimedia Applications

How to...

- Use Windows Media Player
- Take a Quick Look at Windows Movie Maker
- Sketch, Annotate, Draw, and Collaborate with Corel Grafigo
- Make Your Tablet PC a Digital Sketchbook with Alias SketchBook

When a computer like the Tablet PC comes along, offering significant new capabilities and backed by Microsoft, new software is sure to follow. In this chapter and the next, we'll look at some of the great programs that either ship with Windows XP Tablet PC edition, or were significantly updated to take advantage of the Tablet PC, or were written specifically for the Tablet PC.

In this chapter, we look at the two main multimedia applications that come with Windows XP: Windows Media Player and Windows Movie Maker. We also take a look at two excellent drawing programs designed specifically for the Tablet PC: Corel Grafigo and Alias SketchBook.

Use Windows Media Player

Windows Media Player is a digital audio and video player combined with an Internet radio and a media database. Add the ability to play your DVDs and CDs, plus copy tracks from CDs and burn your own CDs (if you have access to a CD-ROM burner), and you've got an all-in-one media center.

The first Tablet PCs to arrive on the market included Windows Media Player 8. Since that time, Media Player 9 has arrived on the scene with a variety of enhancements, including a docking mini-player, new playback modes, and automatic volume-leveling. Before you do anything else, I recommend you download and install Media Player 9. The next section walks you through the process.

 *I know of only one drawback to upgrading to Media Player 9. Media Player 8 users must download a Media Player 9 codec to view any videos you create with Media Player 9.*

Upgrade to Media Player 9

To upgrade to Media Player 9, go to the Windows Media 9 Series Download page at: http://www.windowsmedia.com/9series/Download/download.asp. The page will automatically detect that your Tablet PC is running Windows XP (it doesn't distinguish between the different editions of Windows XP). It then shows you a list of the programs you can download (only Windows Media Player 9 Series was available when I wrote this). Tap the Download Now! button to download Media Player 9. As usual, tap Save to save the downloaded file to your hard disk, then when the download is complete, tap Open to run the setup program.

In general, accepting the default options during setup makes sense. However, there is one place in the installation process where you might want to modify what the setup program suggests. The place I'm talking about is the Customize The Installation Options screen. If you look at the list on the File Types tab in this screen (Figure 12-1), you'll see that Windows Media Player wants to make itself the default player for 11 types of audio and video files.

Accepting these defaults is fine if you plan to let Windows Media Player play most or all of all your multimedia files. But if you already have a favorite player for certain types of files (maybe you use MusicMatch Jukebox to play MP3s, for example), you should look carefully at this list and make sure to clear the check

12

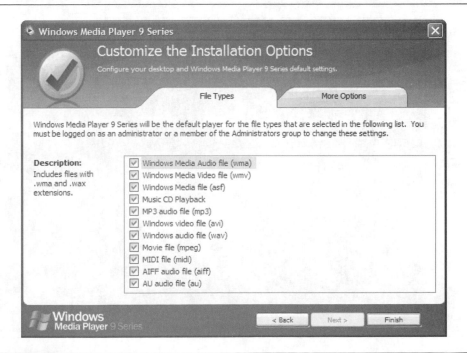

FIGURE 12-1   Use this screen in the setup process to control which types of files Media Player will be the default player for.

boxes for file types you plan to play with other players. If you don't, when you try to open those files by double-tapping them, Windows Media Player will start instead of your preferred viewer.

 *You need to be logged on to your Tablet PC using an account with Administrative rights if you want to change any of the settings in the Customize the Installation Options window.*

Start Using the Media Player

Once you complete the installation process, you're ready to start using Media Player 9. This program really can do a lot, and it gives you tons of capabilities and dozens of options. Unfortunately, this has resulted in a somewhat complicated interface, as you can see from a glance at Figure 12-2. This figure shows the Now Playing view, which is the default view for Media Player.

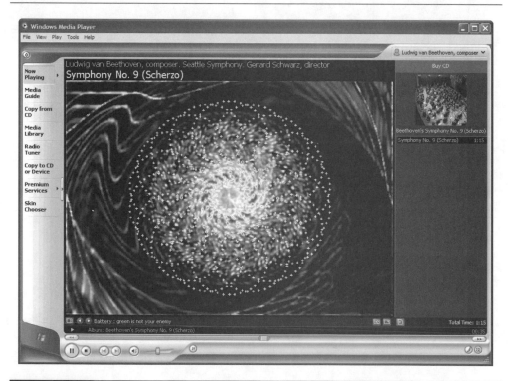

FIGURE 12-2 Media Player 9 offers lots of options and has lots of controls for managing those options.

I'm not going to give you a complete rundown of everything Media Player can do, nor am I going to attempt to describe all the controls and options. Instead, the next few pages will walk you through some of the most common things people do with Media Player. After that, you'll learn how to customize Media Player a bit, and get a list of some of the more useful tips and tricks for getting the most out of the program.

The first step is to become familiar with the main features of the user interface. Looking again at Figure 12-2, the first thing to notice is the bar running down the left side of the window. This is the Features taskbar, and you use it to open the main features of Media Player. Here's a list of the buttons found on the Features taskbar and what they do:

- **Now Playing**   This feature displays the media file that's playing right now. If the file is a video file, the video appears on the video screen, which is the area with the psychedelic pattern in Figure 12-2. If the media file is an audio file, a visualization appears on the video screen. See "Play Audio CDs" later in this chapter for more information on visualizations.

- **Media Guide**   Connects to the WindowsMedia.com web site, which provides you with an array of news, music, and video files to view or download.

- **Copy From CD**   Copies audio tracks from a CD. You can choose from a variety of file formats and bit rates.

- **Media Library**   See "Stock Your Media Library" later in this chapter for more details.

- **Radio Tuner**   Allows you to listen to Internet radio stations.

- **Copy To CD Or Device**   Copies digital audio files and other items from your Media Library to a CD, or to a device like an MP3 player.

- **Premium Services**   Displays a web site containing services you can subscribe to, for a fee.

- **Skin Chooser**   Lets you change the look of the Media Player window. See the "Learn to Skin Your Media Player" section later in this chapter for more details.

Beyond the buttons on the Features taskbar are three others that are adjacent to it. Above the Features taskbar is a button that hides or shows the Media Player

12

menu bar and the borders of the Media Player window. If it is hidden, the menu
bar reappears when you point to an area where the menu bar would normally
be visible.

Along the right edge of the Features taskbar is the Show / Hide Taskbar button.
Tap this to move the Features taskbar in and out of view.

Below the Features taskbar is a Windows logo. Tap that to open the Windows
Media 9 Series web site.

Now that you know how to navigate to the major features of Media Player, it's
time to see what Media Player can do.

Play Audio CDs

Playing an audio CD with Media Player is simplicity itself. Insert the CD into a
CD-ROM drive that's connected to your Tablet PC. If this is the first time you've
tried to play a CD on this machine, a dialog box appears, asking you what Windows
should do with this kind of disc.

To have Media Player start playing automatically when you insert an audio
CD, select Play Audio CD Using Windows Media Player, and set the Always Do
The Selected Action check box. Tap OK and your CD begins to play.

If you have an Internet connection, Media Player downloads album information from the Web and displays that as it plays the music. Depending on the information available about your CD, you may see the Info Center view (Figure 12-3) or a visualization. In Info Center view, you can get whatever information Media Player was able to find on the artist, the album, and more simply by tapping the appropriate button at the top of the video screen.

If a visualization appears, it may look something like the one in Figure 12-2, or it may look quite different. Visualizations are patterns of light and color that appear in the video screen. They change their color and shape with the beat of the music that's playing, and come in themed collections with names like Ambience, Plenoptic, and Musical Colors. For even more variety, some collections are customizable, and you can download new collections from the WindowMedia.com web site.

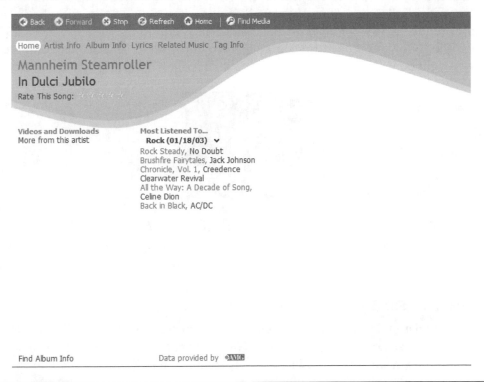

12

FIGURE 12-3   Info Center view lets you see information on the track that's playing, the CD as a whole, as well as other music of interest.

You can manually switch between Info Center view and visualizations with the Select Now Playing Options button at the bottom-left corner of the video screen. Tap the button to open a menu that includes the Visualizations and Info Center View options. Use the Info Center View option to control when the Info Center appears, and Visualizations to determine which visualizations you'll see, download new visualizations, and adjust visualization options.

 To learn how to play audio clips that are stored on your Tablet PC hard disk, read "Play Content from Your Media Library" later in this chapter.

View a Video Clip

Viewing a video clip with Media Player is also simple. The easiest way to give this a try is to tap Media Guide, which brings you to WindowsMedia.com. Here you'll find plenty of audio and video clips. Tap a video clip with the 9 Series logo and Media Player will play that video clip in the video screen for you. The following illustration shows a video clip with the 9 Series logo in the lower-right corner.

 *To learn how to play video clips that are stored on your Tablet PC hard disk, read "Play Content from Your Media Library" later in this chapter.*

Listen to an Internet Radio Station

Just as regular radio stations send out a stream of music and talk to the world, Internet radio stations do the same. Some of these are the Internet side of regular radio stations, while others are Internet-only stations. In any case, Media Player can help you find and play Internet radio stations.

To listen to an Internet radio station, tap Radio Tuner in the Features taskbar. Media Player connects to the Internet, then displays a list of featured stations similar to the one in Figure 12-4. If you see a station you would like to know more about, tap its name. While stations all do things slightly differently, you should see more information about the station, as well as a link that allows you to play the station.

NOTE *Some stations require you to go to their web sites to register before you can listen to them with Media Player.*

If you don't see a station that interests you among the featured ones, you can search for stations by genre (Top 40, Rap & Hip Hop, and so on) or with a keyword search. However you find the station you want to listen to, all you need to do is tap Play to listen.

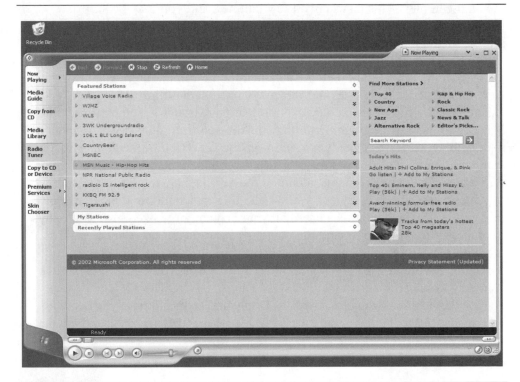

FIGURE 12-4   Use the Radio Tuner feature to find and play Internet radio stations.

Before you can go further with Media Player, you need to start adding content to the Media Library.

Stock Your Media Library

All the activities you've done so far with Media Player have used media that aren't stored on your computer. If you want to do things like listen to music (or view videos) that you previously downloaded, burn your own CDs, copy files to devices like MP3 players, or easily return to favorite Internet radio stations, you need to stock your Media Library.

The Media Library (Figure 12-5) lists all the media that Media Player knows how to play and has access to right now. These are mostly audio and video files stored on your hard disk, but can also include links to Internet radio stations.

Tap the Media Library button on the Features taskbar to start. The first time you open the Media Library, Media Player offers to search your computer for media it can play. This takes only a few minutes, and you may be surprised at all the good stuff that's already available on your Tablet PC. If you agree to the search, Media Player displays the Add To Media Library By Searching Computer dialog box in Figure 12-6.

I recommend you stick with the default option for updating media information, New Files And Existing Files In Library Without Media Information. This will ensure that any files for which media information exists have some information attached to them, without going through the time-consuming process of updating all the library files that already have information. The kind of media information that goes along with each file varies depending on the type of media, but you'll find items like the artist's name, album or movie title, and similar bits.

Once the search is complete, your Media Library should look like the one in Figure 12-5. On the left is a list of all your content, organized in various ways to make it easy for you to find the content you want to play. On the right is more-detailed information about the content you select in the left column. At the bottom of the media Player window are the controls you use for playing the content you select.

To add the tracks you copy from a CD to your Media Library, you need do nothing at all. Media Player automatically adds these tracks to the library under the My Music folder.

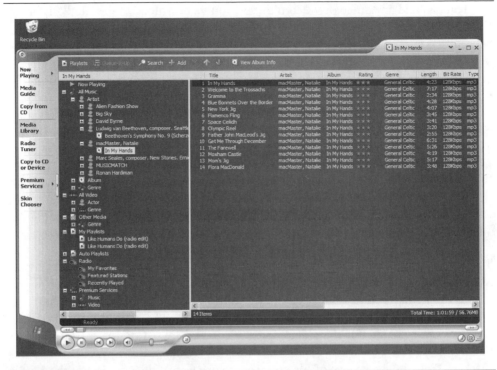

FIGURE 12-5   The Media Library is a central location for keeping track of your media files and Internet radio stations.

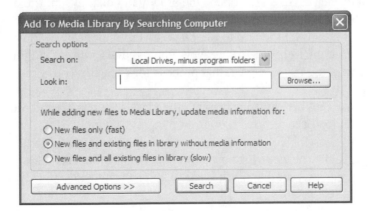

FIGURE 12-6   The options you choose here can have a great effect on the amount of time it takes to add your new media files to the Media Library.

12

You can add any audio or video files that you've download to the Media Library. Find the file on your hard disk and double-tap it. Assuming it's a type for which Media Player is the default player, Media Player starts and begins to play the file. With the file playing, tap File | Add To Media Library | Add Currently Playing Track. This will put a link to this audio or video file in the appropriate section of the library.

To add an Internet radio station to your Media Library, do this. With the station playing in Media Player, tap File | Add To Media Library | Add Currently Playing Track. This will put a link to this station in the My Favorites section of the Radio folder in your library.

With the Media Library stocked, you can play individual files or create playlists.

Play Content from Your Media Library

To play individual files, just find them in the Media Library and double-tap them. Media Player will start playing the file immediately.

To create a playlist, which is a list of multiple media files that are to be played one after another, takes a little more work. Start by tapping the Playlists button, then tap New Playlist. This opens the New Playlist dialog box shown in Figure 12-7.

Next, select the category of file you want to use to sort the contents of the Media Library by selecting that category in the View Media Library By list. Say you chose to sort by Album. The View Media Library By list now shows the names of all the albums in the library. Tap the name of the album that contains the track you want to add to the playlist. This opens the album and displays all the tracks that the Media Player holds for that album.

Find the file you want to add to the playlist. Tap it and Media Player adds it to the playlist on the right side of the New Playlist dialog box. Find the next file you want to add and tap it. Repeat this process for each file you want to add to the playlist.

You can use the three buttons beneath the playlist to change the order of the files in the playlist or to remove files from the playlist.

Once you've assembled your playlist, enter a name for it in the Playlist Name box and tap OK. The new playlist now appears in the My Playlists folder of the Media Library. You can play your playlist the same way you would play an individual file, by double-tapping it.

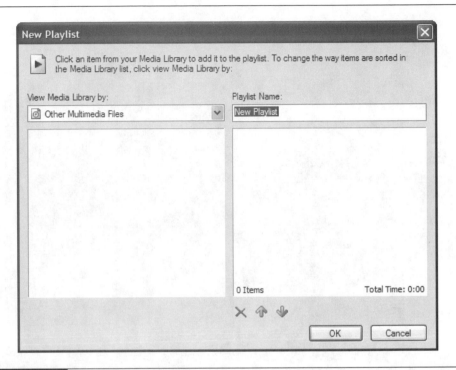

FIGURE 12-7   Use this dialog box to create and save playlists.

Learn to Skin Your Media Player

Somewhere along the line, someone decided that having your programs look the
same all the time was boring, and they decided to do something about it. That
something is called *skinning* an application. When you skin a program, you change
the appearance (the skin) of it, but not the functionality. The program works the
same but looks different, and boredom is banished. Or something like that.

Anyway, as the idea of skinning has caught on, more and more applications
have become skinnable. Media Player is one of those applications. It comes with
two dozen different skins, and you can choose to use any of them with just a few
taps of the pen. To start, all you need to do is tap Skin Chooser in the Features
taskbar. This opens the Skin Chooser feature shown in Figure 12-8. If you look
at the figure, that science-fiction-looking thing on the right is a skin for the
Media Player.

12

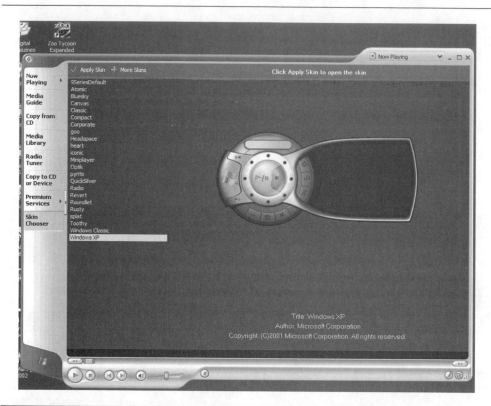

FIGURE 12-8   With the Skin Chooser feature, you can radically alter the appearance of the Media Player window.

Note that there's a list of skin names between the Feature toolbar and the window containing the Windows XP skin. You use the Skin Chooser feature by tapping the name of a skin to see what that skin looks like. When you find the one you want to use, you tap Apply Skin. Windows Media Player instantly transforms itself by using the skin you chose to determine the Media Player's appearance.

Skins are a lot of fun to use, but you do need to keep a few things in mind. It might not always be obvious where all the controls are on the new skin. Not all of the controls will appear on all the skins. It isn't intuitively obvious how you get back from the skinned form to the default form that has the full set of controls.

The key to this last concern (not knowing how to get back to the default form of Media Player) is to memorize this keyboard shortcut: CTRL+1. The CTRL+1 shortcut switches you back to the default skin. You can return to the skinned look with the CTRL+2 keyboard shortcut.

Try These Media Player 9 Tips and Tricks

Here are some tips and tricks for working with Media Player 9. Try them once you're comfortable with the basic workings of Media Player:

- Add a media file to a playlist from My Computer, the Search pane, or other folder windows. Right-tap the media file you want to add to a playlist, then in the shortcut menu that appears, tap Add To Playlist. To add multiple files, select all of them, then right-tap one of the media files and choose Add To Playlist from the shortcut menu.

- Temporarily add items to a playlist with Queue-It-Up. You can temporarily add a song, an entire album, even another playlist to the current playlist. To do it, open the Media Library and find the item you want to add to the current playlist. Right-tap the item, then on the shortcut menu that appears, tap Queue-It-Up. The item is added to the end of the playlist and remains there until you play another item or playlist.

- Use volume leveling for better playback. Volume leveling compensates for the fact that different audio CDs are recorded at different volumes. Media Player 9 computes a volume leveling value for each MP3 or WMA file you create with it. All you need to do is turn it on to get the benefits. To turn volume leveling on, tap View | Enhancements | Crossfading And Auto Volume Leveling. In the Enhancements pane, tap Turn Volume Leveling On. See "How to Add Volume Leveling Values to Files" for instructions on adding volume leveling values to MP3 and WMA files that don't have them.

- Back up your digital media licenses. Backing these up lets you recover if your licenses somehow get lost or corrupted. You can also use the copy to transfer your licenses to another computer (particularly useful if you've been using digital media for some time and want to transfer your existing library to your Tablet PC). To back up your licenses, tap Tools | License Management. In the License Management dialog box (Figure 12-9), tap Change and browse to the folder where you want to store the backup licenses, then tap Backup Now. You can recover the backup copies using this same dialog box.

- Free disk space by automatically deleting files after you copy them to a CD or other device. In the Music To Copy pane, right-tap the file you want to delete and tap Delete From Library in the shortcut menu that appears.

12

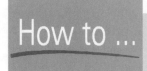 **How to ... Add Volume Leveling Values to Files**

You can get Media Player 9 to add volume leveling values to existing MP3 and WMA files by following these steps:

1. Tap File | Add To Media Library | By Searching Computer.

2. Tap Browse to specify the location of the files you want volume leveling values added to. If you want this done for all the MP3 and WMA files on your Tablet PC, select the C:\ drive as the Location.

3. Tap Advanced Options to display the Advanced Search Options check boxes.

4. Set the Add Volume Leveling Values For All Files check box.

5. Tap Search, and be prepared to wait a few minutes, as this process can take a little while.

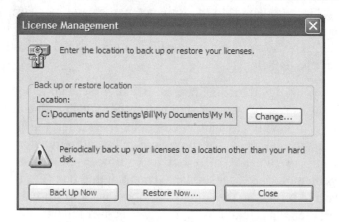

FIGURE 12-9   Backing up your digital media licenses will save you big headaches if there's ever a problem with the original copies.

■ Set Media Player 9 to automatically resize the video window to match the size of the video playing. The Corporate skin will resize the video window to match the size of the video playing, so tap Skin Chooser, then double-tap Corporate to switch to the Corporate skin.

TIP *For even more Media Player tips, check out the Tips and Tricks section of the Media Player help system. Tap Help | Help Topics | Search. Search for the word "tips," then double-tap the Tips and Tricks topic.*

Take a Quick Look at Windows Movie Maker

Windows Movie Maker is another multimedia application that comes as part of Windows XP. As the name implies, Movie Maker is a basic video editing tool. You can use it to convert your analog home videos (your VHS and VHS-C cameras create analog videos, as do various other devices) to digital format, then edit and manage them. While these are great capabilities, your Tablet PC is almost certainly a business tool, and editing home videos isn't a prime use for such a machine. In addition, Tablet PCs aren't powerful enough to give you a really good experience when working with Movie Maker 2, the current version of the program when I wrote this. So this chapter just takes a quick look at Windows Movie Maker. It simply provides an introduction to the program and helps you consider the pros and cons of upgrading to the latest version if you do want to use Movie Maker.

An Introduction to Windows Movie Maker

As stated earlier, Windows Movie Maker is a basic tool for editing and managing digital video files. With it, you can not only convert your existing analog videos into digital format, you can edit them and combine them with other digital media. These other digital media can be other video files, audio files (think of a music soundtrack or a narration of the action in the video), and still images.

To start Windows Movie Maker, tap Start | All Programs | Accessories | Windows Movie Maker. As Figure 12-10 shows, the Movie Maker window is divided into several panes.

The leftmost pane is the Collections list. Collections are groups of items that you will include in a movie. You can add existing audio clips, video clips, and still images into collections. You can also use Movie Maker to import video clips from your video camera.

12

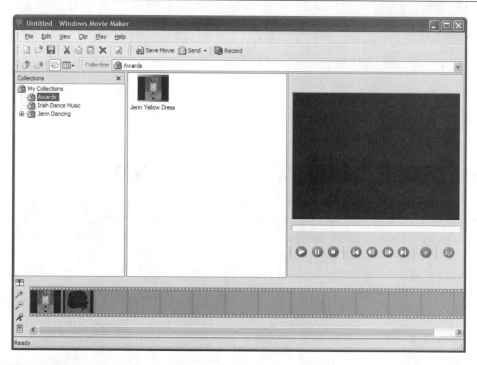

The Windows Movie Maker window has several areas and toolbars that help you do your work.

To the right of the Collections list is the Clips pane, which shows all the clips in a given collection.

On the right side of the window is the Monitor, where you can preview your movie as you work on it.

Across the bottom of the window is the Workspace. The workspace takes the form of a storyboard (the way it looks in Figure 12-10) or a timeline. You use the storyboard to arrange video clips or still images in the order they'll appear in the movie. When you select an audio clip, the workspace changes to a timeline so that you can set the starting and ending times of the audio clip in relation to the rest of the movie. You can also add audio to your movie by narrating it as you watch the action in the monitor.

You start creating a new movie by opening a new project. Then you drag items from your collections onto the storyboard or timeline to create the movie. Once you're happy with the results, you can save the movie and share it with others by e-mail.

Should You Upgrade to Movie Maker 2?

Under most circumstances, there would be no question about whether you should upgrade to Windows Movie Maker 2. Microsoft is always working to make their programs work better and include more features in each release. Here's a partial list of the improvements in Movie Maker 2:

- Support for Windows Media 9

- AutoMovie, which automatically converts your home videos and digital photos into a movie

- Nearly 30 video effects, including blurs and fades

- Dozens of video transitions, titles, and credits

- A classier, easier-to-use interface

With all the great things about Movie Maker 2, you're probably wondering why we're wasting time talking about whether you should upgrade. The somewhat surprising answer is that your Tablet PC may not be powerful enough to run Windows Movie Maker 2.

To see what I'm talking about, open your web browser and point it to this address: http://www.microsoft.com/windowsxp/moviemaker/downloads/moviemaker2.asp. This web page, part of which appears in Figure 12-11, lists the system requirements for Windows Movie Maker 2.

As Figure 12-11 shows, the minimum system requirements include a 600 MHz Pentium III processor or the equivalent, along with at least 128MB of RAM. While all the Tablet PCs that I know of can beat these minimum requirements, they don't do so by much. Add in the additional processing overhead required by the handwriting recognition engine in the Tablet PC, and you can see that running Windows Movie Maker 2 will push most Tablet PCs.

When you move on to the Recommended Computer Requirements section of the page, none of the initial generation of Tablet PCs has that kind of processing power (1.5 GHz), and few can even be upgraded to the recommended amount of RAM (512MB). You will want to take steps to free the maximum amount of RAM and processing power available when you run Movie Maker 2. See the "How to Free Resources for Movie Maker 2" box for some steps you can take.

So now you see where the problem lies, and why automatically upgrading may not be your best choice. You can resolve this problem in a few ways. If you have

12

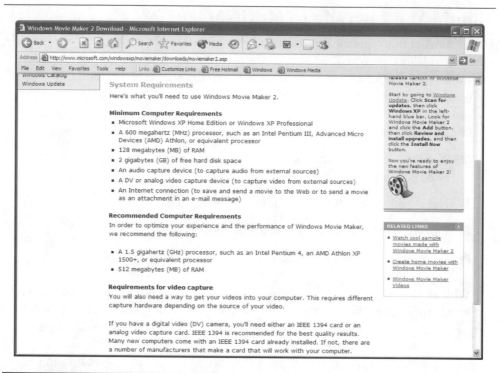

FIGURE 12-11 Windows Movie Maker 2 has steep minimum system requirements that could challenge your Tablet PC.

access to a reasonably powerful desktop computer (one that meets the recommended system requirements for Movie Maker 2), you should consider doing your video editing on that machine.

If you don't have easy access to a powerful desktop machine for video editing, but you're only going to do a limited amount of editing, I suggest you upgrade to Movie Maker 2. Why? Movie Maker 2 may run slower on your Tablet PC than you would like, but you'll have access to all the new features. And slow performance isn't as much of an issue when you're only using the program once in a while.

If you don't have easy access to a powerful desktop machine for video editing, but you plan on doing lots of video editing, you have a tough decision to make. You can:

■ Edit on your Tablet PC using the original Movie Maker and get good performance from the program while simply doing without the new features in Movie Maker 2.

How to ... Free Resources for Movie Maker 2

Since Movie Maker 2 can use all the resources your Tablet PC can give it, you should take steps to free as much of your system resources as you can when you're going to use this application. Here are some steps you can take to do this:

- Close any other applications that you can. You don't want to shut down your antivirus software, but anything else you can live without should be turned off. This isn't the time to be running Media Player or conducting chats with Windows Messenger.

- Upgrade the RAM in your Tablet PC as far as possible. All Tablet PCs come with at least 128MB of RAM. Many come with 256MB. Some Tablet PCs can be upgraded to 512MB of RAM, and one, the Compaq TC1000, can be upgraded to 768MB (although 34MB of that is reserved for the microprocessor's use).

- Disable any special display effects. In the "Configure the Windows Desktop" section of Chapter 3, we talked about various things you can do to make the screen look a little nicer. These are things like displaying web pages on your desktop, or activating ClearType to make fonts look sharper. All these things use a bit of memory and require a bit of the system's processing power. Doing without all of them will free a little more of your system's resources.

12

- Edit on your Tablet PC using Movie Maker 2, and live with whatever performance you get.

- Invest in a desktop computer that meets the recommendations for Movie Maker 2 and do your video editing on that.

- Shop for a third-party video editing program that has the capabilities you want and system requirements your Tablet PC can easily handle.

If you decide to upgrade to Movie Maker 2, start Movie Maker, then tap Help | Windows Movie Maker On The Web. This takes you to the Windows Movie Maker home page shown in Figure 12-12. Tap the Windows Movie Maker

Download link and follow the instructions to download and install Windows
Movie Maker 2.

 *Windows Movie Maker 2 appears in Windows Update. If you don't want
to upgrade to Movie Maker 2, be sure you don't accept the Movie Maker 2
updates that Windows Update offers you.*

 *You can get more help on using Windows Movie Maker and Windows
Movie Maker 2 at the Windows Movie Maker web site. Visit the Get
Started with Windows Movie Maker page at: http://www.microsoft.com/
windowsxp/moviemaker/getstarted/default.asp. You can get information
on everything from choosing a video camera to transferring video to
your camera.*

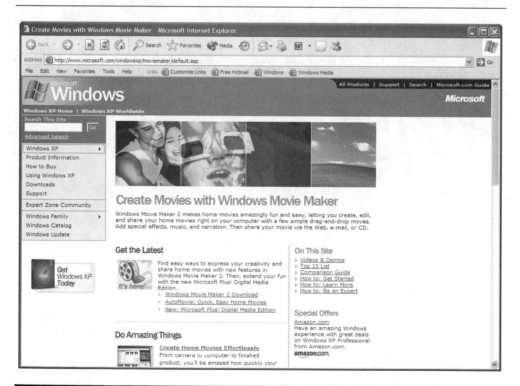

FIGURE 12-12   The Windows Movie Maker home page is a great resource for Movie
Maker users.

Sketch, Annotate, Draw, and Collaborate with Corel Grafigo

Corel Grafigo is a tool designed specifically for the Tablet PC. With it, you can create graphics, exchange ideas, and collaborate on common designs using Microsoft NetMeeting. Grafigo is a business graphics program. As you might expect from such a program, it includes multiple pens, a marker, and an eraser, along with a lasso for selecting objects and a text entry capability. And of course Grafigo supports pen pressure if your Tablet PC has a pressure-sensitive pen. There's also a library of shapes you can select and add to your drawing. Grafigo makes it easy to create drawings like the one in Figure 12-13.

But Grafigo can do a lot more than creating basic drawings. Grafigo features shape recognition, meaning it can automatically turn your sketched ovals, circles, and other shapes into perfect geometric shapes. Handwriting recognition means you can write your comments on a drawing and convert them to printed text in place.

Grafigo's onionskins simulate the practice of making comments on tracing paper laid over a drawing to provide a place to comment without harming the original drawing. When collaborating through NetMeeting, two or more people can work on the same drawing at once, with each making their comments and suggestions on their own onionskin. If the ability to create images and collaborate on the fly is important to you, Corel Grafigo is worth a look.

12

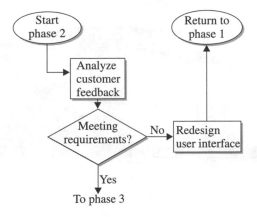

FIGURE 12-13   Corel Grafigo is a business graphics program designed specifically for the Tablet PC.

 **TIP**   *As of January 2003, Corel Grafigo was a free application you could download from the Corel web site at http://www.corel.com/grafigo/.*

Corel also makes available a viewer program (SVG Viewer) that can display Grafigo files on computers that don't have Grafigo installed. You can download it from the Grafigo web site at (http://www.corel.com/grafigo/).

Make Your Tablet PC a Digital Sketchbook with Alias SketchBook

The people at Alias|Wavefront, the publishers of Alias SketchBook Pro, describe their product as a business and personal productivity tool that turns your Tablet PC into a mobile, networked, digital sketchbook. You can use it to create wonderful sketches like Figure 12-14. (Assuming you have the talent, of course. I had to get Alias|Wavefront to send me an image that does justice to their product.)

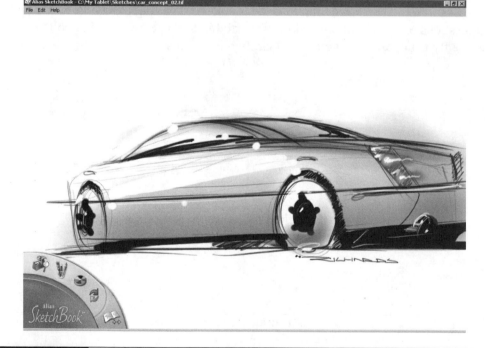

FIGURE 12-14   Alias SketchBook Pro turns your Tablet PC into a digital sketchbook with a unique, pen-oriented interface.

SketchBook Pro gives you a full range of drawing tools, including pressure-sensitive pencils, pens, markers, highlighters, brushes, and airbrushes (if you have a pressure-sensitive pen). And the interface is clearly designed specifically for pen input. Once you get the feel of it, you can change colors, select tools, and do other common actions with a quick flick of the pen.

Another feature of SketchBook Pro is its ability to display and annotate digital photos and other images saved in formats like TIF and JPG. You can use the built-in screen capture utility to grab images of anything on the screen as well. And once you have an image in SketchBook Pro, you can annotate it on the fly, with your mark-ups saved on a separate layer so that the original remains intact. If you need to be able to create sketches and work with images, SketchBook Pro may be just the program you need.

TIP *You can download a limited functionality version of Alias SketchBook Pro from the Alias|Wavefront web site at: http://www.aliaswavefront.com.*

12

Chapter 13

Use Journal and Other Cool Tablet PC Programs

How to…

- Take Advantage of Windows Journal
- Use the Tablet PC Input Panel for Pen Input
- Read Your Favorite Magazines on Your Tablet PC with Zinio Reader
- Explore the World of eBooks with the Enhanced Microsoft Reader
- Experience Mobile Collaboration with Groove
- Enhance Your Productivity with FranklinCovey TabletPlanner
- Try Your Hand at These Tablet PC Power Toys

This chapter continues our look at programs that either ship with the Tablet PC, or were significantly modified for the Tablet PC, or were written from scratch for it. In Chapter 12, we focused on multimedia applications like Windows MovieMaker and Alias SketchBook. Here we're looking at other kinds of programs, ranging from serious business applications to games.

Take Advantage of Windows Journal

We've talked a lot about aspects of Windows Journal throughout this book, starting with an introduction to the application in Chapter 2. In this chapter, we'll pull it all together with a general walkthrough of using Windows Journal, followed by some advanced features you may want to explore, and some tips on getting the most out of Journal.

Learn All the Journal Fundamentals with the Journal Tutorial

Microsoft includes an excellent Windows Journal tutorial in Windows XP Tablet PC edition. Running through this tutorial really will tell you everything you need to know to do basic work with Journal. All those Journal abilities I mentioned in Chapter 2 are covered in the tutorial, including the ability to:

- Organize and search notes
- Modify notes by adding space, even dragging text around the page
- Convert notes to text you can use in other applications
- Mark up images of documents as if they were hard copies
- Share notes with others, even if they don't use Windows Journal

To use the tutorial, tap Start | All Programs | Journal to start Windows Journal. Once Journal is running, tap Help | Journal Tutorial to open the Journal Tutorial window, which looks like Figure 13-1. I suggest you run through the tutorial in the order presented, starting with the multimedia overview: "Basic Notetaking with Journal," right through the list of more detailed topics "Viewing and Organizing Notes" to "Sharing Notes." Running through the entire tutorial and detailed topics won't take you more than 15–20 minutes, but it will teach you what you need to know to use Journal for basic note-taking.

NOTE *At the top of the Journal Tutorial window there's a link to a version of the tutorial that uses only text and images. It's a good choice if you plan to run the tutorial in a place where the sound would be a problem or if you want to proceed through the overview at your own pace.*

Once you finish the tutorial, I recommend you spend some time using Journal for regular note-taking, then check out the following advanced topics.

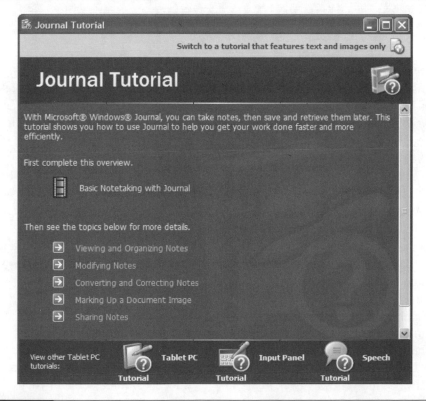

13

FIGURE 13-1   The Journal tutorial included on your Tablet PC is a great way to learn Journal basics.

Explore Some Advanced Journal Topics

If you're comfortable using Windows Journal, and ready to take the next step, here are some things you can try.

 *The Journal help system covers some additional advanced topics beyond the ones here.*

Send Content from a Note in an E-mail Message

In the tutorial, you learned how to send Journal Notes as e-mail attachments with various formats. But instead of attaching an entire Note to your message, you might only want to include some information from your Note in the message. So Journal lets you select Note content and add it to an e-mail message without having to reenter it.

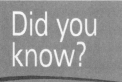

OneNote Is Coming?

As capable and useful as Windows Journal is, it does have some drawbacks. Journal most closely resembles an endless pad of paper. You can use it to take notes on anything, and save or share those notes, but in the end, what you have is the electronic equivalent of a pile of notes on your desk. If you want to find all your notes on a particular subject, you have to dig through that big pile of notes to do it. And Journal has only a clumsy ability to bring information from other sources into your notes. It's sort of like photocopying pages from a reference book, then adding them to that big pile of notes on your desk.

Microsoft is addressing those drawbacks with a new application named OneNote. If Journal is an endless pad of paper, OneNote is an endless notebook, with an unlimited number of pockets to store information, and an unlimited number of sections for organizing information. With OneNote, you can keep all your information organized by subject, project, or whatever organizational scheme you prefer.

OneNote organizes not only information you create, but also information from other applications and sources such as the Web. If you find something interesting in another document or online, you can copy and paste it right into a Quick Note (the URL of the web page information came from automatically gets added too, so you can always find your way back to the source), effectively integrating all your sources of information in one place, OneNote.

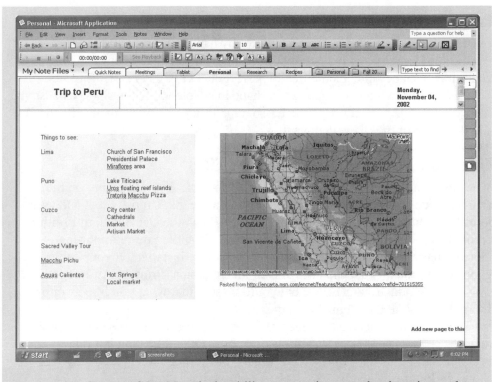

Another feature of OneNote is the ability to organize notes by dragging and dropping them into a logical document for your own use, then e-mail that document to team members, or post it on an internal web site.

When I wrote this, OneNote wasn't quite ready for a public beta test. It is expected to ship sometime around the middle of 2003. From what I've seen so far, this looks like a must-have application for every Tablet PC user.

To copy content from a Note into an e-mail message, you follow these steps:

1. Select the ink that you want to add to your e-mail message.

2. Tap Actions | Convert Selection To | E-mail to open the Convert To E-mail dialog box.

3. Correct the converted text as you would normally.

4. Tap Convert. Journal opens a new message window with the converted text included in it.

13

Create Geometric Shapes in Your Journal Notes

Even though you create your Journal Notes by hand, you can still have perfect squares, circles, ellipses, and straight lines. Journal can easily convert your rough, hand-drawn shapes into geometrically perfect ones.

If you want to include a geometric shape in a Note, draw the shape as best you can by hand. Then select it with the Lasso. Finally, tap Actions | Change Shape To | and the name of the shape you want.

Fine-Tune the Way Journal Imports Files

You can change the way Journal Note Writer formats files depending on the characteristics of the files. If you're importing a file that's mostly text and uses fonts that you have installed on your Tablet PC, then the Use Standard Printing option (the default format) is your best choice. If the file you're importing is mostly images or uses text fonts that you don't have installed on your Tablet PC, you should probably use the Print As An Image option. Print As An Image is slower and produces larger files, but you'll be sure that what you import into Journal looks like the original document.

To change the document image preferences or to change the folder that will receive the imported image, tap Tools | Options | Other, then tap the File Import Preferences button. This opens the Journal Note Writer Properties dialog box shown in Figure 13-2.

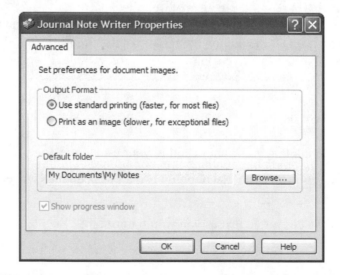

FIGURE 13-2   Use this dialog box to adjust imported image properties for the best results.

 *If you're in the process of importing a document, you can quickly get to the Journal Note Writer Properties dialog box by tapping the File Import Preferences button at the bottom of the Import dialog box.*

Apply These Tips to Work More Efficiently

Here's a list of tips that you can use with Journal to work more efficiently:

- Use the Page bar to navigate through large Notes. If you enable the Page bar (tap View | Page Bar) a segmented bar appears at the bottom of the Journal window. Each segment in this bar represents a page in the Note. If there's at least one flag on a page, its corresponding Page bar segment has an orange bar in it. Tap a page in the bar and Journal displays the equivalent Note page. The Page bar is visible only for Notes that have more than one page.

- Use the Journal Selection Shortcuts. These shortcuts allow you to select items in a Note without having to switch from the Pen or Highlighter to the Lasso. One example of a selection shortcut is to press and hold an item until the mouse icon appears (as if you were right-tapping the item). Lift the pen. The item you were holding becomes selected and a shortcut menu appears with options on what to do with the selected item. You can get a complete list of selection shortcuts in the Journal help system. Type **Selection** in the Index of the help system to find them.

- Take advantage of the Title area for naming your Notes. By default, whatever you write in the Title area of the first page of a Note is used as the filename when you save a Note. By choosing unique and descriptive titles, you can eliminate the need to come up with filenames for your Notes.

- Repair Journal if it continually crashes. Some users have reported problems with Journal crashing on startup. If this happens to you, there's reportedly a fix, although you're unlikely to find it documented anywhere. With Journal closed, tap Start | Run to open the Run dialog box. In the Open text box, type **Journal /REPAIRJOURNAL**, then tap OK. Next, close the Run dialog box and restart your Tablet PC.

Use the Tablet PC Input Panel for Pen Input

It's time to talk about the Tablet PC Input Panel (or simply the Input Panel) again. I know we've talked about it a couple of times already (in Chapters 2 and 10), but there's even more to say about it. In this section, we go into detail on how to use the Input Panel's different pen input modes and make corrections. You'll also learn to customize the Input Panel and look at tips for getting the most out of the Input Panel.

13

 *The Tablet PC Input Panel plays a major role in speech recognition and speech input on the Tablet PC. To learn more about that aspect of the Input Panel, turn to Chapter 15, "Talk To Your Tablet PC."*

But before we go any further, I would like to refer you to the well-done Input Panel tutorial that comes installed on your Tablet PC. While I've covered pieces of the Input Panel wherever they're most relevant to the content in this book, the Input Panel tutorial gives a nice top-to-bottom guide to Input Panel basics. You can view the Input Panel tutorial by opening the Input Panel, then tapping Tools | Help | Tutorial. As with the Windows Journal tutorial, you can choose between a multimedia version and one that uses only text and images.

Explore the Different Pen Input Modes

The Input Panel has five pen input modes. They're all appropriate for different circumstances, so take a few minutes to learn about each of them. I've provided short descriptions of each in the following list:

- **Writing Pad**   The Writing Pad is the one handwriting recognition mode among the five. Just write on the line in your own handwriting and let the handwriting recognition engine in your Tablet PC convert your handwriting into text. You learned about this mode in Chapter 2, under "Enter Text with the Pen." Use this mode if the Tablet PC does a good job of recognizing your handwriting and you need to enter a lot of text.

- **Pocket PC Letter Recognizer**   In this mode, which you tried in Chapter 10, you enter text by writing characters one at a time, into three different areas. One area is for capitalized letters, one for lowercase letters, and one for numbers. Use this mode when you want character-by-character control over what you enter, and you're not entering accented characters.

- **Pocket PC Letter Recognizer, Including Accented Characters**
  In this mode, you enter text as you would for the regular Pocket PC Letter Recognizer, except that you can enter the accent for any accented characters right after entering the character itself. Use this mode when you want character-by-character control over what you enter, and you will be entering accented characters or non-English characters.

- **Pocket PC Block Recognizer**   In this mode, you enter a special symbol for each character, instead of writing the character normally. Once you learn the special symbols for the characters, you may get better character recognition accuracy with this mode. Use this mode if you know the special symbols and want the most accurate character-by-character recognition you can get.

TIP *The Input Panel help system provides a guide to the symbols used with the Block Recognizer. Search for Block Recognizer Reference to see them.*

■ **Keyboard** Keyboard mode lets you enter text by tapping on a picture of a keyboard. Use this mode when none of the others is appropriate or when you need to make corrections to the output of the character recognizer or handwriting recognizer.

The Keyboard and Writing Pad modes are always available in the Input Panel. You reach them by opening Input Panel and tapping the appropriate tab. You must specifically enable the other three modes. Only one of these can be active at a time, and it shares the space allocated to the Writing Pad. To activate one of the character recognition modes, tap Tools | Options | Writing Tools. In the Writing Tools tab of the Options dialog box (shown in Figure 13-3), set the Show Character Recognizer On Writing Pad check box, then select the type of character recognizer you want to use.

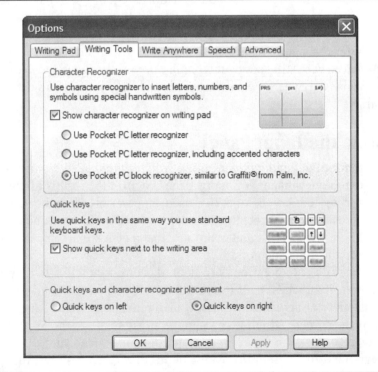

13

FIGURE 13-3 You can enable or disable the character recognizer in the Writing Tools tab of the Tablet PC Input Panel Options dialog box.

Entering text with any of these modes works the same. Tap the spot in a document where you want to enter text, then start writing in the appropriate spot of the Input Panel. The words or characters appear in the document at the spot you tapped.

Experiment with Write Anywhere

Write Anywhere is an advanced feature of the Input Panel that some people find useful, and others find rather confusing. When you activate Write Anywhere, you can write anywhere on the screen where you would normally be able to enter text with the keyboard. What you write in this area is converted to text by the handwriting recognition engine and inserted into the active document exactly as if you were writing in the Input Panel Writing Pad. The Input Panel even provides you with a nice baseline to write on when your pen gets close to the screen. So far, Write Anywhere sounds very useful, doesn't it?

Where Write Anywhere gets confusing is the fact that there may already be things on the screen below the usable writing area. Imagine that you were trying to write something on a piece of glass laid over a document or a web page. That's what it looks like when you use Write Anywhere. It looks like you're writing all over the text or pictures of your active document. The process can be very disconcerting, even though nothing bad happens to the active document.

If Write Anywhere still sounds interesting to you, I suggest you read the "About the Write Anywhere Feature" topic in the help system and then give it a try for yourself.

Customize the Input Panel

You can customize the Input Panel in several ways. One that's very useful is to enable the Text Preview pane. When this pane is active, the results of handwriting recognition appear here instead of at the insertion point in a document. This allows you to see the results and correct them before they appear in your document. To enable Text Preview, tap Tools and make sure that a check mark appears next to Text Preview in the Tools menu.

Another useful customization is to dock the Input Panel. When you dock the Input Panel, it attaches itself to the bottom of your screen and doesn't obscure your view of any applications. It also makes the Input Panel run the full width of the screen, which gives you the most space in the Writing Pad you can have. To dock the Input Panel, tap Tools and make sure that a check mark appears next to Dock in the Tools menu. Figure 13-4 shows the docked Input Panel.

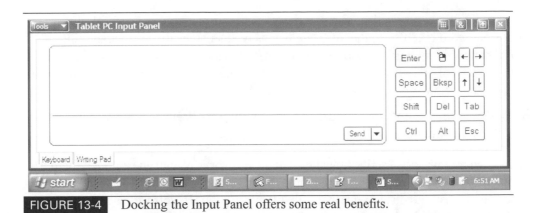

FIGURE 13-4 Docking the Input Panel offers some real benefits.

For any other Input Panel customization, you'll need to go to the Options dialog box. Tap Tools | Options, then select the appropriate tab. Here are two of the most important customizations:

- Quick Keys is a set of buttons that represents important keyboard keys such as ENTER, SPACEBAR, TAB, and the navigation arrows. From the Writing Tools tab, you can turn Quick Keys on and off, as well as control which side of the Writing Pad the keys appear on.

- Title Bar Buttons control whether certain elements of the Input Panel are visible. You can use these buttons to Hide or Show the Pen Input Area (the main window of the Tablet PC Input Panel) and pop up a small Quick Keys pad or a Symbols pad (a block of buttons representing the most commonly needed keyboard symbols). You enable or disable individual Title Bar Buttons on the Advanced tab.

TIP *If you disable Quick Keys on the Writing Tools tab, then go to the Advanced tab and set Show the Quick Keys Pad button on the title bar, you can get the benefits of ready access to the Quick Keys without taking space away from the Writing Pad.*

Make Corrections to Your Entries

As it is probably impossible to create a handwriting recognizer that's 100 percent accurate for every user, there will always be a need to correct handwriting recognizer output. The single most important way to correct recognizer mistakes is with the alternate list. This list contains alternate conversions of your handwritten (or spoken) input.

Using the alternate list, you can replace an incorrect conversion with the correct word taken from the alternate list, as well as enter the correct spelling of the handwritten word. In addition, you can add that spelling to the Input Panel's dictionary of known words, thereby increasing the likelihood that Input Panel will recognize the word correctly in the future.

NOTE   *The alternate list is available only in the Text Preview pane and in certain applications, such as Microsoft Word.*

The best way to describe how the alternate list works is with an example. I wrote a nonsense word, "umbalooie," in the Input Panel's Writing Pad. Input Panel converted it to "cembalos" and displayed it in the Text Preview pane. To correct this mistake, I tap the word "cembalos" to tell the Input Panel I want to replace it. The icon for the alternate list (a small green angular object) appears directly to the left of the word.

Hovering the pen over the alternate list icon causes a down arrow to appear. Tapping that down arrow opens the alternate list shown in Figure 13-5. The list contains a number of alternate spellings for the word, a picture of the handwritten form of the word, and the options to Delete or Rewrite/Respeak the word.

I tap Rewrite/Respeak, then use the Input Panel Keyboard to enter the correct spelling of the word. I could just make the change and move on, but imagine that I'm going to be using this nonsense word a lot and want Input Panel to recognize it in the future. In this case, I can tap the word in the Text Preview pane and open the alternate list again. But this time, instead of a list of alternate spellings, I have the options to Delete or Rewrite/Respeak the word, plus the option to Add 'umbalooie' To Dictionary. Tapping this adds my word to the Input Panel's dictionary of words it knows. The next time I write "umbalooie," Input Panel recognizes it and does the conversion correctly.

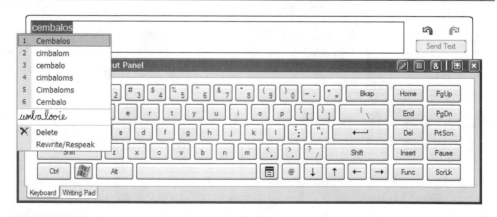

FIGURE 13-5   The alternate list helps you correct misrecognized input.

ritePen Can Enhance Handwriting Recognition?

The Input Panel isn't the only tool that lets you use handwriting to enter text into your applications. A product called ritePen, currently available as a beta product (a product that's being tested by users but is not ready for sale yet), provides full screen handwriting recognition with some significant improvements over the Input Panel.

With ritePen, you're not limited to writing on areas where you could enter text with the keyboard, as you are with Input Panel's Write Anywhere feature. Even better, ritePen can tell when you're trying to manipulate windows or use the pen to navigate instead of to write. So you don't lose the ability to use your pen like a mouse while the handwriting recognition is active.

The ritePen tool also includes a set of sensible and easy-to-learn editing gestures, so you can do basic editing operations on the fly. These gestures include one that pops up a punctuation pane with 36 common punctuation marks, and another that pops up an answer list containing alternatives for every word in the most recently recognized phrase.

For the latest information on ritePen, visit the Pen&Internet web site at http://www.penandinternet.com.

Try These Input Panel Tips

Since you're likely to be using the Input Panel a lot, it's worth the effort to find ways to become as productive as possible with it. This list contains a number of tips worth experimenting with:

- Learn and use the Start Input Panel gesture. See "How to Do the Start Tablet PC Input Panel Gesture" in Chapter 10 if you need a refresher on how to make this gesture.

- Use the correct input mode for the task at hand. The Writing Pad is the best way to enter significant amounts of text with the pen, while the Keyboard (or your favorite character recognizer) is better for entering passwords or other strings of characters that must be exactly right the first time.

- Learn and use the four editing gestures (Backspace, Space, Enter, and Tab) to save time when entering text in the Writing Pad or Write Anywhere.

- Hide the Pen Input Area when you expect to use it again. This leaves the most screen space for your application while leaving the Input Panel readily accessible.

- If you're going to be doing a lot of pen input, consider docking the Input Panel. This gives you lots of room to work and ensures that the Input Panel never covers the contents of an application.

- If your Tablet PC does a good job recognizing your handwriting, consider using the automatic text insertion option with a short time delay.

- If you frequently need to edit your recognized text, consider turning off automatic text insertion. Note that if you do turn off automatic text insertion, you'll need to use the Text Preview pane and tap the Send button in the Writing Pad to get the text into the Text Preview pane. Once there, you can edit it at your leisure, then tap Send Text to enter the edited text into your document.

Read Your Favorite Magazines on Your Tablet PC with Zinio Reader

Computers were once billed as a tool to create the paperless office. Well, as we all know, that never happened. But with a little help from Zinio Reader, the Tablet PC might be able to eliminate your need to subscribe to printed magazines.

Zinio Reader creates exact electronic reproductions of printed magazines. The Zinio version of a magazine, say *Technology Review,* contains everything that the paper version includes: front cover, back cover, advertisements, everything. You can read the Zinio version of a magazine just as you do the paper one, by turning the pages. When you're reading a Zinio magazine on your Tablet PC in the Portrait screen mode, it's almost like reading the real magazine. Figure 13-6 shows a page from a recent issue of *Technology Review* magazine, as displayed by a Tablet PC in portrait mode.

Zinio Reader lets you do more than just view the contents of a magazine. It allows you to annotate the pages of your electronic magazines. You can use the pen to highlight items, or write on the pages as you would in a printed magazine. You can even dog-ear pages (bend down the corner). And of course, you can print pages from a magazine.

But Zinio Reader doesn't just reproduce a paper magazine. It takes advantage of the fact that the magazine is a file on a computer to give you additional capabilities. The Table of Contents of a Zinio magazine is live. That is, you can tap a page number in the Table of Contents and jump directly to that page. You can also zoom in to see more details on a page, or zoom out for the big picture. If you're looking for a particular bit of information, you can search an entire magazine, or follow a hyperlink to the web.

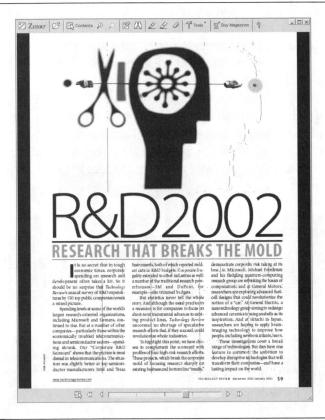

FIGURE 13-6   With a Tablet PC and Zinio Reader, you may never read a paper magazine again.

You can download a version of Zinio Reader for the Tablet PC at the Zinio web site: http://www.zinio.com. Zinio Reader is available free of charge—you just pay for the magazine subscriptions. When I wrote this chapter in January 2003, there were 28 magazines available for reading with Zinio. That number has grown rapidly since the November 7, 2002 launch of the Tablet PC, and you'll likely find a much wider selection of magazines to choose from now.

Explore the World of eBooks with the Enhanced Microsoft Reader

We took a look at the Enhanced Microsoft Reader in Chapter 2, but we stopped short of doing the configuration that needs to be done to use the program fully. We'll do that here, as well as take a look at one great source for free eBooks you can view with Reader. But first, a short recap of what you already know about this program.

What you already know is that Microsoft Reader allows you to read any of the thousands of electronic books (eBooks) that have been formatted for use with Reader. The version of Reader that has been enhanced for the Tablet PC can display eBooks in portrait mode (a much more natural way to read them) and allows you to annotate the pages of your eBooks.

Another useful feature of the Tablet PC version of Reader is the ability to pan and zoom graphics. You can use the ability to examine the details of a picture in an eBook without having to use any external applications. You can also keep the picture open in the Picture Viewer window while you read the eBook. Figure 13-7 shows a page from an eBook, viewed in portrait mode, with the Picture Viewer window open and zoomed on the image from the eBook.

Did you know?

You Can Create Your Own eBooks with Microsoft Word?

Being able to read eBooks with Microsoft Reader is pretty cool. But what if you want to create your own eBooks? Well, you can. I created the eBook shown in Figure 13-7 in less than five minutes. With Microsoft Word 2000 or later, you can download a free add-in that lets you turn Word documents into Reader files with just a few clicks. The add-in is called Read In Microsoft Reader, or RMR for short.

You can download RMR from the Microsoft Reader Download web page at: http://www.microsoft.com/reader/downloads/rmr.asp. Just tap the WordRMR.exe download link on this page, and follow the usual onscreen instructions to download and install RMR. You'll need to close Word and applications that use Word (such as Outlook) before you can complete the installation.

When you restart Word after installing RMR, you'll notice a new toolbar button. It has the Microsoft Reader logo on it, and if you hover the cursor over it, it is named Read. To convert a Word document to Reader format (a .lit file), just tap this button and answer any questions that appear. In a few minutes, your Word document is saved as an eBook.

When you use RMR to convert a Word document to an eBook, you will lose formatting that isn't Reader-compatible. But if you just want to get a basic Word document into eBook format quickly (and for free), RMR can do the job.

If you want to do a more thorough job of creating an eBook, go to this page to find complete guidelines and more tools for eBook authors: http://www.microsoft.com/reader/downloads/default.asp.

FIGURE 13-7   The Tablet PC version of Microsoft Reader supports portrait mode reading of eBooks along with a pan and zoom window for images.

Configure the Tablet PC Buttons to Work with Microsoft Reader

To use Microsoft Reader easily without a keyboard, you need to configure the hardware buttons to provide the equivalent of the PAGE UP and PAGE DOWN keys. Microsoft Reader uses the PAGE UP and PAGE DOWN keys to page forward and backward through an eBook, but by default, Tablet PC hardware buttons aren't set up to function that way.

The problem here is that there are only a very limited number of hardware buttons and button combinations that you can change. On my Acer, there are six combinations, and they're all already assigned. You'll probably have to make some tough decisions to come up with the hardware buttons to assign to the PAGE UP and PAGE DOWN keys. You do have the option to configure buttons to act in different ways depending on the screen orientation. So you could set it up so that certain buttons act like the PAGE UP and PAGE DOWN keys when the Tablet PC is in one of the portrait orientations, and keep their previously assigned actions when in other screen orientations.

13

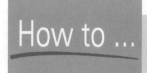 **Reconfigure a Hardware Button**

Reconfiguring hardware buttons is a multiple-step process. First you need to open the Tablet And Pen Settings dialog box to the Tablet Buttons tab. To do this, right-tap the Tablet And Pen Settings icon in the notification area, then select Properties in the shortcut menu that appears and go to the Tablet Buttons tab.

Next, you need to decide whether the change you make will apply regardless of the screen orientation, or only for a particular screen orientation. Once you've decided, follow these steps to implement the change:

1. Select the screen orientation you want your change to affect in the Button Settings For list. By default, changes apply for all screen orientations.

2. Tap the name of the button you want to configure in the list at the bottom of the dialog box. The Button Location and Detailed View images in the dialog box change to show the button or button combination that you've selected.

3. Tap Change to open the Change Tablet Button Actions dialog box. The name of the button you selected appears at the top of the dialog box, right above an Action list.

4. Find the name of the action you want the button (or button combination) to perform in the Action list. If you select Launch An Application or Press A Key Or Key Combination in this list, additional options appear in the Settings area of the dialog box. Since you're configuring the hardware buttons for Microsoft Reader, select Press A Key Or Key Combination.

5. Tap Clear in the Settings part of the dialog box, then tap once in the Keys text box to highlight the word (None).

6. Press the key you want the hardware key to act as.

7. Tap OK to return to the Tablet Buttons tab.

Repeat the process for each hardware button you want to reconfigure.

I find that having the button actions change depending on the screen orientation is too confusing, so I sacrificed the two actions I use least and replaced them with PAGE UP and PAGE DOWN, but there are lots of options and the choice is up to you.

Download Free eBooks

We haven't got to the other big task with Microsoft Reader—but there is still plenty you can do with Reader before you worry about activating the program. In particular, you can download and read thousands of free eBooks. Perhaps the best resource in the world for free eBooks is the Electronic Text Center at the University of Virginia. In addition to a collection of tens of thousands of texts and images available in SGML and XML formats that Microsoft Reader cannot read, they make available nearly 2,000 free eBooks in Microsoft Reader format. Figure 13-8 shows a page from *The Marvelous Land of Oz,* one of the eBooks available there. To peruse their eBook library, go to: http://etext.lib.virginia.edu/ebooks/.

 *Permission to print the following image was granted by the Electronic Text Center (http://etext.lib.virginia.edu) at the University of Virginia, copyright 2002 Rector and Visitors of the University of Virginia.*

So you can get lots of public domain eBooks for free. But if you want the latest and greatest, you'll usually have to pay for your eBooks. And that's where Microsoft Reader Activation comes into the picture.

13

FIGURE 13-8   This is a page from one of the nearly 2,000 eBooks available at the University of Virginia's Electronic Text Center.

The FrogPad Will Offer One-Handed Typing for Your Tablet PC?

While all this handwriting recognition and character recognition stuff sounds great, what if you just can't get the hang of writing on the screen of your Tablet PC? Are you doomed to using a boring old keyboard? Maybe not.

There may be a middle ground for you between no keyboard and a full keyboard. Mind you, I haven't used one of these myself (at least not yet), so I can't give you a first-hand report, but you may want to investigate the FrogPad Keyboard.

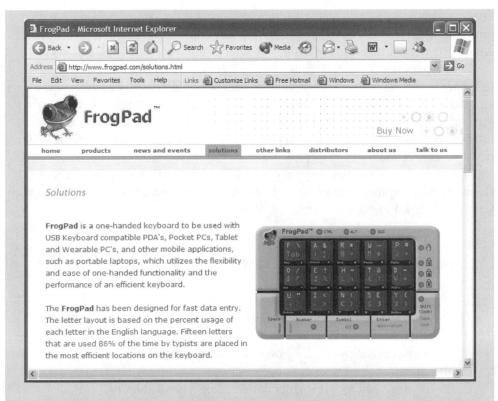

The FrogPad Keyboard is a form of one-handed keyboard. Using just 20 multipurpose keys, the device replaces a full keyboard. The design has reportedly been optimized for fast data entry by putting the 15 letters most commonly used in English words in the most efficient locations. If the FrogPad Keyboard works as advertised, it may be exactly what you need. Watch for it.

Activate Microsoft Reader and Shop for eBooks

Activation is a process where Microsoft connects your Microsoft Passport account (currently called .NET Passport account) to identifying information about your computer, then uses this information to create an Activation Certificate that's stored on your computer. Why? It's all part of a copy-protection scheme for eBooks. Many eBooks are sold with encryption and with only the owner having the right to read them. To enforce this, Microsoft forces you to read such books only on computers that are tied to your .NET Passport account. This means you can't buy or read protected eBooks without getting a .NET Passport. You can't give a protected eBook to someone else to read when you're done with it (as you might do with a printed book). You can't even read a protected eBook you own on any computer where you haven't activated Microsoft Reader with your own .NET Passport.

If you're concerned with your privacy rights, this explanation has probably set off all sorts of alarm bells in your head. Microsoft has created quite an extensive Activation FAQ (Frequently Asked Questions) page that addresses most of the questions you're likely to have about activation. I suggest you go to http://www.microsoft.com/reader/support/faq/activation.asp#1 and read the FAQ if you're concerned.

If you do decide to activate your copy of Reader, here's how you go about it. Open Internet Explorer and go to http://das.microsoft.com/activate, and log in with your .NET Passport sign-in name.

If you don't have a .NET Passport, you'll need to sign up for one (it is just called a Microsoft Passport on this page) before you can buy any protected eBooks.

The activation process is billed as a one-click process (once you have that .NET Passport), but it can take a bit more effort than that (you may need to enter your .NET Passport password, for example) and it can take a while for the process to actually finish.

Once you have Microsoft Reader activated on your Tablet PC, you're ready to go shopping for premium eBooks. There are lots of places to shop. You can visit Microsoft's own eBook catalog (at http://www.mslit.com/) to see what they're selling directly. Or you can follow the links on Microsoft's eBookstores page (http://www.microsoft.com/reader/us/shop/default.asp) to visit major eBook sellers (Figure 13-9 shows the names of some of the major book sellers who now sell eBooks). And the ePublishers page (http://www.microsoft.com/reader/us/shop/publishers.asp) on the Microsoft web site contains links to many of the top eBook publishers. And of course you can buy eBooks at Amazon.com.

Experience Mobile Collaboration with Groove

Groove Workspace (Figure 13-10) is desktop collaboration software. With Groove, multiple people can work in shared spaces, sharing files and collaborating on projects, in real time, across firewalls, with complete security.

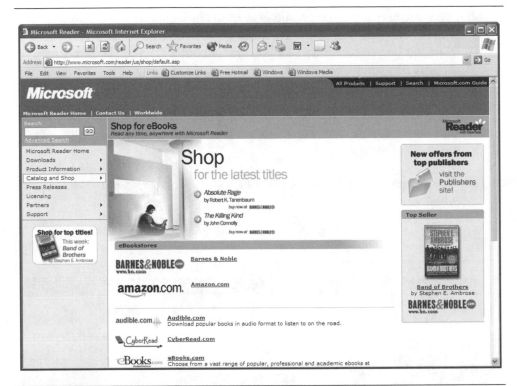

Visit this page on the Microsoft web site for links to major booksellers who sell eBooks.

While Groove has been around since well before the Tablet PC arrived (I've used the Groove Workspace on my last few book projects), it's an application that's well suited to the Tablet PC:

- Groove Workspace automatically synchronizes information in its shared spaces whenever it has an Internet connection. This is a natural fit with the Tablet PC's integrated wireless networking.

- With Groove Workspace on your Tablet PC, you can establish a direct peer-to-peer connection with another Groove Workspace user, even if you don't have regular Internet or network access.

- Ink Chat (Figure 13-10) and other Groove Workspace applications under development, support inked and spoken input.

13

■ Groove Workspace uses 192-bit encryption to secure its always-on connections with shared spaces, meaning you can be in touch with your team and your spaces wherever you are without worrying about the security of your information.

■ When you're not connected, you can continue to work with your local copies of the information in your shared spaces. When you have a connection again, Groove Workspace automatically synchronizes your changes with the other members of the shared space.

NOTE   *You can download a trial version of Groove Workspace from http//:www.groove.net.*

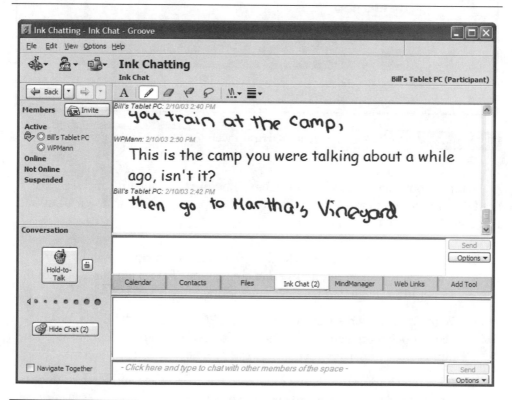

FIGURE 13-10   Groove Workspace is well suited to the mobile, collaborative nature of the Tablet PC.

Enhance Your Productivity with FranklinCovey TabletPlanner

The FranklinCovey TabletPlanner brings the famous paper-based FranklinCovey planner system to the Tablet PC. With this application, you get the layout and organization of the paper-based system, along with the benefits of digital ink and handwriting recognition.

The TabletPlanner interface appears as an opened paper planner, complete with eight tabbed sections. These tabbed sections are:

- Calendar
- Notes
- Guide
- Values
- Goals
- Finances
- Key Info
- Contacts

The Calendar section's interface gives you easy access to a Daily Task List, your Appointment Schedule, and Daily Notes (see Figure 13-11). You can write in the Daily Notes section as if you were writing on a Windows Journal page.

TabletPlanner Was Featured at the Tablet PC Launch?

The FranklinCovey TabletPlanner was one of the featured applications at the Tablet PC launch in New York City on November 11, 2002. Stephen R. Covey himself, author of *The 7 Habits of Highly Effective People,* was on hand to discuss the theme of scheduling your activities around your priorities and to explain how the Tablet PC and FranklinCovey TabletPlanner make this easier than ever.

13

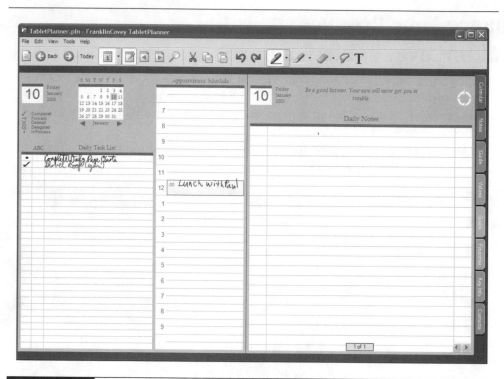

FIGURE 13-11 The Calendar view in the FranklinCovey TabletPlanner looks very much like the original paper version.

In the Daily Task List and Appointment Schedule, when you tap a spot the TabletPlanner opens a window for you to enter your information and relevant settings, such as an appointment's start and end times. Tap in the 4:00 P.M. slot and the window will considerately open with a default starting time of 4:00 P.M. and ending time of 5:00 P.M. These windows give you room to write comfortably and make it easy to enter the relevant information quickly.

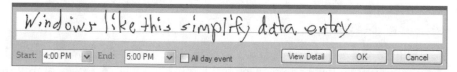

In addition to easy data entry, the TabletPlanner uses handwriting recognition and a custom set of gestures to quickly record the priority and status of tasks. The FranklinCovey system uses various marks to show the status of tasks, with alphanumeric codes to show the priority of each task. Write an alphanumeric code in the proper column, and the TabletPlanner automatically recognizes it, converts it to text, and allows you to sort incomplete tasks based on this priority code.

The task status gestures (see Figure 13-12) are a great adaptation of the Tablet PC's handwriting recognition abilities. The TabletPlanner recognizes a set of gestures that corresponds to the status of your tasks, and when you enter those gestures in the first column of the Task List, it automatically recognizes them, converts them to their text equivalents, and applies the indicated status to the task.

TabletPlanner takes advantage of the fact that the Tablet PC is always doing background handwriting recognition to convert your handwritten information to text. Why? To make it searchable. Tap the Search icon in the toolbar, then write or type your search term in the Search For box and tap Search to find the TabletPlanner information you're looking for.

Stay in Sync with Corporate Data

While easy handwritten data entry is certainly a useful feature, it's even more useful to be able to synchronize your data with your corporate information systems. TabletPlanner covers that contingency with its ability to synchronize data (contacts, calendar entries, tasks) with Microsoft Exchange.

TabletPlanner uses Exchange's Outlook Web Access connector to synchronize the data. While this requires your network administrators to run the Outlook Web Access connector and provide a connection from Exchange to the Web, it provides

Symbol	Gesture	Meaning
✓	Draw a check mark, drawing from left to right.	Task completed.
→	Draw an arrow with a straight line, and then add the tip of the arrow on the right end.	Task moved forward to the next day. Task will automatically appear on the next day's task list.
✖	Draw an X.	Task deleted.
G	Draw a G.	Task delegated.
•	Draw a circle.	Task in process. This indicates that you are working on the task. "In Process" tasks are automatically forwarded until their status is changed.

13

FIGURE 13-12   The FranklinCovey TabletPlanner's Task Status system understands and acts upon gestures that represent the status of a task.

an important benefit. Since TabletPlanner synchronizes across the Web, you can synchronize your data anywhere that your Tablet PC can get a connection to the Web. This provides far greater flexibility than any synchronization scheme involving a direct connection to your corporate network.

Tie All Your Information Together with eBinder

Another way that the TabletPlanner can simplify your life is by binding together all your information in one place. No longer does your information need to be scattered between these TabletPlanner Notes, and those Word documents, and the other Excel worksheets. The eBinder feature is able to gather copies of those documents and turn them into Notes stored on the TabletPlanner Notes tab. You can bind together pages from virtually any application that can print, rename the bound notes as appropriate, and move them to another tab to further organize them.

To get pages into eBinder, you need to run the application that created the document, then "print" the pages to something called the FranklinCovey TabletPlanner printer. The TabletPlanner installation program installs this virtual printer on your Tablet PC when you install TabletPlanner. Nothing you send to the FranklinCovey TabletPlanner printer is actually printed. Instead, it is turned into a TabletPlanner Note and stored with the rest of the TabletPlanner Notes.

To show you how this pseudo-printing works, I'll send the FranklinCovey TabletPlanner home page from the Web (located at http://www.franklincovey.com/tabletplanner/index.html) to the FranklinCovey TabletPlanner printer. I do this by opening the page in Internet Explorer, then tapping File | Print and selecting FranklinCovey TabletPlanner from the list of possible printers, then tapping Print.

I then go back to the TabletPlanner and look at the Notes section. The name of the web page now appears in the Notes section Contents list, and if I select it, a copy of the web page appears as a Note as shown in Figure 13-13.

Once you have information stored as Notes, you can easily rename the Notes (tap Edit | Rename) or drag them to a different tab to further organize your information.

View a Demo and Download a Trial Version

FranklinCovey has you covered if you're interested in learning more about TabletPlanner or perhaps want to download a 30-day trial copy. The company provides an interactive demo that you can view online or download from http://www.franklincovey.com/tabletplanner/index.html. You can also download a 30-day trial copy of the product from the same page.

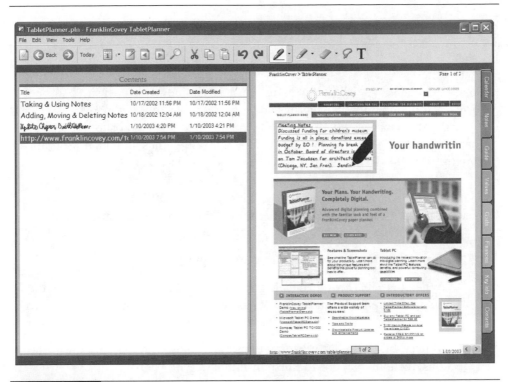

FIGURE 13-13   If you can print it from an application, you can almost certainly add it to the TabletPlanner as a Note.

NOTE

By the time you read this, Version 2.0 of TabletPlanner should be available. Among other improvements, the new version synchronizes with Microsoft Outlook, making it suitable for people who don't connect their Tablet PC to a Microsoft Exchange server.

13

Try Your Hand at These Tablet PC Power Toys

In Chapter 10, you visited the Microsoft PowerToys for Tablet PC web page to download a copy of the Writing Recognition Game. In Chapter 11, we went back to that page to grab the Snipping Tool. I'm sure you noticed that there were several other interesting-looking PowerToys to be had on that page as well. In this section, we'll look at additional PowerToys that were available when I wrote this (more may well have been added since then). If you need a refresher on how to download and install PowerToys, see "How to Download and Install PowerToys" for instructions.

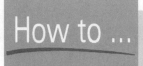 **Download and Install PowerToys**

Downloading and installing PowerToys on your Tablet PC is easy. You should, however, remember that PowerToys are not officially supported by Microsoft. If one doesn't work for you, you won't be able to get technical support on it. That said, here are the steps to download and install games and other programs from the Tablet PC PowerToys page.

1. Go to the Microsoft PowerToys for Windows XP Tablet PC Edition web page at: http://www.microsoft.com/windowsxp/tabletpc/downloads/powertoys.asp.

2. Find the setup file for the PowerToy you wish to download.

3. When the File Download dialog box appears, I recommend you save the setup program to your hard disk before running it. Tap Save, then specify the path to the folder where you want to save the setup program.

4. When you finish downloading the setup program, run it and follow the onscreen instructions to finish installing the PowerToy.

Once you install a PowerToy, you can run it from the PowerToys for Tablet PC folder. To reach this folder, tap Start | All Programs | PowerToys For Tablet PC | and the name of the PowerToy you want to run.

 Be careful when installing PowerToys. More than one of them use the same name ("Setup.exe") for their setup program. This means you can overwrite one or more of the setup programs if you try to download all the PowerToys before installing any of them. You should either store each setup program in its own folder or install your PowerToy before downloading the next.

Thumbnail View

Windows Journal uses its own new file formats, .jnt and .jtp, which most Windows applications don't recognize. Thumbnail View is a PowerToy that extends the built-in Thumbnail view within folders so that you can see thumbnail views of Journal files the same way you can see thumbnail views of images. While this isn't a major new capability, it's nice to see these Tablet PC–specific files more closely integrated into the operating system.

Thumbnail View is a great little tool, since all you need to do is install it and forget it. Figure 13-14 shows the thumbnail view of a folder containing various types of files after I installed Thumbnail View. The two files on the right, CMS Loan Agreement— Bill Mann.jnt and ToDoList.jtp, represent the two types of Journal files.

Tablet Pool

Imagine, if you will, a photorealistic game of pool where your Tablet PC pen serves as the pool cue, and you can play by yourself, against the computer or against other people locally, on a network, or connected through the Internet. Now add in all the little details like stick angle, the ability to vary the force and English you apply when you hit the ball, authentic sound effects, and of course accurate physics. You've just imagined Tablet Pool, a free pool game for Tablet PCs.

The photorealistic quality of the game's graphics makes Tablet Pool fun to look at (see Figure 13-15), while the sound effects and the variety of play options keep it interesting. You can play three different games: Casual Pool, 8-Ball, and 9-Ball, and you can set the conditions for winning as you see fit.

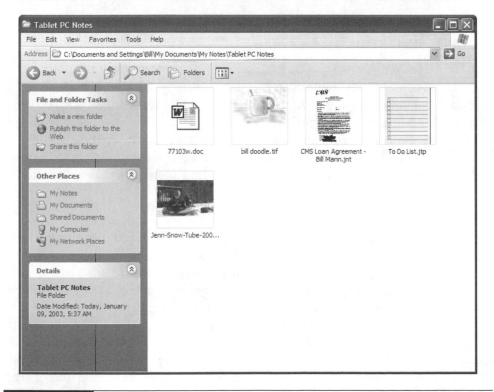

FIGURE 13-14 Thumbnail View extends the Thumbnail view in folders to show Windows Journal files.

13

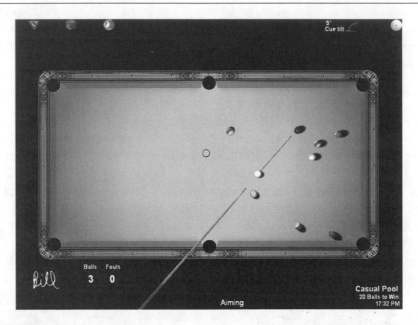

FIGURE 13-15   Tablet Pool turns your Tablet pen into a cue in a photorealistic game of pool.

When it comes to opponents, you have lots of variety. You can choose between computer-controlled players with skills ranging from Novice to Guru. Or you can play another human for a real challenge.

While this game is well done, I did find the interface a little confusing. It may take you some time to figure out the interface and develop the skills needed to play well, but if you're interested in pool, you should find Tablet Pool worth the effort.

Puzzle Game

Puzzle Game is a simple game where the objective is to attach all the puzzle pieces together to solve the puzzle as quickly as possible. Each puzzle consists of a photographic image broken into anywhere from 4 to 49 pieces. To assemble the puzzle, you need to move pieces and rotate them so that they are in the correct position and orientation relative to the other puzzle pieces. If you've ever done a jigsaw puzzle, consider this a jigsaw puzzle on your Tablet PC.

Puzzle Game comes with five images that you can use as puzzles, each of which can be chopped up into varying numbers of parts depending on the difficulty level you choose. Figure 13-16 shows Puzzle Game with one of the included puzzle images. The figure also shows one of the optional components of Puzzle Game—the Key. You can have the Key visible to help you work on the puzzle, or you can hide the Key to make things that much tougher for yourself.

You move pieces by tapping and holding in the center of a piece, then dragging it to its new location. To rotate a piece, you drag one of the edges. This takes a bit of getting used to but allows you to do everything you need to do in the game with only the pen.

One feature of Puzzle Game that's particularly nice is the ability to use your own images in the puzzle. The game is limited as to the file types it can display (.bmp, .jpg, .gif, and .png are the only image formats supported right now), but it sure is fun and easy to turn one of your own pictures into a puzzle—Figure 13-17 shows one created from a .jpg photo of my daughter. Just tap Game | Select Picture, and use the Open dialog box to find and select the picture you want to use. That's all it takes.

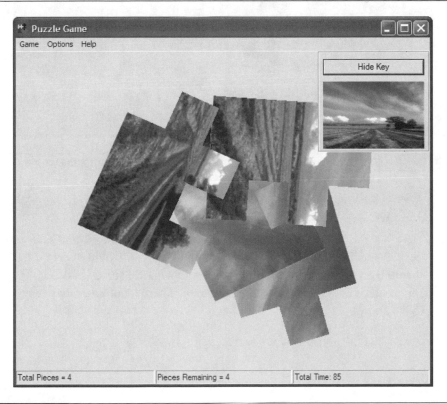

FIGURE 13-16 Puzzle Game makes jigsaw puzzles on your Tablet PC.

13

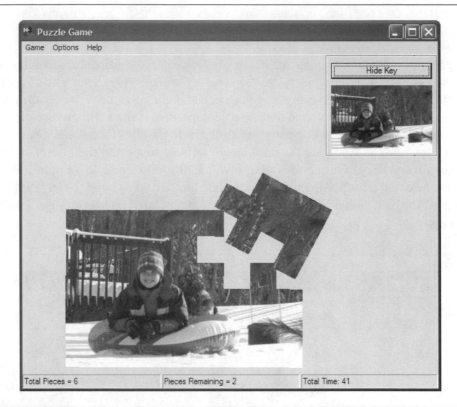

FIGURE 13-17   Puzzle Game can make puzzles out of your own pictures too.

Tic Tac Toe

Do you play Tic Tac Toe? If so, now you can play on the Tablet PC and save some paper. The Tic Tac Toe PowerToy works about the way you would expect it to. You play against the computer, and write your X's or O's on the screen instead of typing them. Your goal, of course, is to get three in a row. There's nothing fancy here, as Figure 13-18 shows.

FIGURE 13-18   Play Tic Tac Toe against your Tablet PC with this computerized version of the classic game.

Okay, there is one thing fancy here. If you make a mistake while writing X or O in a spot, you can resolve it by tapping the Clear button, which appears in the square while you're making your move. Handwriting recognition, a Clear button to fix mistakes, and an always-ready computer opponent could make this the ultimate Tic Tac Toe game.

Chapter 14

Extend Office XP with the Tablet Pack

How to...

- Download and Install the Office XP Pack for Tablet PC

- Use Handwriting in Word Documents

- Use Handwriting in Excel Spreadsheets

- Use Handwriting in PowerPoint

- Take Advantage of the Tablet Pack Extension for Windows Journal

Since Office XP (also called Office 2002) came into existence long before Windows XP Tablet PC edition was ready, Office XP didn't ship with built-in support for the Tablet PC's unique features and capabilities. To address this

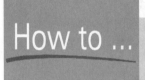 ## View the Tablet Pack Demo

You can follow these simple steps to view the Tablet Pack demo on the Microsoft Web site:

1. Go to the Office XP and Tablet PC Web page. To do so, open Internet Explorer and go to this address: http://www.microsoft.com/office/tabletpc/.

2. Tap the See a Tablet Pack demo link found somewhere on this page. At this writing, the link is in a box on the right side of the page, but this location is subject to change.

See a Tablet Pack Demo
Watch how Tablet Pack can enhance how you use Office XP programs on Tablet PCs.

problem, Microsoft released the Office XP Pack for Tablet PC (the Tablet Pack), a free download that provides some basic ink capabilities to Word XP, Excel XP, and PowerPoint XP. In addition to enhancing these Microsoft Office staples, the Tablet Pack extends Windows Journal to allow you to use Journal notes in Outlook XP and import Outlook XP meeting information into your Journal notes.

This chapter shows you how to download and install the Tablet Pack, and examines the way the Tablet Pack enhances Microsoft Office (and Windows Journal) on the Tablet PC.

NOTE   *To take advantage of the Tablet Pack, you must have one or more of the relevant Office XP applications (Word, Excel, PowerPoint, or Outlook) installed on your Tablet PC.*

If you would like to see a nice demonstration of the Tablet Pack and its effects on Office XP on the Tablet PC, try the online demo Microsoft provides. The "How to View the Tablet Pack Demo" box shows you how to get there.

Download and Install
the Office XP Pack for Tablet PC

Right now, the Office XP Pack for Tablet PC is available only as a download, although its capabilities will be integrated into future versions of Microsoft Office. The file you need to download is over a megabyte in size, and according to Microsoft it will take about eight minutes to download with a slow modem, so this shouldn't be a real burden for you.

Before you begin downloading the Tablet Pack, you should be sure that Office XP Service Pack 2 (SP2) or higher is installed. If you're not sure of this, open one of your Office XP applications, then tap Help | About. At the top of the About box, you'll see the name of the application, along with a string of digits representing the release number. Following this number you will find the number of the most recently installed service pack, as shown in Figure 14-1.

If you don't have Service Pack 2 or higher installed, please do that before continuing.

CAUTION   *You may need to upgrade your antivirus software after you install Service Pack 2. Check your antivirus software maker's web site for details.*

14

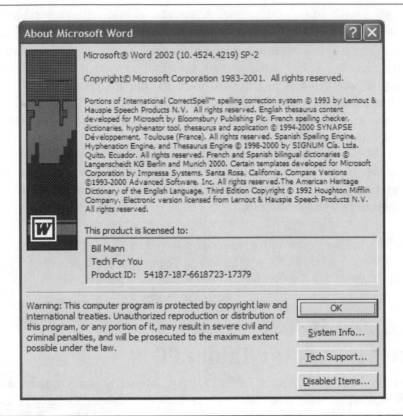

FIGURE 14-1   Look in this dialog box to see that Service Pack 2 (SP-2) or higher is installed before downloading and installing the Tablet Pack.

Once you're sure you have Service Pack 2 or higher installed, you should close any open Office XP program (Word, Excel, PowerPoint, or Outlook) as well as Windows Journal. When these are all closed, you're ready to begin.

1. Using Internet Explorer, go to the Office Pack section of the Microsoft Office Download Center by browsing to this address: http://office.microsoft .com/downloads/2002/oxptp.aspx. This opens the Tablet Pack download page shown in Figure 14-2.

2. Tap the Download Now button to download opsetup.exe, the Tablet Pack setup program.

3. Internet Explorer may pop up a dialog box warning you that this file could be dangerous. Ignore this warning and tap Save to download opsetup.exe to your hard disk. In the Save As dialog box that appears, specify the folder you want the download stored in, then tap Save to begin downloading.

TIP *It can be helpful to create a folder where you can store downloaded programs like this one whenever you download them. I use a folder named Temp Install as the destination for all my downloads. That makes it easy to find the file if I need it again.*

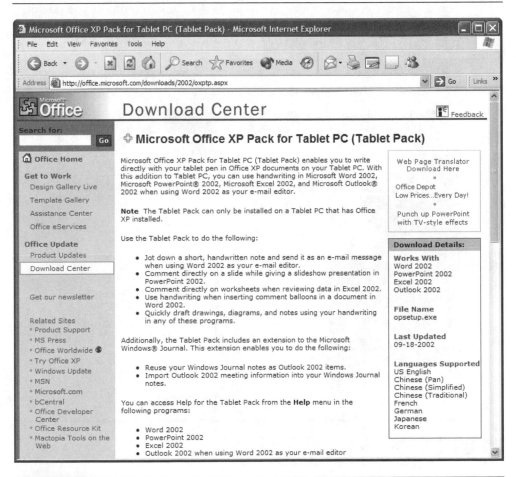

FIGURE 14-2 You get your free copy of the Tablet Pack from the Microsoft Office Download Center on the Web.

Installing the Tablet Pack is also easy. Here are the steps you follow:

1. Once Internet Explorer finishes downloading opsetup.exe, it should give you the option to Open the downloaded file, which starts the installation process. If Internet Explorer does not give you the option to open the file, go to the folder where you stored it and double-tap the opsetup.exe icon to start the installation.

2. Follow the onscreen instructions provided by the Installation Wizard.

3. When you reach the final screen of the Installation Wizard (see Figure 14-3), you'll find a check box named Start The Tablet Pack Tutorial. If you do not clear that check box, the Installation Wizard launches Internet Explorer and runs the Tablet Pack Demo described at the beginning of this chapter.

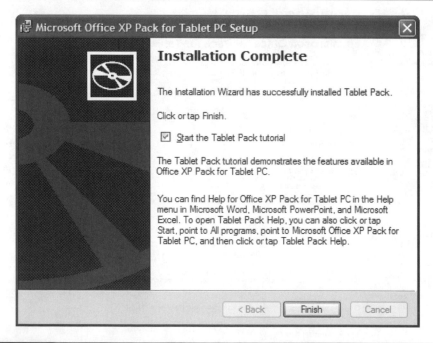

FIGURE 14-3 Clear the Start The Tablet Pack Tutorial check box if you don't want to see the Tablet Pack Demo on Microsoft's Web site.

Uninstall the Tablet Pack

While the Office Pack shouldn't give you any real problems, it does have at least one annoying quirk, and there's always the chance that you'll want or need to uninstall it. If so, you can do so using Add Or Remove Programs. Tap Start | Control Panel | Add Or Remove Programs. In the Currently Installed Programs list, select Microsoft Office XP Pack For Tablet PC. Tap the Remove button, then follow the onscreen instructions to uninstall the Office Pack.

Repair Your Tablet Pack Installation

If something happens to corrupt or otherwise damage your installation of the Tablet Pack, you can follow the original installation process to repair the problem. When you run opsctup.exe with the Tablet Pack already installed, the Installation Wizard presents you with a Repair button instead of an Install button. Tap the Repair button to complete the repair.

Use Handwriting in Word Documents

One of the disadvantages of creating documents (like this book) electronically is that you can't write on them. This can be a particular headache when reviewing documents, as you sometimes would like to just whip out your trusty red pen and scribble a note on a page. With the Office Pack, you can go one better than that. You can insert handwritten notes into a Word document instead of writing them on the document. What's the difference? There are some big differences:

- Handwritten (inked) notes inserted into a document become part of the document instead of something written on a hard copy of the document. If you e-mail me a document to edit, I can add my comments to it and e-mail it back, with comments included.

- Notes added to a document are editable, instead of unchanging red marks on a piece of paper.

- An inked note added to a document can be deleted with a few taps of the pen.

The Office Pack allows you to add handwritten notes to documents in two ways. You can add inked content to the body of a document with the Ink Drawing And Writing Area command. You can insert comments with the Ink Comment command.

14

Add Handwritten Content in an Ink Drawing and Writing Area

When you use the Ink Drawing And Writing Area command to add handwriting to a document, it works very similar to inserting a graphic in a document. A movable and resizable box appears at the entry point (the point where you placed the cursor in the document). Within this box, you can draw or write using the pen as shown in Figure 14-4.

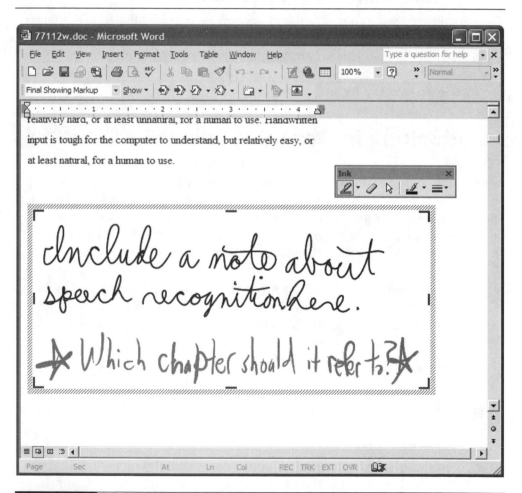

FIGURE 14-4 Insert handwritten content in the body of a Word document with the Ink Drawing And Writing Area command.

NOTE   *If you are using Word in Normal view and you insert an Ink Drawing and Writing area, Word switches to Web Layout view so it can display the change. If Word is in Print Layout view when you insert an Ink Drawing and Writing area, it remains in Print Layout view.*

When the Ink Drawing And Writing Area is selected, Word also displays the small Ink toolbar visible in Figure 14-4. This toolbar gives you control over the basic characteristics of the ink within the area. Working from left to right, you can choose the pen you use to write, erase ink within the area, select ink with the Selection tool, change the ink color, and change the ink style (line width). The Eraser option in the toolbar erases entire ink strokes, while you can use the eraser on the back of your pen (if it has one) to erase whatever spot you touch with it.

If you change the document that the Ink Drawing And Writing area is part of, the area sticks with the point where you inserted it into the document. In other words, if the document changes in length, the inserted area moves with the spot where you inserted it.

To insert an Ink Drawing And Writing area into a document, tap the point where you want to insert the box, then tap Insert | Ink Drawing And Writing. When you're done writing in this area, deselect it by tapping any spot in the document that's outside the Ink Drawing And Writing area.

Add Handwritten Comments with the Ink Comment Command

Adding handwritten (inked) comments to a document is similar to adding an Ink Drawing And Writing area. Tap the point in the document where you want to insert the comment, then tap Insert | Ink Comment. A Comment box like the one in Figure 14-5 appears in the margin of the document.

If you look closely at Figure 14-5, you can see that a line runs from the Comment box to the exact spot where the cursor was when I inserted the comment. This feature allows you to have multiple Ink Comment boxes that refer to the same line of a document without confusion.

NOTE   *If you are using Word in Normal view and you insert an Ink Drawing And Writing area, Word switches to Web Layout view so it can display the change. If Word is in Print Layout view when you insert an Ink Drawing And Writing area, it remains in Print Layout view.*

Although it is hard to read in the figure, Ink Comments can have titles, as this one does. This feature can come in very handy if you're going to be talking

14

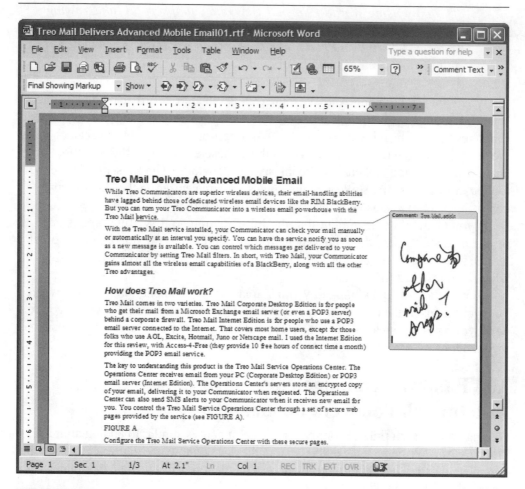

FIGURE 14-5   Insert a comment at an exact spot in a Word document with the Ink Comment command.

about a particular comment, as well as looking at it in the onscreen version of the document.

You have the same choice of writing tools in an Ink Comment that you have in an Ink Drawing And Writing area: Pen, Eraser, Selection Tool, Ink Color, Ink Style (line width).

Use Handwriting in E-mail

The Tablet Pack lets you include handwritten material in your e-mail messages if you are using Outlook XP (Outlook 2002) and are using Word XP as your e-mail editor. This allows you to send handwritten e-mail, make handwritten replies to messages you receive, or send a sketch to someone. If you're creating a new message, replying to one, or forwarding one, ink is now a viable e-mail option. Any recipient using Internet Explorer 6 or later can view the ink messages you send.

> **NOTE** *In this section, we're talking about using handwriting in e-mail messages in the form of ink. You can also use handwriting from Windows Journal in e-mail messages. However, the handwriting from Journal is converted into text before being added to the e-mail message. It isn't retained as ink.*

Even with the Tablet Pack, there are limits on the ways you can use ink in e-mail messages. You can use ink only in the body of a message—you can't write in any of the other fields, so you can't just write someone's e-mail address.

> **NOTE** *If you use Rich Text Format (RTF) for your e-mail messages, the inked portion of your message may not appear when you reply to handwritten messages that have multiple recipients. Ink works best with HTML-format e-mail.*

You must be using Word XP as your e-mail editor for inked e-mail to work. See "How to Use Word As Your E-mail Editor" to set this up if you haven't already done so. With Word as your e-mail editor, follow these steps to insert handwritten material in a message:

1. Fill in the header of your message and any typed content in the body of the message as you would normally.

2. Tap the point in the message where you want to insert handwritten content.

3. With the cursor in the right location in the body of the message, tap Insert | Ink Drawing And Writing. The Ink Drawing And Writing area appears.

4. Write in the Ink Drawing And Writing area, then send your message when done.

The person who receives your message should be able to see it exactly as you wrote it, assuming their e-mail editor can display HTML or RTF messages. Figure 14-6 shows a message containing both text and handwriting, as it appears on a non–Tablet PC. While the recipient can't respond in handwriting, he can at least view the message as you meant it to be seen.

14

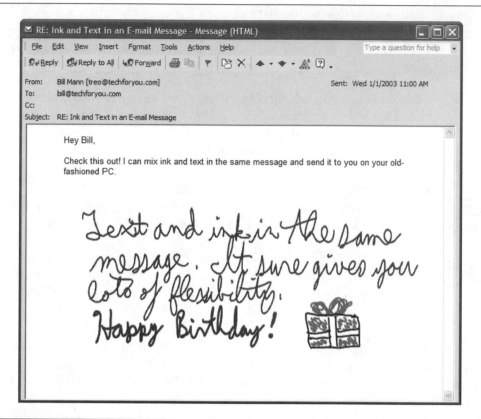

FIGURE 14-6   You can send handwritten messages to people who don't use a Tablet PC without any problem.

How to ... Use Word As Your E-mail Editor

If you want to use Word as your full-time e-mail editor, you can set this up by following this procedure. If you're not sure whether you are already using Word as your e-mail editor, follow the procedure anyway. It'll take only seconds.

1. Start Outlook if it isn't already running.

2. In the main Outlook window, tap Tools | Options to open the Options dialog box shown in Figure 14-7.

3. Tap Mail Format if the Mail Format page isn't visible, then in the Message Format section of the page, set the Use Microsoft Word To Edit E-mail Messages check box if it isn't already set.

4. While you have the Options dialog box open, make sure that the Compose In This Message Format option is set to HTML or Rich Text (RTF).

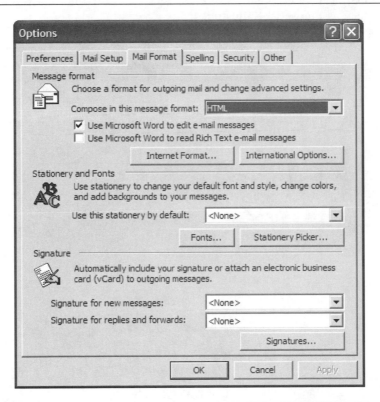

FIGURE 14-7 Set Word as your e-mail editor and HTML or Rich Text as your message format if you want to be able to use ink in e-mail.

14

If you like the ability to include handwritten comments in e-mail messages, you'll love the Snipping tool. The Snipping tool for Tablet PC lets you select anything on the screen, write on it, then cut it out and save it, or e-mail it to someone. See "Try the Snipping Tool" in Chapter 11 for more information.

Use Handwriting in Excel Spreadsheets

Adding handwritten content to an Excel spreadsheet is very similar to adding handwritten content to a Word document. All you need to do is tap a spot in the worksheet where you wish to add handwritten text, then tap Insert | Ink Drawing And Writing. The Ink Drawing And Writing area works the same in Excel as it does in Word, meaning you have the same Ink toolbar and can move or resize the area as needed. You can also have more than one Ink Drawing And Writing area in a worksheet, as Figure 14-8 illustrates.

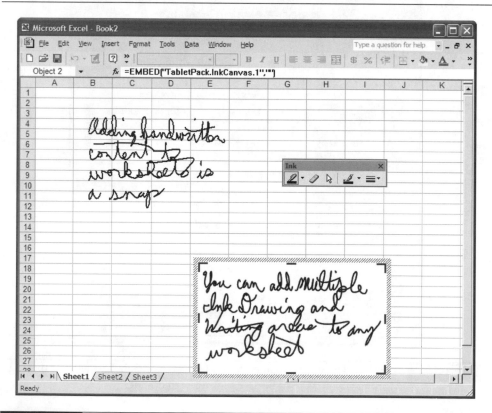

FIGURE 14-8   The Tablet Pack lets you add multiple Ink Drawing And Writing areas to Excel worksheets.

If handwritten content obscures worksheet data that you need to see, move the Ink Drawing And Writing area (by tapping in it to activate it, then dragging a border) or resize (by activating it, then dragging the area's sizing handles).

 When you resize an Ink Drawing And Writing area in Excel, the ink inside the area doesn't resize with it. You can't reduce the size of an area below the size of the ink in the area.

Use Handwriting in PowerPoint

The Tablet Pack allows you to add inked comments to your PowerPoint presentations while editing them. Even better, you can add comments while you're showing your presentation. This allows you to emphasize points or address audience comments right in the presentation.

Add Ink While Editing

If you want to add inked comments to a presentation while you are creating or editing it, you insert an Ink Drawing And Writing area just as in Word and Excel. You can add inked content this way when you are working in Normal view, Notes Page view, or Master view. Tap the slide at the point where you want to enter the handwritten material, then tap Insert | Ink Drawing And Writing. You get the familiar Ink toolbar and Ink Drawing and Writing area shown in Figure 14-9.

Add Ink While Presenting

The ability to add inked comments to a PowerPoint presentation, while you're presenting it, is a great example of the future of the Tablet PC. It gives you a way to do something that was easy and natural when presenting overheads but became difficult or impossible when we started using PCs for our presentations. It keeps the benefits of PowerPoint, while reclaiming a lost benefit of pre-PC presentation technology.

14

NOTE *The capabilities described in this section replace the Pen feature that is built into PowerPoint XP.*

To write on your presentation while you present it, you need to change the pointer into a pen, marker, or highlighter. To do this, right-tap the screen to open the slide show shortcut menu, then tap the tool you want to use (Ballpoint Pen, Felt Tip Pen, or Highlighter). This makes the pointer function like that tool, and

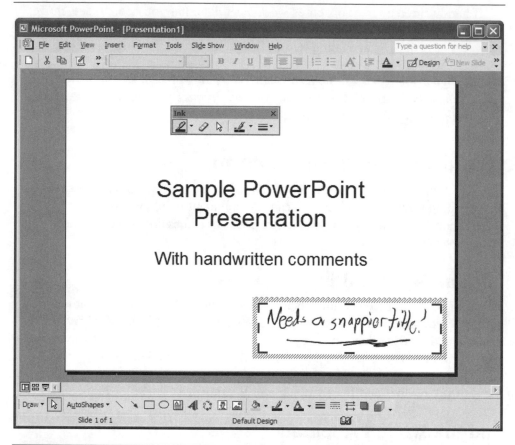

FIGURE 14-9   You can easily add handwritten content to a PowerPoint presentation you're creating.

causes a subset of the Ink toolbar to appear. Write anywhere on the presentation as necessary. The entire screen is an active drawing area. Figure 14-10 shows a slide from an active presentation that I've just scribbled all over without exiting the presentation.

NOTE   *You can also follow the same procedure to use the pointer as an ink eraser, or to erase all the ink on a slide instantly.*

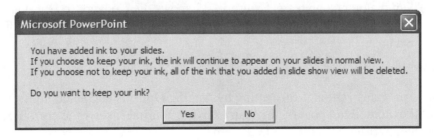

Forget to give the slide a name →Slide 2

- Adding handwritten content to a presentation while you're presenting it, is very slick.
- This could really improve the productivity and interactivity of presentations.

Especially when you can write on the presentation as you present it!

FIGURE 14-10   Being able to write anywhere on a presentation while you're presenting it can really be useful.

The abbreviated Ink toolbar contains the Ink Color button and an Arrow button. Tap the Arrow button to convert the writing tool back into a pointer and resume your normal presentation.

When you end a slide show during which you added ink to one or more slides, PowerPoint gives you the option to save or discard the ink. If you save it, it becomes part of the presentation and is available whenever you edit the presentation. If you don't save the ink, it is immediately lost.

14

Microsoft PowerPoint ☒

You have added ink to your slides.
If you choose to keep your ink, the ink will continue to appear on your slides in normal view.
If you choose not to keep your ink, all of the ink that you added in slide show view will be deleted.

Do you want to keep your ink?

[Yes]   [No]

Take Advantage of the Tablet Pack Extension for Windows Journal

In addition to its other capabilities, the Tablet Pack gives Microsoft Journal and Outlook XP the ability to share information with each other. Specifically, it allows you to:

- Use handwritten information from Journal in Outlook appointments, contacts, e-mail messages, or tasks

- Insert Outlook meeting information into a Journal note

Use Journal Information in Outlook XP

I use Journal whenever I need to take notes. Then I find myself reading chunks of that information from the Journal notes and typing it into Outlook items like Calendar entries. The Tablet Pack can help eliminate that chore by allowing you to insert information from notes into Outlook items. Since Outlook doesn't understand handwritten information when it comes to things like e-mail addresses or meeting times, Journal automatically converts the handwritten information to text, and gives you the option to correct it before inserting the converted text into Outlook.

To insert Journal information into an Outlook item, open Journal to the note containing the information, then follow these steps:

1. Select the information you want to insert in an Outlook item.

2. In Journal, tap Actions | Convert Selection To, then tap the type of Outlook item you want to include the information in. A Convert To Outlook item dialog box appears. Figure 14-11 shows the Convert To Outlook Appointment dialog box with some text converted from the handwriting in a note.

3. Correct the recognized text.

4. Apply any optional formatting by tapping Options and selecting from the menu that appears, then tap Convert. Journal inserts the converted handwriting into the Outlook item.

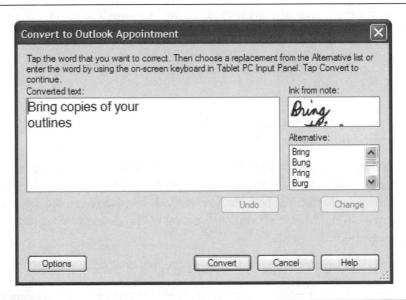

FIGURE 14-11   Correct handwriting recognition in the Convert To Outlook item dialog box before inserting into an Outlook item.

Where the converted text appears in the Outlook item depends on the type of item it is. The converted text appears

- In the message body for e-mail Messages

- In the comments area for Appointments and Contacts

- In the Subject for Tasks

Insert Outlook Meeting Information into a Journal Note

If you use Windows Journal to take notes at meetings, you might find yourself copying information from the meeting notice out of Outlook and into the Journal note, in order to keep all the information about the meeting together. The Tablet Pack lets you extract the information from a meeting notice and insert it into a Journal note without reentering it. The rest of this section explains how.

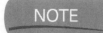 *The meeting must already appear in your Outlook Calendar before you can transfer its information into a Journal note.*

Start by opening the Journal note that you want to use. Then follow these simple steps:

1. In Journal, tap Insert | Outlook Meeting Information. This opens the Insert Meeting Information dialog box.

2. Choose the meeting you want to work with by selecting the appropriate date from the Date list, then the appropriate meeting from the Meeting list. When you do this, the information that will be inserted in the Journal note appears in the Meeting Summary section of the dialog box, as shown in Figure 14-12.

3. Tap OK to insert a text box containing the information into the Journal note.

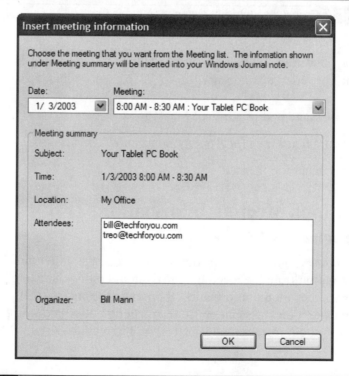

FIGURE 14-12   Use the Insert Meeting Information dialog box to select meeting information to include in a Journal note.

Figure 14-13 shows the Journal note with the meeting information inserted. You'll notice that the text that came from Outlook is integrated right into the note so you can do things like write on it or highlight it.

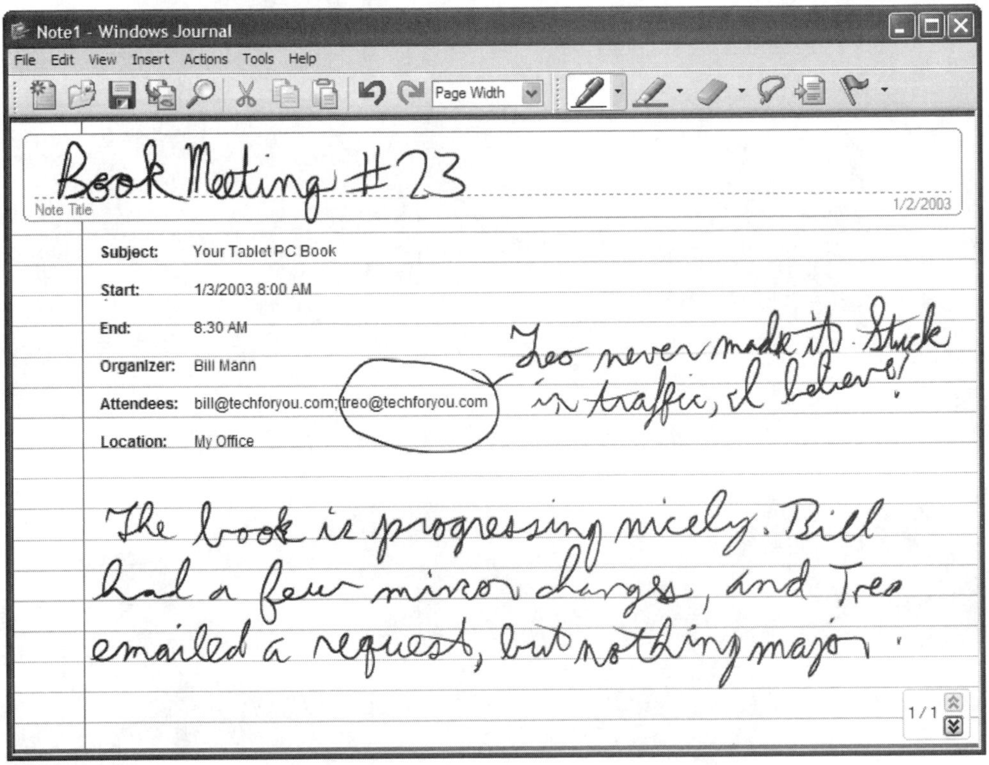

FIGURE 14-13   This Journal note contains meeting information taken from an Outlook Meeting item.

Chapter 15

Talk to Your Tablet PC

How to...

- Understand Speech Recognition Basics
- Use Tablet PC Speech Recognition
- Use These Tips for Speech Recognition in Specific Applications
- Try These General Speech Recognition Tips and Advanced Options

Although it tends to get less attention than handwriting recognition, speech recognition is another important way to get information into your Tablet PC. In this chapter, we'll start with a look at the basic concepts of speech recognition. From there, we'll cover using speech recognition on the Tablet PC in general, along with specific tips for specific applications. Once you're comfortable with all that, you can explore the advanced features and general tips at the end of the chapter.

Understand Speech Recognition Basics

Spoken input (speech recognition) is another form of *natural interface.* Science fiction stories abound in which the humans of some far-distant future communicate with their computers by speaking to them using normal spoken language. Since humans learn to speak and understand speech in our infancy, it was assumed that automatic speech recognition (ASR) would be simple.

Over the last couple of decades, we've learned that the things we thought would be easy for computers, such as handwriting and speech recognition, are quite hard. The things that are easy for us are hard for computers, and the things that are hard for us, like mathematical and logical reasoning, turned out to be relatively easy for our computers.

NOTE   *Handwriting recognition, the other type of natural interface that you can use with your Tablet PC, is covered in Chapter 10.*

Check Out This Speech Recognition Timeline

Research into automatic speech recognition has been underway at research labs and major corporations like AT&T and IBM for more than 60 years. It's only in the last few years that all the work in speech recognition, semiconductors, and computer science has combined to give us something like practical speech recognition technology in a package small enough and cheap enough that individuals can use it. To give you some idea of the scope of the effort that got us here, this timeline shows some of the steps in the progression:

- **1922**   The Elmwood Button Company produces the first speech recognition system. It was, believe it or not, a totally electromechanical toy dog. For more on Rex, see the "Did You Know How Radio Rex, The First Speech Recognition System, Worked?" box later in this chapter.

- **1959**   Researchers at MIT's Lincoln Laboratories develop a system that can identify vowel sounds with 93 percent accuracy.

- **1966**   Researchers at MIT's Lincoln Laboratories develop a system that can match *utterances* to a list of 50 words with more than 80 percent accuracy.

- **1968**   The science fiction movie *2001: A Space Odyssey* is released. The movie featured an artificially intelligent ship's computer named HAL, which communicated with the crew using speech recognition.

- **1970s**   The *Hidden Markov Modeling* (*HMM*) approach is developed by a researcher at Princeton University. HMM eventually became a key component in the majority of speech recognition systems.

- **1971**   DARPA, the Defense Advanced Research Projects Agency, establishes the Speech Understanding Research unit, which funds speech recognition work at MIT; Carnegie Mellon University; Stanford Research Institute; and Bolt, Beranek, and Newman (BBN), as well as other facilities.

- **1982**   Dragon Systems founded. This company did much of the early work in commercial speech recognition systems.

- **1995**   Dragon Systems releases first *discrete word dictation recognition system* for consumers.

- **1996**   BellSouth launches the first voice portal, Info By Voice (originally called Val).

- **1997**   Dragon Systems releases NaturallySpeaking, the first *continuous speech dictation system* for consumers.

- **1998**   Microsoft invests in Lernout & Hauspie, another speech recognition leader.

- **1999**   Microsoft acquires Entropic, which at the time produced what was perhaps the most accurate speech recognition system in the world.

15

- **2000**   Lernout & Hauspie acquires Dragon Systems.

- **2000**   TellMe introduces the first worldwide voice portal. You could dial this system from anywhere and ask for information such as stock prices or the weather forecast for any location.

- **2001**   ScanSoft purchases NaturallySpeaking and most related speech recognition intellectual property from Lernout & Hauspie. This is the technology that provides the *speaker-independent recognition* capabilities of OmniForm described in the "Did You Know OmniForm Features Speaker-Independent Recognition?" later in this chapter.

- **2001**   Microsoft adds speech recognition technology to the Developer version of Office XP.

As the timeline shows, research into speech recognition has been underway for many decades, with technology of use to the general public coming on the scene only within the last few years. A number of terms appear in this timeline that you're probably not familiar with. They will be described in next section, "Learn a Little about How Speech Recognition Works."

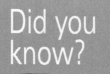

How Radio Rex Worked?

According to the stories I have been able to find, Radio Rex was quite the ingenious little toy. He consisted of a small toy dog attached to an iron base. That base was held within Rex's dog house by an electromagnet. A spring pushed against Rex so that if the electromagnet was turned off, Rex would spring from his house.

Rex was a speech recognition system because the current for the electromagnet flowed through a simple construction that could be made to vibrate by sound energy at a frequency of around 500 cycles per second. When someone called loudly for Rex, the sonic energy produced by saying the vowel sound caused enough vibration to interrupt the flow of current to the electromagnet, allowing Rex to spring from his house.

Learn a Little about How Speech Recognition Works

While each speech recognition system has its own unique features and ways of doing things, it's possible to give you a general idea of how they work. The speech recognition process begins when a system detects an utterance. An utterance is a stream of speech separated from other utterances by silence. The utterance, which is in the analog form of sound waves, is converted to digital form so that it can be processed.

Once the utterance is in digital form, the system begins to search for patterns that it recognizes. One way of doing this is with Hidden Markov Modeling (HMM), which breaks the utterance into tiny segments, then makes predictions about the next segment. Using HMM or other techniques, the system eventually comes up with its best guess as to what phonemes, words, or phrases make up the utterance.

Discover the Types of Speech Recognition Systems

Several different types of speech recognition system are possible. Early ASR systems were discrete word systems. That means that the system required each utterance to be a single word. This approach makes recognition easier for the system, since word predictions can be made on the assumption that each utterance is a discrete word. That's great for the system, but for this approach to work, the person using the system must…talk…like…this, with clear pauses between each word.

Continuous speech systems allow the user to speak more or less normally. In continuous speech, an utterance is most likely to be a group of words, a phrase, even an entire sentence. Continuous speech greatly increases the workload of the ASR system, since the system must decide where individual words begin and end within an utterance, as well as figure out which words they are.

Another way you can divide speech recognition systems is between voice command systems and dictation systems. A voice command system can recognize only a limited number of predefined words or phrases. Since the number of possibilities is limited and known, the system can more easily determine what you said to it. This results in relatively high accuracy for recognizing the acceptable commands.

A dictation system has to be able to accept whatever you say to it and convert that into correct words, phrases, and sentences. Since you can say anything you want to a dictation system, it must be able to recognize any arbitrary utterance. This requires a more powerful and flexible system. Dictation systems are generally more flexible but less accurate than voice command systems.

Yet another way to divide speech recognition systems is between speaker-independent systems and user-specific systems. A speaker-independent system

15

is designed to accept spoken input from anyone who speaks the language the system is designed for. Because of the wide variation in the way humans speak, a speaker-independent system must be able to accept and recognize a wide variety of spoken input.

A user-specific system is optimized to accept spoken input from a particular person. This optimization often takes the form of an enrollment process, where the target user speaks predefined text to the system so that it can analyze the way the user speaks known words. Using this information, a user-specific system can modify its workings (can be trained) to increase the likelihood of correct recognition for that user. This generally results in recognition accuracy for the target user that is better than the accuracy achieved by a speaker-independent system. On the other hand, a user-specific system is likely to have much lower accuracy when recognizing speech from someone else.

The Tablet PC speech recognition exhibits many of the characteristics you just learned about. In particular, it is a continuous speech, user-specific system that has both a voice command mode and a dictation mode. It optimizes the speech recognition system for a specific user by training itself during the enrollment period. This system goes one step further by using information gleaned when you correct its mistakes during use, to further optimize its performance.

Another aspect of many dictation speech recognition systems, including the one in your Tablet PC, is the use of a dictionary. This dictionary contains a list of words that the system "knows." The speech recognition system uses the dictionary to help it guess at the spoken input it receives. As a result, if a word is in the system's dictionary, it is more likely to be recognized accurately.

 *You'll learn how to add words to the Tablet PC's Speech Recognition dictionary when you run the Speech tutorial described under "Run the Speech Tutorial" in the next section.*

Use Tablet PC Speech Recognition

Now that you understand the basics of speech recognition, it's time to try some modern speech recognition software yourself. In this part of the chapter, you'll get the Tablet PC speech recognition system ready to go, then start putting it to use in your daily work.

Train the Speech Recognizer

Before you can give spoken input to your Tablet PC, you must train the speech recognizer to recognize your voice. You talk to the Tablet PC through the Input

Panel. To enable speech recognition, you open the Input Panel and tap Tools | Speech. This opens the Input Panel Speech bar. The Speech bar appears at the top of the Input Panel and is divided into the three sections shown in Figure 15-1.

The first section of the Speech bar contains the Dictation and Command buttons. These buttons are dimmed if you haven't completed the speech recognition enrollment process, which I'll describe momentarily. The middle section of the Speech bar is a status area that shows the status of speech recognition. The last section contains the Start Speech button. Tap this button when you want to speak to your Tablet PC.

If this is the first time you've enabled speech recognition, the system pops up the Speech Recognition Enrollment dialog box shown in Figure 15-2. This dialog box requires you to adjust your microphone and train the speech recognizer, which should take about ten minutes.

The Microphone Wizard guides you through the first part of the enrollment, where you read a sentence so that the Wizard can adjust the volume level of your microphone and check the quality of your voice input. It's important that you do this in a quiet environment and take the time to read the sentence clearly and without rushing.

If you don't take the time to read clearly, or if your microphone isn't the best quality, you can't get the best possible recognition results, as the dialog box in Figure 15-3 indicates. If you plan to do a lot of voice input on your Tablet PC, you should seriously consider investing in a high-quality USB microphone or headset.

The Microphone Wizard walks you through a test of the positioning of your microphone, then leads you into voice training. In voice training, you read aloud to your Tablet PC so that it can learn your voice. You must complete at least one speech training session before you can use speech input, but the more you do, the

15

FIGURE 15-1   Use the Speech bar of the Input Panel to control speech input to your Tablet PC.

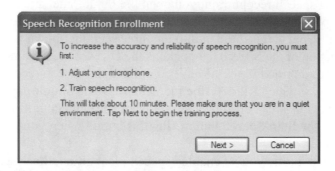

FIGURE 15-2   You must go through the speech recognition enrollment process before your Tablet PC will accept spoken input.

faster your Tablet PC learns your voice. Carefully read and heed the instructions in each of the Wizard's windows to get the best results from the training.

After you work your way through each voice training session, the system adjusts your speaker profile with the training data gathered during the session (see Figure 15-4). This is the information that allows the speech recognition system to learn how you speak, which increases the recognition accuracy.

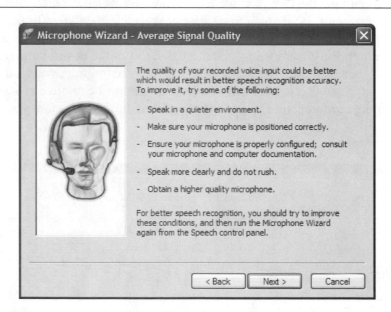

FIGURE 15-3   It takes careful speech and high-quality equipment to get good speech recognition results.

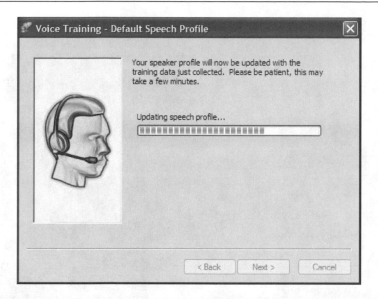

FIGURE 15-4   Every time you complete a voice training session, the system updates
your speaker profile to increase its recognition accuracy.

Even if you're done with voice training sessions for now, don't exit the Wizard
yet. Your Tablet PC is ready to accept spoken input from you. To really get the feel
for how this works, I suggest you open a blank Notepad document and work through
the Speech tutorial before trying to use speech input in a "real" document. To open
a blank Notepad document, tap Start | All Programs | Accessories | Notepad. Once
you have a blank document open, run the Speech tutorial.

Run the Speech Tutorial

Running through the Speech tutorial won't take you too long, but it will give you
a good understanding of basic speech recognition on your Tablet PC. To use the
tutorial, tap Start | All Programs | Tablet PC | Tablet PC Tutorials | Speech Tutorial
to open the Speech Tutorial window, which looks like Figure 15-5.

I suggest you run through the tutorial in the order presented, starting with the
multimedia overview, "Using Speech," right through the list of more detailed
topics "Dictating and Correcting Text" to "Using Input Panel and Adding Unique
Words." Tap Tutorial Home at any time to return to the main Speech tutorial page.

15

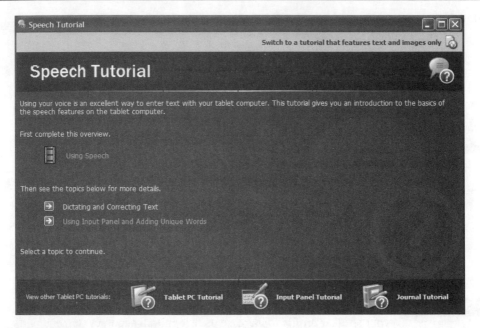

FIGURE 15-5 The Speech Tutorial is a great way to learn the basics of speech input on your Tablet PC.

 At the top of the Speech Tutorial window there's a link to a version of the tutorial that uses only text and images. It's a good choice if you plan to run the tutorial in a place where the sound would be a problem or if you want to proceed through the overview at your own pace.

Start Using Speech Recognition in Your Daily Work

Now that you've completed the speech recognition enrollment process and the Speech tutorial, it's worth repeating the basic steps of dictating text before going further. Start by taking another look at the Speech bar in the Input Panel. As this illustration shows, the Dictation and Command buttons are no longer dim, the status area displays a status message ("Not listening"), and the Start Speech button has been replaced by a Speech Tools menu.

With the cursor in the blank Notepad document, use the pen to press and hold the Dictation button in the Speech bar. Wait until the status area displays the word "Listening," then speak a phrase into the microphone. As you speak, the status message changes from Listening to Dictating. Lift the pen when you're done dictating. This stops the Input Panel from listening and prevents accidental data entry. A moment after you lift the pen, the converted text appears in the Notepad document.

> **TIP** *If you're working in a quiet environment, and you're going to be entering a lot of information by voice, you can tap the Dictation button instead of holding it down. When you tap the button, the Input Panel switches into Dictation mode, and it remains in that mode until you tap the Dictation button again.*

I suggest you spend some time mastering the basic speech recognition techniques you learned in the tutorial before trying the more advanced options and tips covered at the end of this chapter. One thing I have trouble with when using speech recognition on my Tablet PC is remembering the proper forms of the general voice commands. When I forget one, I refer to the Input Panel Voice Command Reference in the help system. Refer to the "How to View the Input Panel Voice Command Reference" box for instructions if you find you need help remembering the commands too.

> **TIP** *If you're unhappy with the speech recognition accuracy you're getting, try completing additional voice training sessions. You can conduct a training session at any time by tapping Start | Control Panel | Sounds, Speech, And Audio Devices | Speech | Train Profile.*

Another way to see what voice commands you have available is to look in the What Can I Say dialog box shown in Figure 15-6. This dialog is a context-sensitive guide to the commands that are available for the active program (the one you're dictating to or barking commands at).

You can open the What Can I Say dialog box in one of two ways. You can go to the Speech bar and tap Speech Tools | What Can I Say, or you can hold down the Command button and say, "What Can I Say?"

The commands in the What Can I Say dialog box are organized into categories that you can expand to see the individual commands. You may have to do a little poking around to find what you want, but the Input Panel commands that you can use with the active program all appear here.

15

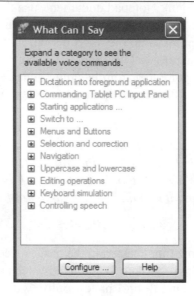

FIGURE 15-6   The What Can I Say dialog box lists the voice commands that are available to you in the active document.

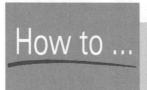

NOTE   *As explained in "Speak to Microsoft Office Applications" later in this chapter, you can also speak commands to Microsoft Office applications by holding down the Command button and speaking the name of a menu item, button, or other visible control.*

How to ...

View the Input Panel Voice Command Reference

Here are the steps to follow to view the Input Panel Voice Command Reference:

1. Open the Input Panel if necessary.

2. Tap Tools | Help | Help Topics.

3. Tap Search, and search for the phrase "command reference." This returns a list of general topics as well as topics containing command references.

4. Select Input Panel Voice Command Reference in the topic list, then tap Display. This displays the topic you're looking for.

Use These Tips for Speech Recognition in Specific Applications

Now that you know how to use speech recognition on your Tablet PC in general, it's time to learn about the idiosyncrasies of using speech recognition with specific applications. This section covers speech recognition with Microsoft Office applications, Internet Explorer, and Windows Journal.

Speak to Microsoft Office Applications

You can dictate text to Microsoft Office applications such as Word and Excel using the Input Panel. You can also control those applications simply by speaking the name of any active button, menu, or control. For example, assuming Word is the active application, and the Standard toolbar is visible, you could open a new blank Word document by holding down the Command button on the Input Panel Speech bar and saying "New Blank Document." New Blank Document is the name of one of the buttons on Word's Standard toolbar, so you can give that command by speaking the name of the button.

While this all works simply and efficiently, there are a few points you need to keep in mind when using the Input Panel for voice input to Microsoft Office applications:

- Do not activate the speech recognition software that comes as part of Microsoft Office. Let the Input Panel's speech recognition system do all the work.

- The commands that you can enter by holding down the Command button on the Speech bar and speaking the name of a visible button, menu, or other control are in addition to the commands that appear in the "What Can I Say?" dialog box.

- In most cases, using both the pen and the speech recognition system to edit text you've dictated is more effective than just using speech.

- Watch out for the Text Preview pane. While the basic Office applications can show the alternate list, some of their add-ins cannot. If you configured the Text Preview pane to appear when the alternate list isn't available, you may find the pane appearing at unexpected times. For example, if you are dictating a document in Word, and you decide to add an Ink Note, the Text Preview pane can suddenly appear, which can be confusing at the least. The pane won't go away on its own, so you'll need to close it before you can continue entering text directly into your application.

15

Speak to Internet Explorer

You can enter text and speak commands to Internet Explorer in much the same way you do to Microsoft Office applications, except that Internet Explorer never displays the alternate list, so you need to use the Text Preview pane when dictating to it.

Speak to Windows Journal

You can use speech recognition with Windows Journal, but the value of doing so is limited. Journal is made for inked input, and you can't dictate inked input. This leaves you with the ability to use voice commands and dictate into text boxes you insert in a note. Even the ability to use voice commands is less useful than it might be, since to do so, you'll need to move the pen from the writing area of Journal to the Command button on the Input Panel Speech bar, speak your command, then move the pen back to where you were writing. It would be easier to just tap the command you want to use.

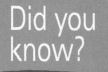

OmniForm Features Speaker-Independent Recognition?

OmniForm is an electronic forms program from ScanSoft, Inc. ScanSoft has created a Tablet PC version of OmniForm that not only accepts inked data entry in form fields, but also speaker-independent voice navigation of forms. Speaker-independent voice navigation means that you can speak commands like "next page" or "check" and OmniForm will understand them, without requiring any training. The ScanSoft speaker-independent voice system works with the built-in Tablet PC microphone, and it can handle a noisy environment.

I saw this for myself at the Tablet PC launch event. The ScanSoft representative merely handed me a Tablet PC in the middle of the crowded and noisy exhibition hall, and let me start talking. I was able to navigate through the sample form perfectly, despite the noisy environment, and despite never having trained (or even spoken to) the system OmniForm was running on.

As you can see here, the forms that you can generate and fill out with OmniForm can be quite complex, and the ability to navigate them by voice while typing or writing in them can be very handy.

In addition to OmniForm, ScanSoft is upgrading several of their other programs with Tablet PC support. For a complete rundown of Tablet PC support in ScanSoft programs, visit their Tablet PC Productivity Applications web page at: http://www.scansoft.com/tpc/.

15

Try These General Speech Recognition Tips

Here are some general tips that will help you get the best results from speech recognition:

- Optimize the environment for each speech recognition session. To get the best results, you want to make the relevant aspects of the physical environment of each session as much as possible like the environment you used for voice training. That means you want a quiet environment with the same microphone placed in the same position as when you trained the system. Likewise, you want to speak in the same way you did when you trained the system.

■ Be sure to pronounce your words clearly, but don't separate them into distinct syllables. The speech recognition system works better with whole words than with words broken down into separate syllables.

■ Try to dictate an entire paragraph at a time, then go back and use your pen to help make corrections. The pen allows you to jump directly to any spot in a paragraph and quickly select words, making the combination of voice and pen a potent one.

■ Turn off the speech recognition software when you're not using it. Whenever the status area says Listening or Dictating, your Tablet PC is trying to process speech input. This takes a lot of processing power that could be dedicated to whatever you're actually doing—and runs down your battery.

■ Consider closing applications you aren't using when you want to use speech recognition. This will make the maximum amount of processing power available for recognition.

■ Always add specialized words to the dictionary. If your work calls for a specialized vocabulary that your Tablet PC doesn't recognize, adding those words to the dictionary will greatly increase speech recognition accuracy when you're dictating. And don't forget to add your company's name, and your boss's!

■ Don't start talking until the word Listening appears in the status area and you hear a tone notifying you that the system is ready to listen.

■ Finally, don't let someone else use speech recognition when they're signed on to your Tablet PC under your user name. The system will try to recognize their voice, and begin training itself to recognize them. This will hurt your recognition results.

Try These Advanced Speech Recognition Options

Once you're comfortable using speech recognition for basic dictation and Input Panel commands, you can experiment with the more advanced features described in this section.

Use Text Formatting Voice Commands

In the Speech tutorial, you learned how to dictate text to the Input Panel and how to issue spoken commands to the Input Panel. But the Input Panel also understands over 30 spoken formatting commands that are supported by at least some applications. To find out which of these formatting voice commands are understood by the program you're working in right now, you can use the "What Can I Say" command to see a list of all the voice commands that are valid given the program you are working with now.

To see the complete list of formatting voice commands, search for the phrase "formatting voice commands" in the Tablet PC Input Panel help system. Figure 15-7 shows a few of the over 30 formatting voice commands that the Input Panel understands.

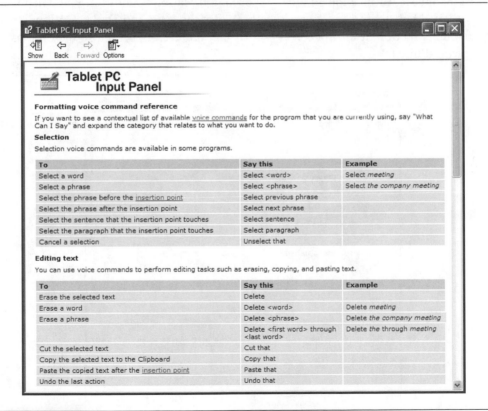

FIGURE 15-7   The Input Panel help system contains the full list of formatting voice commands the Input Panel understands.

Use System Software Voice Commands

Just as the Input Panel recognizes certain spoken text formatting commands (when supported by the current program), it also recognizes some spoken system software commands. These commands, which allow you to do things like switch to another open program, or open a new file, may or may not be available at any given time. To find out which of these system software commands are available right now, you can use the "What Can I Say" command.

Customize the Way Speech Recognition Works

You can customize the way your Tablet PC works to make using voice input easier for you. You can mix and match any of the four customizations described here to meet your needs.

Turn on Speech Notification Sounds   Speech notification sounds tell you when the Input Panel is listening and when it isn't. To turn these on, tap Tools | Options. In the Sounds section of the Speech tab shown in Figure 15-8, set the sound options you would like to use.

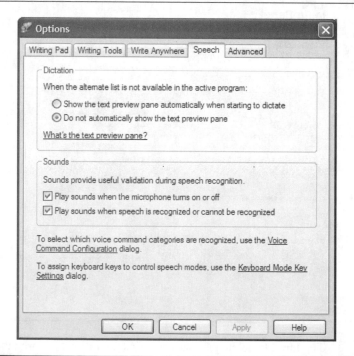

FIGURE 15-8   Use speech notification sounds to know when the Input Panel is ready to process your spoken input.

Set the Text Preview Pane to Automatically Open When Necessary   Some programs won't display the alternate list when you select a word that you've dictated. To address this situation, you can have the Input Panel automatically use the Text Preview pane with programs that behave that way. When you speak to such programs, your dictation will automatically go into the Text Preview pane, where you do have access to the alternate list for correcting mistakes.

To set the Text Preview pane to automatically open for programs that don't display the alternate list, tap Tools | Options. In the Dictation section of the Speech tab, select Show The Text Preview Pane Automatically When Starting To Dictate.

Reduce the Number of Commands the System Must Recognize   The more different words a speech recognition system must understand, the greater the chance that it will make a mistake. The opposite is also true. You can increase the system's ability to recognize the commands you speak by reducing the number of different commands it needs to recognize. You can do this by turning off recognition for command sets you won't use.

For you to do this, the Speech bar must be visible. If necessary, open the Input Panel, then tap Tools | Speech to display the Speech bar. Next tap Speech Tools | Voice Command Configuration. This opens the Voice Command Configuration dialog box shown in Figure 15-9. The dialog box lists the categories of voice commands that are available, along with very short descriptions of the kinds of commands in each category. Clear the check boxes next to the categories of commands that you don't plan to use.

Make Commands Available During Dictation   By default, the Controlling Speech set of commands is available when you're using Dictation mode as well as Command mode. You can make the rest of the commands in the Working With Text set available during Dictation as well. This can save you from having to frequently switch modes, but it can also reduce your recognition accuracy. The only way to know whether this trade-off is worthwhile for you is to give it a try.

To make the Working With Text commands available during Dictation, the Speech bar must be visible. If necessary, open the Input Panel, then tap Tools | Speech to display the Speech bar. Next tap Speech Tools | Voice Command Configuration. This opens the Voice Command Configuration dialog box. Without clearing the check box next to the name, select the Working with Text category. This activates the Details button at the bottom of the dialog box.

Tap Details to open the Working With Text – Details dialog box. Check Enable During Dictation to make all the active Working With Text commands available in Dictation mode. If you know you won't be using some of the command sets available in this dialog box, disable them now. Doing so will reduce the impact of

15

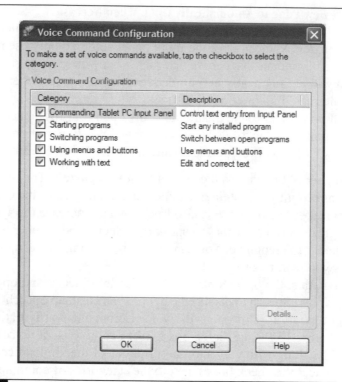

FIGURE 15-9   Disabling sets of voice commands you don't use can increase the recognition accuracy for the commands you do use.

making Working With Text commands available in Dictation mode by reducing the total number of commands you make active.

Use Different Speech Recognition Profiles for Different Situations

When you train the speech recognition system to recognize your voice, you do so in a specific environment. The acoustics of the space you're working in, the ambient noise level, even the presence of other people can affect the training of a speech recognition profile. Your voice presumably stays much the same over time, but your environment can change. Say you move to a new building, or a new office in the same building. This changes the environment more or less permanently.

You can address a permanent change of environment by allowing your Tablet PC to adapt over time. A better solution is to create a new speech recognition profile and retrain the speech recognition system in this new environment. Or perhaps you do a lot of work in two different environments, say your office at work and your home office. In this case, it would be nice to have two profiles, one for each environment.

You can indeed create multiple speech recognition profiles. You'll need to train any new profiles in the environment where you'll use them, and you'll need to remember to switch the active profile when you change environments, but if you want the best speech recognition in differing environments, multiple speech recognition profiles is the way to go.

NOTE *All the speech recognition profiles created under a specific user login account use the same dictionary, so you don't have to re-create the dictionary every time you create a new profile.*

To create a new profile, tap Start | Control Panel | Sounds, Speech, And Audio Devices | Speech. On the Speech Recognition tab (Figure 15-10), look in the

FIGURE 15-10   Use this dialog box to create speech recognition profiles, and choose the one you'll use in any given environment.

15

Recognition Profiles area. All the speech recognition profiles for this user account appear in the Recognition Profiles list, with the active profile checkmarked.

Tap New to start the Profile Wizard, which guides you through creating a new profile. You want to do this in the environment where you'll use the profile, since part of the creation process is training the new profile. The Wizard automatically sets the new profile as the selected profile when you're done.

To change profiles, you return to this dialog box (Start | Control Panel | Sounds, Speech, And Audio Devices | Speech), go to the Speech Recognition tab, and tap the profile you want to use.

Part IV

Fix What Ails Your Tablet PC

Chapter 16

Prevent Problems with Regular Maintenance

How to…

- Maintain Your Tablet PC Hardware
- Maintain Your Disk Drive
- Schedule Maintenance Tasks
- Maintain Optimum Performance

Over time, the performance of any computer tends to decline. The hard disk fills up, unused programs and icons accumulate, and parts get dirty, dusty, and out of calibration. Like anything else you own, your Tablet PC needs some sort of regular maintenance to keep performing at its best. This chapter covers some of the most important preventive maintenance tasks you can perform to keep your Tablet PC in shape.

Using Antivirus Software Is a Key Maintenance Task?

One of the best forms of preventive maintenance you can perform on your Tablet PC is to use antivirus software. Literally thousands of viruses, worms, Trojan horses, and other hostile programs are out there, all specifically designed to give you grief. If your Tablet PC gets infected with one of these pests, the consequences can range from annoying or obscene messages appearing on your screen, to the complete obliteration of the files on your computer.

Fortunately, your Tablet PC almost certainly came with antivirus software installed. Take the time to learn about the antivirus software installed on your computer. It should have the ability to automatically connect to the Internet and download the information it needs to detect and contain the latest hostile software.

If antivirus software is installed and running on your machine, you'll find an icon for it in the notification area. Right-tap that icon and open the program for more information on it.

Maintain Your Tablet PC Hardware

A little basic maintenance of the physical structure of your Tablet PC will go a long way toward keeping it functioning properly. After all, this is a machine that's expected to be used more, and venture into more environments than the normal notebook computer. That makes it more likely to get dirty, dusty, and generally beat up than a normal notebook computer.

The first thing you need to do is occasionally clean the computer screen and keyboard. The screen is likely to get dirtier than you're used to, because you lean your hand against it as you write with the pen. Although you should always check the manuals that came with your computer for specific instructions, normally you will clean your Tablet PC's screen by wiping it with a static-free cloth. Avoid cleaning fluids or even water unless specifically directed by your computer's documentation.

Clean the keyboard the same way. If the keys are very dirty, you might want to use a slightly damp cloth to clean them, but don't use a lot of water or cleaning fluids. You can also use one of the commercially available compressed air cleaning kits to blow the gunk out of a keyboard.

Because the screen and pen combination on your Tablet PC is a physical system, it can get out of alignment. If you notice that you're having trouble tapping items on the screen, it's time to recalibrate. We went over this process in Chapter 3, but in case you've forgotten, here's how you calibrate the screen:

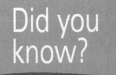

Ruggedized Tablet PCs Are Available?

If you work in environments in which your computer needs to be tough as well as smart, you're in luck. Two companies, Walkabout Computers, Inc. and Xplore Technologies, make Tablet PCs that meet or exceed various military environmental test standards (MIL-STD 810). These are seriously tough machines. When I spoke to representatives of these companies, they told stories of machines routinely enduring three-foot drops onto concrete, being submerged in creeks, even being run over repeatedly by large trucks.

16

■ Right-tap the Tablet and Pen Settings icon in the notification area. In the shortcut menu that appears, tap Properties. On the Settings tab shown in Figure 16-1, tap the Calibrate button (located in the Calibration section). Follow the onscreen instructions to recalibrate the screen. When performing this process, remember these two important points:

■ When tapping the calibration points, hold the pen the way you normally would when writing on that spot on the screen. The calibration will be more effective if you do.

■ You need to calibrate the screen in each orientation you use.

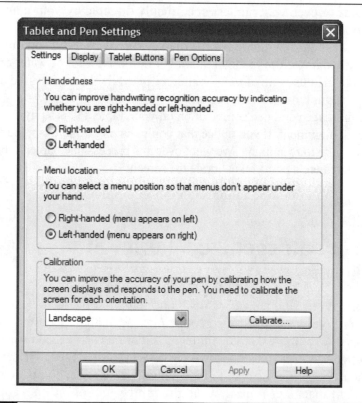

FIGURE 16-1   You may occasionally need to recalibrate the screen using the Calibration section of the Tablet and Pen Settings dialog box.

 *If your Tablet PC pen contains a battery, you should change that at least once a year, or sooner if directed by the manufacturer. A weak battery in your pen could result in erratic behavior.*

Clean and protect the exterior of your Tablet PC, because it is likely to be touched much more than a regular desktop or notebook computer. It is also likely to be exposed to more harsh environments than the other kinds of machines. Keep any port covers closed when you're not actively using that port. When it gets dirty, wipe the machine with a static-free cloth or perhaps a slightly damp one. And consider a protective case that will shield the outside of the machine while still allowing you to write on the screen.

Acer has a case that not only protects the exterior of their TMC100 series Tablet PCs (see Figure 16-2), but makes the machine easier to hold while you're working with it.

Figure 16-3 shows the clever way this case allows you to hold the computer and write at the same time. You should be able to find similar cases for other brands of Tablet PCs too.

FIGURE 16-2   A well-designed case can leave your Tablet PC protected while still fully usable.

16

FIGURE 16-3 Consider buying a protective case for your Tablet PC to shield it from damage (and perhaps make it easier to use).

Maintain Your Disk Drive

Perhaps the single area where maintenance matters the most and where you can do the most is the disk drive. As an electro-mechanical device, the disk drive is vulnerable to problems that cause the corruption of data stored on the drive. In addition, the day-to-day use of your computer can gradually degrade the performance of your disk drive, and therefore your system as a whole.

In this section of the chapter, you will learn how to detect and deal with disk errors, defragment your hard disk, and free disk space with Disk Cleanup.

Detect and Deal with Disk Errors

Once in a while, something will get messed up on your disk drive. For whatever reason, some of the data on your hard disk will get corrupted. Windows comes with a utility that can detect and correct many of these errors. The error-checking tool is the modern descendant of ChkDsk, a program that did the same job for DOS-based computers.

To start the error-checking tool, tap Start | My Computer. Then right-tap the icon for the disk drive. Tap Properties in the shortcut menu that appears. In the Properties dialog box, tap the Tools tab, then Check Now. The Check Disk dialog box shown in Figure 16-4 appears.

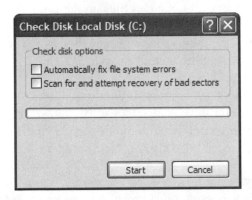

| FIGURE 16-4 | Find and fix disk errors with this error-checking tool. |

I recommend that you select both these options: Automatically Fix File System Errors, and Scan For And Attempt Recovery Of Bad Sectors. Selecting only Automatically Fix File System Errors is faster, but it can result in the loss of a bit of your disk drive's storage capacity as bad sectors accumulate on the disk.

In most cases when you tap OK, Windows tells you that it cannot check the disk now because the error-checking tool needs exclusive access to some Windows files. You have the option to schedule the error-checking for the next time you start Windows, or to abandon the checking. Tap Yes to schedule the check for the next time you start Windows.

When you do restart Windows, your computer will partially restart, and then you'll see some messages about checking the disk for errors. After the error-checking tool completes its work (this can take several minutes), Windows finishes starting.

Some kinds of system problems will cause Windows to automatically run the error-checking tool the next time your system starts, so this part of the process may look familiar to you.

Defragment Your Hard Disk

When Windows stores a file on your hard disk, it often needs to store parts of that file in physically different locations on the disk to take advantage of the space that is available. Files like this are said to be *fragmented*. Fragmenting a file doesn't hurt anything, and as a user, you normally can't tell the difference between fragmented files and those that are not fragmented.

16

Over time, the number of fragmented files on the disk grows, increasing the chances that new files will also need to be fragmented to fit. Fragmented files take longer to access, and as the fragmentation of the disk as a whole increases, you'll eventually notice slower performance from your Tablet PC.

The solution to the problem of file fragmentation is to occasionally run the Disk Defragmenter utility that comes with Windows. Disk Defragmenter works by rearranging files on the disk drive so that they are no longer fragmented. At the same time, Disk Defragmenter consolidates all the free space on the drive into one large contiguous area, which reduces the chance that future files will be fragmented.

Because defragmenting a disk drive can take a long time (hours for a large, heavily fragmented disk), you may want to run Disk Defragmenter overnight.

To start Disk Defragmenter, tap Start | All Programs | Accessories | System Tools | Disk Defragmenter. The Disk Defragmenter window opens, as shown in Figure 16-5.

Your first step is to tap Analyze. This causes Disk Defragmenter to analyze the selected disk drive to determine its level of fragmentation. At the end of this analysis, Disk Defragmenter opens a dialog box that will likely tell you your hard disk needs to be defragmented.

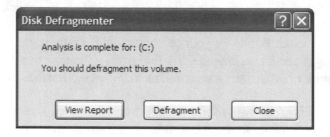

In this dialog box, you can tap View Report to get details on the amount of fragmentation on your hard disk, along with a bunch of other statistics. But you really needn't bother. If Disk Defragmenter says your disk needs to be defragmented, I heartily recommend you do it and don't worry about the detailed analysis.

To defragment the disk, tap Defragment. After a moment or two of whirring and clinking, Disk Defragmenter begins defragmenting your disk. At the beginning of this process, the disk usage maps shown in the window look very much alike, if not identical. Not to worry. As the defragmentation process continues, the Estimated Disk Usage After Defragmentation map begins to change to reflect the new organization of

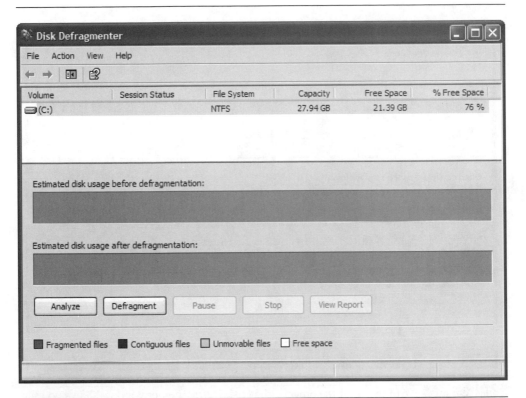

FIGURE 16-5   Disk Defragmenter can reorganize the files on your hard disk to improve your Tablet PC's performance.

information on your hard disk. Look in the status bar at the bottom of the window to see the percentage complete and the file currently being defragmented.

> *If your disk drive has less than 15 percent of free space left, it will ask you whether you want to proceed with defragmentation. Your best bet at this point would be to delete unneeded files to give Disk Defragmenter more room to operate. See "Free Disk Space with Disk Cleanup" for more information.*

Once the defragmentation process is complete, you'll see a dialog box announcing the fact, and the Disk Defragmenter window (Figure 16-6) shows the before and after results. My disk wasn't too badly fragmented at the start of the process, so the difference isn't profound. The more fragmented your disk was when you started, the more obvious the difference in the maps.

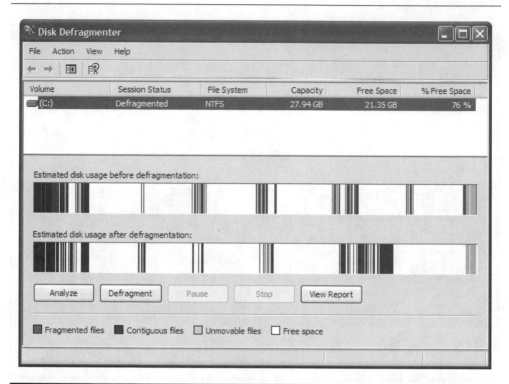

FIGURE 16-6 At the end of the process, the Disk Defragmenter window shows you the results of its work.

Free Disk Space with Disk Cleanup

Despite the fact that hard disks store more information than ever before, it is possible for your Tablet PC to run low on disk space. This problem may be even more likely to occur than it was with the last computer you used. For one thing, the disk drive in your Tablet PC may store less information than the one in your desktop computer. For example, my Acer has a 28GB (gigabyte) drive, while the one in my desktop computer is 40GB.

Another reason you may need to be concerned about disk space is that ink takes more storage space than text. That means all other things being equal, inked documents will be larger than documents using regular text.

NOTE *See "How to Determine How Much Disk Space Is Available" if you want to learn how to check the amount of disk space you have available. Try it right before and right after you run Disk Cleanup to see how much space this utility reclaims for you.*

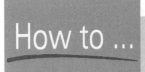 **Determine How Much Disk Space Is Available**

It takes only a few seconds to determine how much space is available on your Tablet PC's hard disk. Just follow these steps:

1. Tap Start | My Computer. The My Computer window appears. In the View pane you should see some folders, along with an icon representing the hard disk. It's normally named Local Disk (C:), although the drive letter may be D: or even E: depending on which peripherals you have connected.

2. Right-tap the icon for the disk drive. In the shortcut menu that appears, tap Properties. The Local Disk Properties dialog box appears.

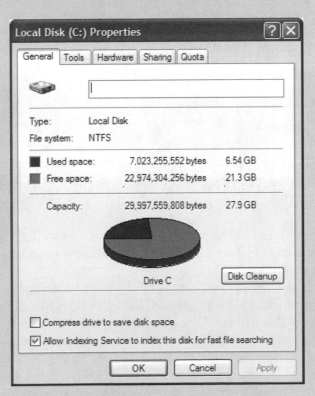

16

3. Tap the General tab if it isn't already visible, and then look at the Free Space value. This tells you how much disk space remains available. In the illustration, the Free Space value is 22,974,304,256 bytes, or 21.3GB. Plenty of space.

If you check the free space and find that you have only 1 or 2GB left, it's definitely time to free some space. Although gigabytes of free space sounds like a lot, it really isn't.

Disk Cleanup is a utility that can free some additional space on your hard disk by eliminating various types of unneeded files for you. In the course of normal operation, your computer generates all sorts of temporary files, along with files that are no longer needed. Examples include files in these places:

- Temporary Internet Files folder
- Recycle Bin
- Deleted Items folder
- Various Temporary folders
- Offline web pages

 Offline web pages are pages from web sites that are stored on your hard disk so you can view them even when your Tablet PC isn't connected to the Internet.

By deleting files like these from your hard disk, as well as by compressing infrequently used files, Disk Cleanup can often liberate hundreds of megabytes, even gigabytes, of disk space.

To start Disk Cleanup, tap Start | All Programs | Accessories | System Tools | Disk Cleanup. Assuming your Tablet PC has only one hard disk (as do all the Tablet PCs available at this writing), Disk Cleanup begins by immediately calculating how much space it can liberate by deleting the files in various locations. This may take a few minutes, during which time the dialog box shown in Figure 16-7 is visible. This dialog box provides little immediately useful information, but it does show you that your computer isn't in a coma, or otherwise not responding during the time that Disk Cleanup is examining your system.

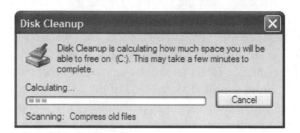

FIGURE 16-7   Disk Cleanup scans your hard disk to calculate potential space savings, allowing you to decide what to delete.

Once Disk Cleanup finishes its analysis of your hard disk, the main Disk Cleanup dialog box appears. This dialog box is divided into two tabs: Disk Cleanup and More Options. For the moment, you want to look at the Disk Cleanup tab (Figure 16-8).

FIGURE 16-8   This tab shows you how much disk space will be recovered by deleting each of the file types in the list.

16

Set or clear the check boxes in the Files To Delete list to tell Disk Cleanup which types of files you want it to remove. If you're not sure what a particular type of file represents, tap the name of the type and then check the Description area below the list. This area briefly describes the type of file you selected. Tap View Files on this tab to see a list of the specific files that will be deleted or compressed.

To eke out even more usable disk space, tap the More Options tab. This tab (Figure 16-9) points you to three major opportunities to free significant amounts of disk space. The first opportunity is the chance to delete Windows components that you're not using. This can free lots of space, and poses little risk because you can always reinstall components you need later.

The second opportunity is to uninstall programs you haven't used in a while. Tap the Clean Up button in the Installed Programs section of the Disk Cleanup tab, and Windows opens the Add or Remove Programs window to the Change Or Remove Programs list shown in Figure 16-10.

FIGURE 16-9   You can reclaim significant amounts of disk space using this tab, but don't delete files you actually need.

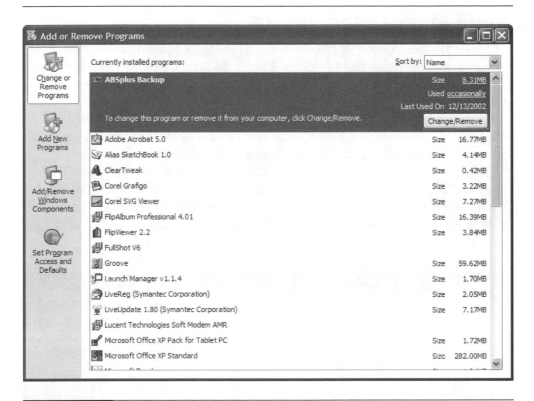

FIGURE 16-10   You can free disk space by uninstalling programs you don't use.

Tap a program to see how much space it occupies on the hard disk and when you last used it. If you decide to uninstall it, tap the Remove button (which sometimes appears as the Change/Remove button) and follow the onscreen instructions.

 *You may need to provide the original CD to uninstall certain programs, including portions of Microsoft Office XP.*

The third and final opportunity to liberate space is to delete all but your most recent restore point (see "Use System Restore to Quickly Recover from Problems" in Chapter 18 for more on restore points). This can free up huge amounts of space, at the cost of limiting recovery options to the single most recent restore point. To do this, tap the Clean Up button in the System Restore section of the More Options tab.

16

Schedule Maintenance Tasks

The sheer number of possible system maintenance tasks could make keeping your system running its best a real headache. The Scheduled Tasks utility can prevent this headache. Scheduled Tasks allows you to assign maintenance tasks, or any program, to run on the schedule you specify, with the settings you choose.

To start Scheduled Tasks, tap Start | All Programs | Accessories | System Tools | Scheduled Tasks. When you do, the Scheduled Tasks window shown in Figure 16-11 appears. When tasks are scheduled, they appear in the View pane on the right.

To add a task, double-tap the Add Scheduled Task icon in the View pane. This launches the Scheduled Task Wizard, which walks you through the scheduling process. After a welcome screen, the Scheduled Task Wizard presents you with a list of programs it can run on a schedule. This list can be quite extensive, containing

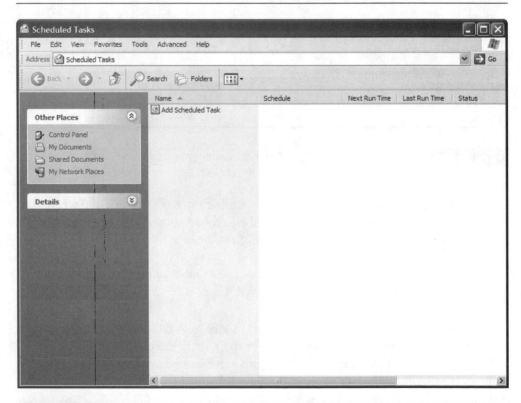

FIGURE 16-11   Use Scheduled Tasks to ensure that important maintenance tasks get run automatically.

many dozen programs from which you can choose. Figure 16-12 shows the wizard and a small fraction of the programs it can run on my Tablet PC.

The wizard gives you the option to run a program at any of the following times:

- Daily

- Weekly

- Monthly

- One time only

- When your computer starts

- When you log on

 *For Scheduled Tasks to do its work, it must be running. Because your Tablet PC will likely be turned off or hibernating when you're not using it, options that assume the machine is always running may not be good choices.*

FIGURE 16-12   The Scheduled Task Wizard walks you through the process of scheduling a program to run automatically.

16

Continue working your way through the wizard. Depending on the program you choose to run, the wizard may ask you to enter a user name and password, which it then uses to run the program as if it were started by that user.

When you come to the end of the wizard, it will present you with the option to open the advanced properties for this task. Select this option, and the wizard opens the Disk Cleanup dialog box shown in Figure 16-13. You can change any properties of the scheduled task from the tabs in this dialog box.

 *You can quickly get to this dialog box by right-tapping the icon for the task in the Scheduled Tasks window, then tapping Properties in the shortcut menu that appears.*

If you decide to cancel a scheduled task, you can do it by selecting the task in the Scheduled Tasks View pane, then tapping Delete This Item. If instead you want

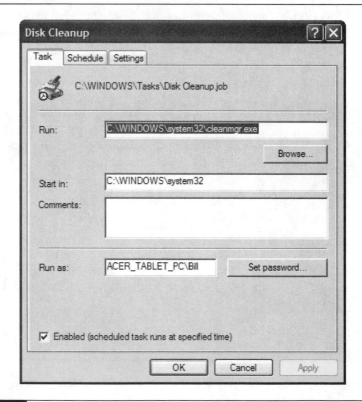

FIGURE 16-13   Every scheduled task has a properties dialog box like this one.

to stop the task from running without actually deleting it, open its properties dialog box, and then clear the Enabled check box on the Task tab.

The Advanced menu in the Scheduled Tasks window offers you several additional options. One you might find particularly useful notifies you when a scheduled task has not been run. To activate this option, open Scheduled Tasks and tap Advanced | Notify Me Of Missed Tasks.

Maintain Optimum Performance

You can perform a few tasks to optimize the performance of your Tablet PC. A Tablet PC in general has a smaller hard disk, a slower processor, and less memory (RAM) than a high-end desktop system or notebook computer. At the same time, your Tablet PC has to handle all the needs of Windows XP Professional, plus the additional burdens of pen input and handwriting recognition. As a result, you may find that your Tablet PC runs slower than your desktop or notebook computer. If so, you can experiment with the following ways to optimize the machine's performance:

- Add memory
- Tune display settings
- Adjust processor and memory settings
- Resize the paging file

Add Memory

The best way to increase the performance of your Tablet PC is to add memory. Windows XP Tablet PC edition can take advantage of as much memory as you can give it, reducing the amount of time it spends waiting to retrieve information from the hard disk. You'll need to consult the documentation that came with your Tablet PC to see if you can upgrade the memory, and if so, how.

Tune Display Settings

Although adding memory is the best way to improve the performance of your Tablet PC, tuning the display settings can definitely help. Windows can tweak several settings to make the image you see on the screen look better. But all of these effects (smoothing fonts with ClearType, for example) use processing power. You can turn off many of these effects to increase performance at the expense of aesthetics.

16

The place to tune display settings is the Visual Effects tab of the Performance Options dialog box, which appears in Figure 16-14. To get there, tap Start, then right-tap My Computer. On the shortcut menu that appears, tap Properties | Advanced. On the Advanced tab, tap the Settings button in the Performance section, and then tap Visual Effects if that tab isn't visible.

The Visual Effects tab offers four options that balance appearance against performance. Your system will probably be set to the first option: Let Windows Choose What's Best For My Computer. To get the best possible performance, select Adjust For Best Performance instead. This will turn off all the visual effects, including font smoothing and the display of the contents of folders while you move them. Tap Apply to see what your screen looks like with the setting you chose.

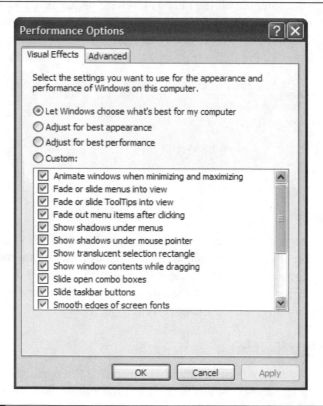

FIGURE 16-14   You can improve overall system performance by disabling most visual effects.

If eliminating all visual effects is too extreme, you can compromise by tapping Custom, then setting and clearing the visual options you want in the list.

> NOTE *Two of the options in the effects list are kind of confusing. Use Common Tasks In Folders isn't a visual effect at all. Instead, clearing this option turns off the list of tasks that normally appears on the left side of folders and other windows. Use Visual Styles On Windows And Buttons turns on or off the distinctive curved window and button corners that are standard in Windows XP.*

Adjust Processor and Memory Settings

Your next option for improving performance is to adjust processor and memory settings. In general, changes you make here will have limited effects on your Tablet PC experience—if your system runs slowly or takes a long time to recognize handwriting, changing these settings won't work miracles. But if you like to experiment to try for the absolute optimum performance, you can try adjusting these settings and see what happens.

The place to tune processor and memory settings is the Advanced tab of the Performance Options dialog box, which appears in Figure 16-15. To get there, tap Start, then right-tap My Computer. On the shortcut menu that appears, tap Properties | Advanced. On the Advanced tab, tap the Settings button in the Performance section, and then tap the Advanced tab if it isn't visible.

The options for adjusting processor and memory settings are very similar. In each case, you can give priority to the programs you are running, or to other tasks. Normally, you'll want the processor and memory scheduling to give priority to your programs, because your programs are what you're interacting with when you are using your Tablet PC.

However, sometimes you might want to change these settings. Handwriting recognition is an ongoing background task on a Tablet PC. If you use handwriting a lot, and the handwriting recognition on your machine seems too slow, you might want to try changing the Processor Scheduling setting to give priority to background services. This will give more processor time to the handwriting recognition engine, and may speed up your system.

If you tend to use only a few applications on your Tablet PC at a time, you may want to experiment with changing the Memory Usage setting. Giving the system cache priority can improve performance if you use only a few applications at a time, but use them with large files.

16

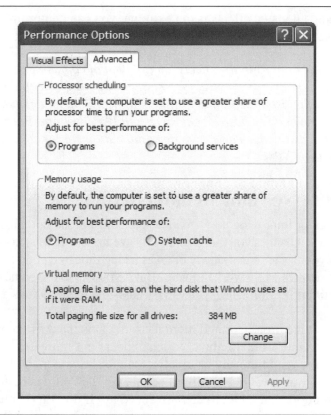

FIGURE 16-15   You can make some helpful adjustments to your processor and memory settings on this tab.

Resize the Paging File

The *paging file* is an area on your hard disk that Windows sets aside to use as virtual memory. When the programs you are running require more memory than your computer has available, Windows moves chunks of your programs to and from virtual memory as necessary to give the running applications the memory they need. The advantage of virtual memory is that your system doesn't fall down if you try to run too many programs at once. The disadvantage of virtual memory is that although your computer doesn't fall down, it really slows down. Virtual memory is far, far slower than real memory, and when your computer uses it, performance plummets.

Normally, Windows manages the paging file by itself, allocating enough disk space to handle almost any situation. And normally, you don't want to mess with this arrangement. You might want to manually adjust the size of the paging file in only two situations: The first situation is when your computer has more than one hard disk, which is seldom the case with a Tablet PC. The second situation is when you are running very low on disk space. In that case, you may want to reduce the size of the paging file to free some disk space. That limits the number of programs you can run, but it's a trade-off you can consider.

To change the size of the paging file, you need to get back to the Advanced tab of the Performance Options dialog box. Once again, you can get there by tapping Start, then right-tapping My Computer. From there, tap Properties | Advanced. On the Advanced tab, tap the Settings button in the Performance section, and then tap the Advanced tab if it isn't visible. In the Virtual Memory section of the page, tap Change to open the Virtual Memory dialog box, which should look very similar to Figure 16-16.

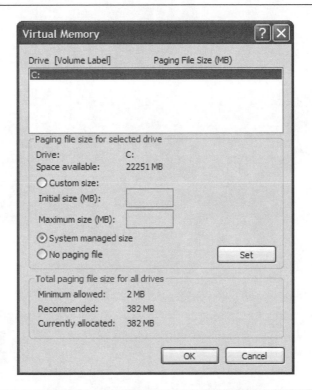

FIGURE 16-16   You can adjust the size of the paging file to free more disk space, but don't take this step lightly.

16

The figure shows that the paging file on my machine's single disk drive is being automatically managed by Windows, and is currently using 382MB of disk space. If you need some of the disk space occupied by the paging file, you can set Custom Size, and then enter an initial size and maximum size for the paging file. You can eliminate the paging file completely, but I recommend against it unless you've got a gigabyte or more of memory stuffed into your Tablet PC. Tap Set to make the change. You'll have to restart Windows before the change will go into effect.

Chapter 17

Back Up Your Tablet PC

How to...

■ Understand Your Tablet PC Backup Options

■ Use Backup to Protect Your System and Personal Data

■ Use System Restore to Quickly Recover from Problems

■ Prepare Your Tablet PC for Possible Problems

Sooner or later, most of us have a problem with our computer that causes the loss of some data or even the loss of the ability to start Windows. This is true even with Windows XP Tablet PC edition, which is the most stable version of Microsoft Windows ever. Backing up your computer is a necessity if you want to recover from such a problem without major headaches.

This chapter introduces the major forms of backup available on the Tablet PC. I've provided some tips on which type of backup to use when, and ended the chapter with some steps you can take to protect yourself from disaster when and if it strikes your computer. I hope that you'll never have to rely on your backups to recover from a problem but, in case you do, the information in this chapter should maximize your chances of recovering without too much trouble.

Did you know?

Your Tablet PC Is at Risk?

A number of industry analysts have pointed out that Tablet PCs are more likely to get damaged than regular notebook computers. And, if you think about it, it's easy to understand why. Tablet PCs are designed to be used more of the time and in more environments than regular notebook computers. I know mine goes places that my old notebook didn't, such as to the Tablet PC launch in New York, where I carried the thing around all day, taking notes as if it was a paper notebook. A regular notebook computer would have been totally impractical in that setting. Likewise, I use my Acer in meetings where plunking away at a regular notebook would be considered rude. Then there was that breakfast meeting at the local diner last week, and so on. Using a Tablet PC a higher percentage of the time increases the wear and tear on the machine.

Then there's how you carry the thing. I can't speak for anyone else, but I end up holding the computer with one hand while wielding the pen with the other, all the while asking questions, taking notes, or otherwise not paying any attention to the computer itself. The odds of my dropping the computer, or getting it knocked out of my hand, are much higher than the odds of something similar happening to a notebook computer that's sitting squarely on a desk or other flat surface with both my hands right there.

What this means is that your Tablet PC is more likely to suffer a fatal accident than a notebook or desktop computer. What that means is backing up your Tablet PC is extremely important.

Understand Your Tablet PC Backup Options

When it comes to backing up your Tablet PC, you have two main options: regular backups and system restores. Regular backups are what you probably think of when you think about backing up your computer. They involve creating a copy of your personal data and other information, and then storing it somewhere so you can retrieve some or all of the stored information at a later date.

System restores involve storing the state of certain elements of your system, such as the registry and the current versions of some applications. It doesn't back up your personal data and it doesn't replace regular backups. Consider System Restore a complement to regular backups.

The rest of this chapter explains the differences, and shows you how and when to use them.

Use Backup to Protect Your System and Personal Data

Backup is a powerful utility built into Windows that lets you back up (create a copy of) information stored on your Tablet PC. You can store this copy anywhere, preferably in a different physical location. If the information on your hard drive is damaged or lost, you can use the back up to restore the lost information. Use Backup when you want to save your personal data, as well as other files and folders.

The Backup utility handles both backing up and restoring. Normally you'll want to use the utility's Backup or Restore Wizard for either activity. But Backup also has an Advanced mode where you have access to all the options of the Backup or Restore Wizard without the wizard.

Let the Backup or Restore Wizard Do the Work

The best way to back up your Tablet PC (unless you're an advanced user) is with the Backup or Restore Wizard. As its name indicates, the wizard (shown in Figure 17-1) can either back up files and settings, or restore them. When using the wizard to back up, you have the option to back up just your own documents and settings, the documents and settings of every user of this computer, all the information on the computer, or the specific items you choose.

 *Your user account must have Administrator rights to back up all information on the computer.*

The trade-off for these options is time and storage space. Backing up your own documents and settings is the fastest way to go, and this uses up relatively little storage space. Backing up everyone's documents and settings can be a lot slower (depending on how many users there are), and can occupy a good deal of space on

FIGURE 17-1   The Backup or Restore Wizard can make it easy to do a manual backup of your important information.

the hard disk. Backing up everything on the computer takes even more time and the backup occupies even more disk space.

Obviously, the disk space required when you manually choose what to back up varies but, in general, this is the slowest backup option of all because of the time needed to select the items to be backed up.

To start the Backup or Restore Wizard, tap Start | All Programs | Accessories | System Tools | Backup. Once you tell the wizard you want to back up information and tell it what kind of backup you plan to do, it allows you to store the backed up information on your Tablet PC, on another computer connected to yours by a network, or on removable media like floppy or Zip disks.

Backups can take a while, so while the backup is in progress, Windows displays the Backup Progress dialog box that appears in Figure 17-2. Along with vital information like the name of the backup file it's working on, the dialog box also shows the estimated time remaining before the backup is complete.

To restore information you've previously backed up, start the Backup or Restore Wizard, tell it you want to restore information, and then let it help you select and restore the information.

	Backup Progress	? X

| | | Cancel |

Drive:	C:
Label:	Backup.bkf created 12/18/2002 at 7:29 PM
Status:	Backing up files from your computer...
Progress:	▮▮▮▮▮

| | Elapsed: | Estimated remaining: |
| Time: | 1 min., 57 sec. | 9 min., 48 sec. |

| Processing: | C:\... Settings\Bill\Desktop\Captures\F03-26.tif |

	Processed:	Estimated:
Files:	730	10,080
Bytes:	128,274,690	772,926,708

FIGURE 17-2   Keep track of the status of a backup operation and find out how much longer it'll take with the Backup Progress dialog box.

17

 *If you want to control backups and restores directly, without the help of the Backup or Restore Wizard, you can easily do so. Start the wizard normally, and then tap Advanced mode to manually control backups and restores.*

Use Automated System Recovery

If you want a way to automatically recover from a situation where you can't start Windows, Automated System Recovery is the answer. You create a boot floppy disk and store a copy of your system's key files. If you have a problem that prevents Windows from starting, you can connect the floppy drive to your computer and start the system from the floppy disk. The floppy disk then restores the state of your system from the backup stored on the copy.

To do this, you'll need a floppy disk (and a floppy drive that can connect to your Tablet PC). With those in hand, start the Backup or Restore Wizard by tapping Start | All Programs | Accessories | System Tools | Backup. On the wizard's second screen, select Backup Files And Settings. On the next screen, select All Information On This Computer (see Figure 17-3). This tells the wizard

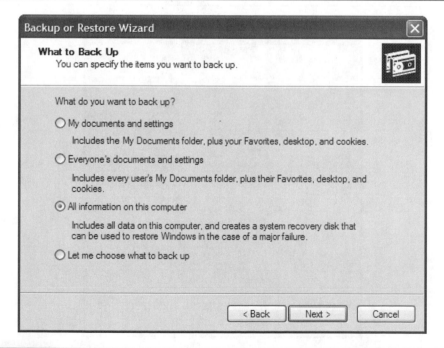

FIGURE 17-3　Back up all the information on your Tablet PC and create a System Recovery Disk so you can recover from a catastrophic failure.

to back up all the data on the computer and to create a System Recovery Disk you can use for an Automated System Recovery.

 *If your Tablet PC didn't come with a floppy disk drive, you can buy a plug-and-play drive with a USB interface for around $50.*

Follow the instructions provided by the wizard to finish creating the System Recovery Disk and the copy of your computer's information.

Use the Advanced Backup Mode

In the *Advanced Backup mode,* you can directly control backups and restores without the help of the Backup or Restore Wizard. To do this, start the Backup or Restore Wizard normally (tap Start | All Programs | Accessories | System Tools | Backup). On the wizard's Welcome screen, clear the Always Start In Wizard Mode check box to start in Advanced Backup mode in the future. Then tap Advanced Mode to open the Backup Utility Advanced Mode window shown in Figure 17-4.

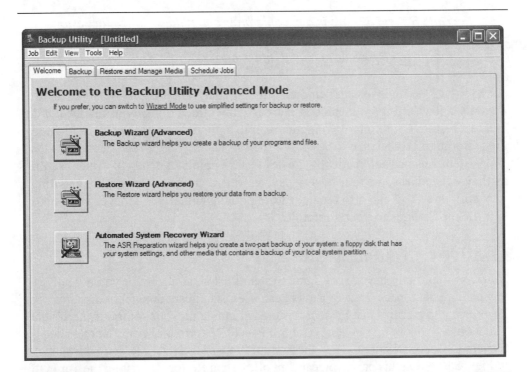

FIGURE 17-4   In the Advanced Backup mode, you can interact with Backup's three wizards without the help of the Backup or Restore Wizard.

17

From this window, you can directly launch the Backup Wizard, Restore Wizard, or the Automated System Recovery Wizard. If you want even more control, you can directly control which files get backed up or restored using the appropriate tabbed pages. I suggest you don't go to this level of control and, instead, stick with using the Backup, Restore, and Automated System Recovery Wizards. Their choice of settings is sufficient for most situations, and you can probably find better uses for your time than managing the details of your backups and restores.

Use System Restore to Quickly Recover from Problems

System Restore is a wonderful capability. Using *System Restore,* you can recover from problems such as bad applications, mysterious incompatibilities, or the corruption or deletion of an important application. System Restore can reset your Tablet PC's system settings to the state they were in before the problem reared up and started making life miserable for you. System Restore is easy to use, too.

 *While System Restore is a capable program, it doesn't save or restore your personal data. You need some sort of backup program like Windows Backup to store your personal information.*

System Restore is installed and running on your Tablet PC by default. There are only a few settings you can configure and only three things you can have it do: create a restore point, return your computer to a previous restore point, and undo the restoration you last did.

System Restore automatically creates restore points (a group of system settings as they existed at some time) every day, as well as before events, like installing new software. You can also create restore points manually whenever you make significant changes to your Tablet PC.

Configure System Restore

You won't normally have to configure System Restore at all. But if you're really low on hard disk space (System Restore can use a significant amount of disk space) or if you want to confirm that System Restore is running on your computer, here's how you would go about it. Tap Start | Control Panel | Performance And Maintenance | System | System Restore to open the System Properties System Restore tab shown in Figure 17-5. On this page, you can turn off System Restore by setting the Turn Off

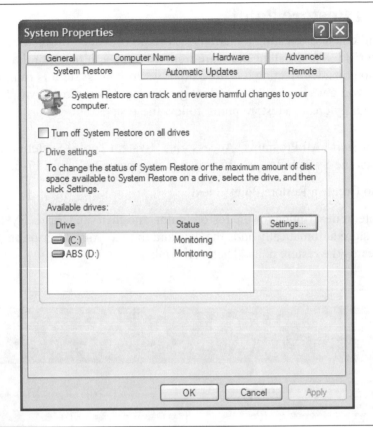

FIGURE 17-5   If you need to configure System Restore, this tab is the place to start.

System Restore On All Drives check box, or select one of the drives System Restore is monitoring and tap Settings to configure System Restore on that drive.

 *Another way to get to the System Restore tab is to tap Start, right-tap My Computer, and then tap Properties | System Restore.*

On the Drive Settings page, you can adjust the amount of space that is allocated to System Restore on this drive. Reducing the amount of space allocated to System Restore will free disk space, but may reduce the number of restore points you can have.

If the drive you're looking at is the system drive (typically the C: drive), you can't disable System Restore for this drive without disabling it for all drives. If the drive you're looking at isn't the system drive, you can turn off System Restore for this drive using a check box on the Settings page.

17

Create a Restore Point

You should consider creating a manual restore point when you're about to do something risky like installing software from a source you're unfamiliar with. You should also consider creating a restore point when your system is running great. This gives you a way to get back to that great state if you move away from it.

To manually create a restore point, follow these steps:

1. Tap Start | All Programs | Accessories | System Tools | System Restore to open the System Restore Wizard, which appears in Figure 17-6.

2. Tap Create a Restore Point | Next.

3. Enter a description for the restore point, and then tap Create. System Restore automatically adds the date and time to your description, and creates the restore point. That's all it takes.

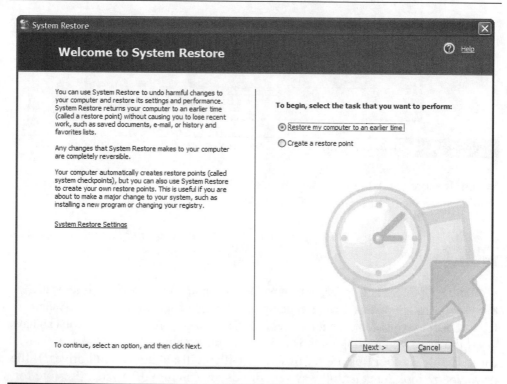

FIGURE 17-6   With the System Restore Wizard, you can manually add new system restore points or return the system settings to an earlier point.

Return the System to a Previous Restore Point

If something goes haywire and you want to return your system to an earlier state, you can follow these simple steps:

1. Tap Start | All Programs | Accessories | System Tools | System Restore to open the System Restore Wizard.

2. Tap Restore My Computer To An Earlier Time | Next. The Select a Restore Point window shown in Figure 17-7 appears.

3. On the calendar, tap the date containing the restore point you want to use (any date with at least one available restore point appears bold in the calendar).

4. Tap the name of the restore point you want to use, and then tap Next. The Confirm Restore Point Selection window appears.

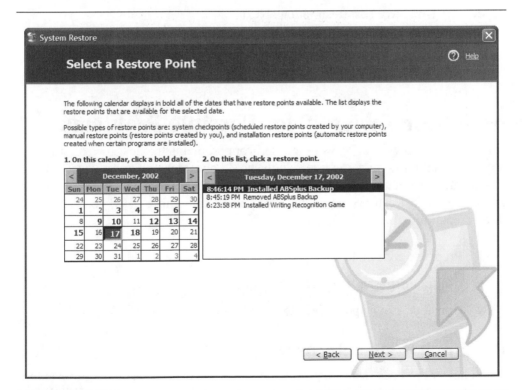

FIGURE 17-7   Use the calendar and restore point list to choose which restore point gets restored.

5. Confirm the name of the restore point you want to use. Heed the warnings in this window, and save all your work and close all your applications before tapping Next. Windows will shut down for a short while as it resets the system to the selected restore point.

TIP   *You can get into System Restore from Safe mode, too. When restarting your computer in Safe mode, it should ask you if you want it to run System Restore.*

Undo the Return to a Previous Restore Point

You may find that returning to a previous state isn't what you wanted to do after all. If that happens, you can undo the restore by following these steps:

1. Tap Start | All Programs | Accessories | System Tools | System Restore to open the System Restore Wizard.

2. Tap Undo My Last Restoration | Next.

3. You'll again be advised to save all work and close all applications before continuing. When you tap Next, Windows shuts down for a while as System Restore undoes the last restoration.

Prepare Your Tablet PC for Possible Problems

Now that you know some ways to recover from problems like lost files or crummy programs that mess up your system, you should consider preparing your Tablet PC for such problems. Aside from backing up your personal data regularly and creating System Restore points whenever you do something risky, you can take three precautions:

- Prepare a System Recovery Disk

- Configure Startup and Recovery settings

- Consider using a portable automatic backup system

Prepare a System Recovery Disk

If you haven't already done so, prepare a System Recovery Disk and a full backup of your computer. This will allow you to recover in those cases where Windows just won't start. You can find more information on System Recovery Disks and the Automated System Recovery they make possible, in the section titled, "Use Automated System Recovery," earlier in this chapter.

Configure Startup and Recovery Settings

If your Tablet PC experiences a major problem that causes it to stop running, you'll want it to take certain steps that will make recovery and troubleshooting easier. The computer should already be set up to take the most common steps, but it's worth a minute or two to check and be sure. After a disaster is no time to find out that your computer isn't collecting debugging information or doesn't display recovery options.

To check your computer's startup and recovery settings, tap Start | Control Panel | Performance And Maintenance | System | Advanced. Then tap Settings in the Startup and Recovery section. This opens the Setup and Recovery dialog box in Figure 17-8.

You should make sure that your system is set to display recovery options when necessary. You'll want them displayed for at least 30 seconds, so you have time to respond before the system tries to restart normally.

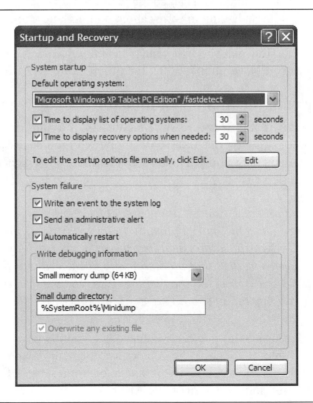

FIGURE 17-8   Check this dialog box before a disaster strikes your Tablet PC.

You'll also want to make sure that the computer writes an event to the system log when a problem occurs because that will help technicians address the problem. Similarly, you want to make sure that the system does a memory dump, which also provides information for the technicians. The small memory dump records the minimum amount of information needed to debug a problem while using up the least disk space to store information. This is sufficient in most cases, although if you have recurring problems, you may, instead, be asked to select a kernel or complete memory dump.

Consider Using a Portable Automatic Backup System

If you accept that it's important to back up your Tablet PC regularly, then it would be nice to have an automatic backup system, one that makes doing the backup as easy as possible. If you travel a lot with your Tablet PC, a portable automatic backup system is what you need. What we're talking about here is a hard disk in a box that you can connect to your Tablet PC wherever you are to get an automatic backup of its hard disk. With such a thing, you can continue to back up your computer while you're on the road, without having to worry about burning and storing CD-ROMs or carrying around stacks of floppy disks.

CMS Peripherals, Inc. was the first vendor to announce such a system, doing so in a press release on November 7, 2002, the official Tablet PC launch date.

Travel Safely with the ABSplus Automatic Backup System

The *ABSplus hardware and software system* consists of a hard drive in a small (six inches by three inches by one inch) case, along with the necessary cables and software. The device is plug-and-play, and ships with the software on the drive, as well as on the included CD-ROM.

I got to use an early release of the Tablet PC version of the product. While it needed some more polishing to be ready for prime time, the system effectively accomplished its primary task, creating a physically separate bootable disk that automatically backed up my Tablet PC hard disk whenever I connected the two together. The version of the device that you can buy today should have all the kinks worked out.

To put the ABSplus system to work, you need only supply power to the drive and connect it to your Tablet PC. But before you do that, the manufacturer recommends that you temporarily disable any antivirus software on your Tablet PC. Once you've disabled your antivirus software, turn on the ABSplus drive. You computer will detect the drive and display a list of the files that are currently loaded on the drive.

Double-tap setup.exe in the list to start installing the automatic backup software. From there, you follow the onscreen directions to finish configuring the system. As part of this process, the setup program installs the ABSplus Launcher on your computer. This small utility runs in the background and runs the backup software when you connect the ABSplus drive to the Tablet PC. Once everything is set up properly, the ABSplus reformats its own disk drive to match the drive in your Tablet PC. It then copies all the relevant data from your computer, resulting in a backup of your Tablet PC's entire hard disk.

The ABSplus system only needs to make a complete backup of your computer once. After that, whenever you connect the ABSplus drive to your Tablet PC, it scans your computer's hard disk and only backs up files that have changed or been added since the last backup.

To restore files that have been backed up to the ABSplus, connect the system to your computer, and then cancel the backup which will automatically begin. Next, tap Start | My Computer, and then right-tap the icon representing the ABSplus drive. In the shortcut menu that appears, tap Explore to view the contents of the ABSplus drive. This will be nearly identical to the contents of your Tablet PC hard disk, as Figure 17-9 shows.

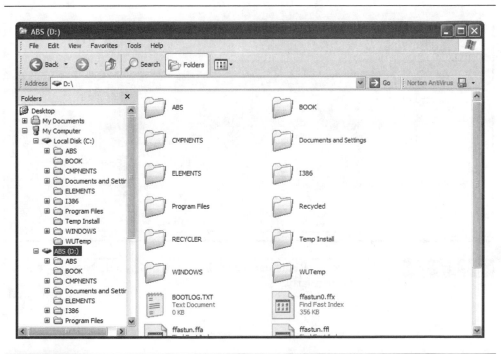

17

FIGURE 17-9   The ABSplus system creates a replica of your Tablet PC hard disk so you can easily restore lost or damaged files.

You should be able to use the ABSplus automatic backup system with all its default settings. One setting you might want to configure is the Reminder. This option reminds you when it's time to back up your hard disk again. To activate the Reminder, right-tap the ABSplus Launcher icon in the notification area. On the shortcut menu that appears, tap ABSplus Backup Settings.

When the ABSplus Backup Settings dialog box appears, tap Options | Advanced Options. This opens the dialog box in Figure 17-10. In the Reminders section, set the Remind Me To Backup check box, and then set the number of days you want between backup reminders. The ABSplus software will then pop up backup reminders on the interval you specified.

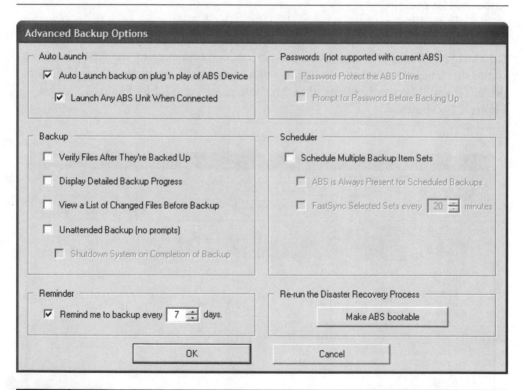

FIGURE 17-10   Setting backup Reminders can help ensure that you do back up your Tablet PC regularly.

Chapter 18

Use the Tablet PC's Tools to Solve Problems

How to...

- Use the Help and Support Center
- Use Other Tools for Diagnosing Problems
- Solve Specific Problems
- Get Help with Remote Assistance

While Windows XP Tablet PC edition is arguably the best, most stable version of Microsoft Windows ever, that doesn't mean you'll never have any problems. If you do run into trouble, this chapter points you to tools you can use to diagnose and fix the problem.

Get Familiar with the Help and Support Center

The Windows XP Help and Support Center is a valuable starting point when you need to diagnose and fix problems. Conceptually, it's a central location for information about Windows and the programs and utilities that come bundled with it. To open the Help and Support Center, tap Start | Help and Support.

The exact appearance of your computer's Help and Support Center will depend on which model of Tablet PC you have, but it should look something like the one in Figure 18-1. If the form of the Help and Support Center looks familiar, it's because the center is implemented as a set of web pages stored on your Tablet PC and displayed in a customized Internet Explorer window. This allows manufacturers to customize the center for their systems.

The left-hand column in the Help and Support Center usually consists of links to major help topics, while the right side usually has links to other major resources, some on your system and some on the Internet. Let's look at some Help and Support Center resources that could be particularly useful to you when dealing with problems.

Get Right to It with the Fixing a Problem Link

Tapping the Fixing A Problem Link takes you to a page similar to the one in Figure 18-2. This page gathers together tools and information for dealing with broad categories of problems, such as Application and Software Problems, or Hardware and System Device Problems.

FIGURE 18-1   The Windows XP Help and Support Center is a good place to look for tools and information to fix problems with your Tablet PC.

Tap the category you're interested in and you'll jump to a page structured similarly to the one in Figure 18-3. While the detailed information will, of course, vary, the View pane of each page will be divided into three sections: Fix A Problem; Pick A Task; and Overviews, Articles, And Tutorials.

18

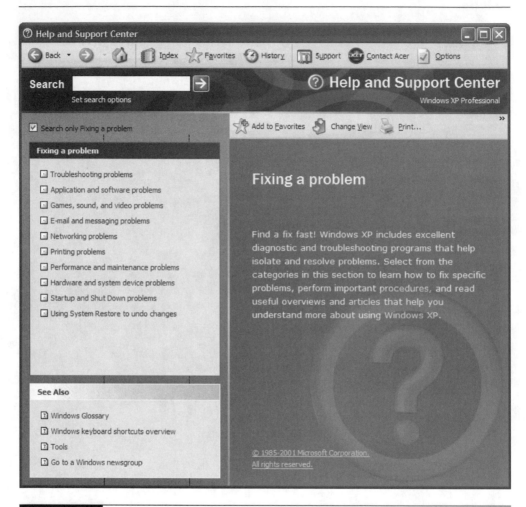

FIGURE 18-2   The Fixing A Problem section of the Help and Support Center can help with all sorts of problems.

Run Dr. Watson When Required

Dr. Watson is a utility that creates a log of the state of your computer when an error occurs. This log includes information like a description of the error and a list of the things that were running on your computer when the error occurred. Using this information, support personnel can try to diagnose and fix the problem.

I recommend you don't do anything with Dr. Watson unless you're directed to do so by a technician or other support personnel helping you with a problem. If you still want to learn more about Dr. Watson, you can get information by tapping Fixing

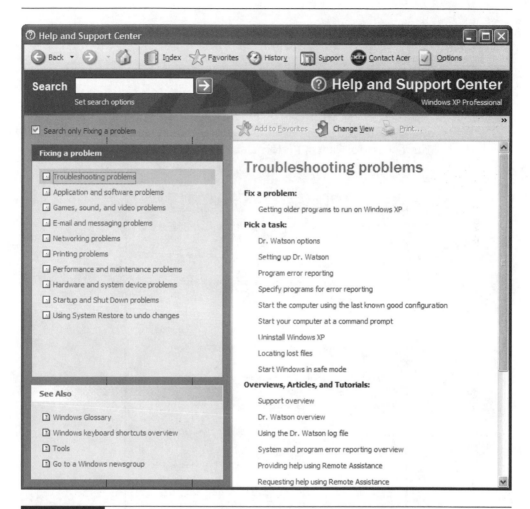

FIGURE 18-3   With the amount of information available on major types of problems, you have a good chance of solving them yourself.

A Problem on the Help and Support Center home page. You should see several links to information related to Dr. Watson.

Use Windows Update to Fix Problems

In Chapter 5, we talked about Windows Update as a way to ensure that you have the latest versions of the relevant device drivers on your Tablet PC. If you run with that concept a little, you can see how Windows Update can be a tool for fixing system problems.

18

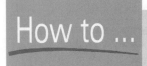 **Set Up and Use Automatic Updates**

Setting up your Tablet PC to automatically check for updates is a simple process. To configure your Tablet PC to automatically check for updates:

1. Tap Start | Control Panel | Performance And Maintenance | System | Automatic Updates.

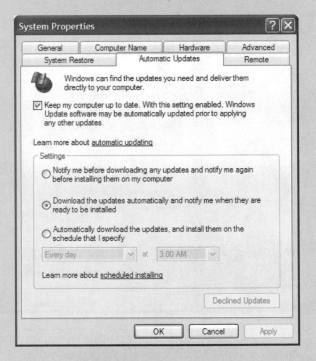

2. On the Automatic Updates tab, set the Keep My Computer Up To Date check box.

3. In the Settings section of the page, tell Windows how you want it to behave when it detects updates.

4. Tap OK to finish setting up automatic updates.

If you do this, your computer periodically checks the Windows Update site for updates relevant to your system. If your computer finds them, it displays a balloon message near the notification area, telling you updates are available and giving you a quick route to them. You can review each of the updates and tell Windows which to install by setting or clearing the check boxes for each individual update.

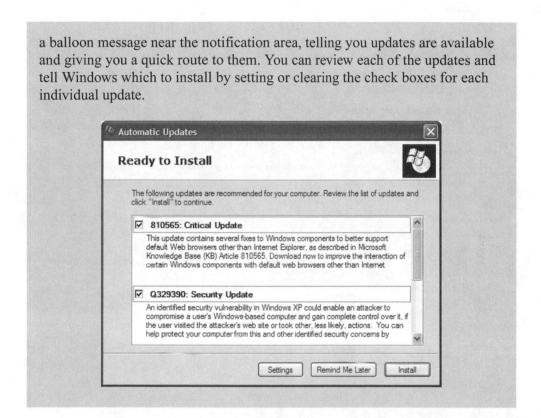

As I'm sure you're well aware, computer programs have bugs. No program that does anything significant is without some bugs, even if only obscure ones. That includes the utilities, applications, and other programs related to Windows XP Tablet PC edition. Microsoft is continually releasing updates and service packs for its software (as are all other major software publishers).

The problem you're experiencing may be caused by a bug in Windows XP Tablet PC edition, and that bug may be fixed by an available update or service pack. Because Windows Update will tell you which service packs and updates you need to install, using it could fix your problem.

You can run Windows Update from the Help and Support Center home page. Tap the Windows Update link to see the window in Figure 18-4. The key feature of this window is the Scan For Updates link in the View pane. Make sure your Tablet PC has an active connection to the Internet, and then tap Scan For Updates.

Once Windows Update completes its scan of your computer, it displays a list of the updates it thinks you should download and install on your computer. Once the scan is complete, Windows Update displays a list of the updates that are applicable

18

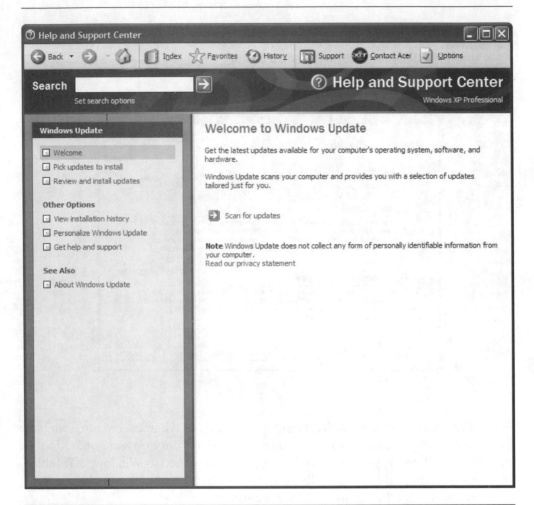

FIGURE 18-4   Windows Update can fix what ails your Tablet PC by helping you install new versions of programs that may include a fix for your problem.

to your computer (if any). Tap Review And Install Updates to find out more about the updates recommended for you, and to choose which you want to install now.

You can free yourself from the need to manually search for updates on the Windows Update page by setting up your computer to accept automatic updates. See the section, "How to Set Up and Use Automatic Updates," for instructions.

If service packs or critical updates should be installed, Windows Update guides you to deal with them first, before installing any of the noncritical changes. Figure 18-5 shows two critical updates that should be made on my Tablet PC before I worry about the driver update that's also applicable.

You should be aware that making changes to your computer with Windows Update may necessitate restarting it. You don't have to restart the system right away, but the changes won't go into effect until you do, and you won't be able to install further updates until you do.

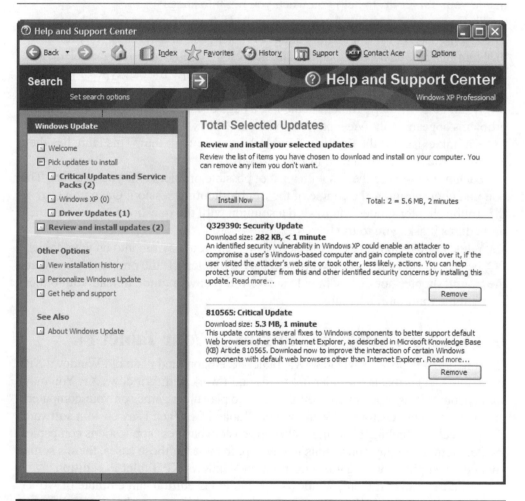

18

FIGURE 18-5   When you tap Review And Install Updates, Windows Update provides explanations of each change it thinks you should make and lets you choose whether or not to make them.

Solve Problems with the Troubleshooters

The Windows Help system contains quite a few troubleshooters. *Troubleshooters* are interactive, step-by-step guides to solving some of the most common Windows problems. Each troubleshooter starts at the most basic level, asking general questions about the problem, and using your answers to those questions to try and pinpoint the problem. Each step along the way, the troubleshooter will provide you with things to try either to solve the problem or narrow it down until the troubleshooter can recommend a solution. It's a little like having a technical support person stuffed inside your Tablet PC to help you when you run into snags.

To find and run a troubleshooter, start at the Help and Support Center home page. Then tap Fixing A Problem. In the Fixing A Problem list, find the category your problem fits into (an application problem, networking problem, printing problem, and so forth), and then tap the link for that category. The page for that type of problem will have a troubleshooter you can try. I'll use a printing problem as an example.

When I tap Printing Problem in the list, a page of information specific to printing problems appears in the View pane. Looking under Fix A Problem in the View pane, I see a link exists for the Printing Troubleshooter, so I tap that. This launches the Printing Troubleshooter shown in Figure 18-6.

Each troubleshooter begins with a list of possible problems for you to select. The one you choose guides the course of the troubleshooting session. Once you start, the troubleshooter guides you toward a solution with the questions it asks and the procedures it asks you to try.

While troubleshooters can't solve every problem you may run into on your Tablet PC, be sure to check them first when you have a problem. If the problem is one that the troubleshooter does know how to solve, you'll have a guide to lead you to the fix with the minimum of trouble.

Get Your Old Programs to Run on Your Tablet PC

One important issue with Windows XP Tablet PC edition (and plain old Windows XP, for that matter) is that some older programs don't work with Windows XP. You may well encounter this problem yourself if you try to play older games on your computer or if you try to use custom software on your Tablet PC. When I say custom software, I'm particularly thinking about things like the custom business applications companies create internally or pay consultants to develop. In either of those cases, there's some chance the application or game won't run on Windows XP Tablet PC edition.

To address this problem, Windows XP Tablet PC edition can emulate or work like earlier versions of Windows. The emulation enables you to have your Tablet PC act like Windows 95 and 98, Windows Me, 2000, and NT 4.0. In addition, you

FIGURE 18-6   The Printing Troubleshooter is just one of the many interactive
troubleshooters included in the Windows XP Tablet PC edition
Help system.

can adjust the video settings to try and re-create the video mode the old application
was designed for. To help you set up and configure the emulation, Windows XP
Tablet PC edition includes the Program Compatibility Wizard.

Use the Program Compatibility Wizard

To start the Program Compatibility Wizard, tap Start | All Programs | Program
Compatibility Wizard. Follow the wizard's instructions to identify the application

18

you're having trouble with, specify the version of Windows the application works with, and set the display mode to use when the application is running.

 *Using the Program Compatibility Wizard to run old antivirus, backup, or similar programs is a bad idea. Such programs are often tightly integrated with a specific version of Windows, and using the wizard to make them run on your Tablet PC is very risky. Doing so could conceivably result in the loss of all your data and the corruption of your operating system. You should invest in Windows XP versions of such programs.*

Once you've made your setting changes, the wizard enables you to test the application using those settings before making them permanent.

Set Compatibility Manually

If you find that the application still doesn't work right with the settings you chose, you don't need to go back into the Program Compatibility Wizard to adjust them. You can set a program's compatibility mode manually.

To set a program's compatibility mode manually, right-tap the program's icon, and then tap Properties in the shortcut menu that appears. Tap the Compatibility tab to see the same set of options the wizard presented you, but all on a single page, like the one in Figure 18-7. Change the settings as necessary, tap OK, and then run the application to try it with the new settings.

Use Other Tools for Diagnosing Problems

The Help and Support Center isn't the only place to find tools for diagnosing problems on your Tablet PC. This section takes you to some of those other tools.

Investigate Problems with System Information

The *System Information* window provides detailed information about the configuration of your computer. This information is particularly useful when your Tablet PC is having problems, and the technicians may use System Information to help troubleshoot the problem. System Information also has a menu full of additional tools you can use when trying to diagnose and recover from problems.

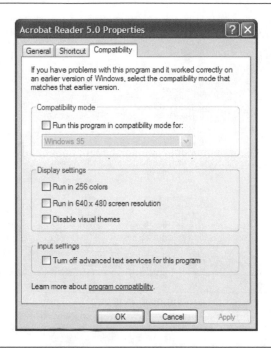

FIGURE 18-7   Use the Compatibility tab of a program's Properties dialog box to adjust compatibility settings manually.

You can start System Information by tapping Start | All Programs | Accessories | System Tools | System Information. This opens the window shown in Figure 18-8.

As you can see in Figure 18-8, the configuration information provided by System Information is divided into several broad categories. If you're getting phone support and the technician asks you for some information, you'll likely be able to find it somewhere in System Information.

Solve Specific Problems

Some problems are common enough to merit specific mention in this chapter. They're not necessarily bad problems and, in fact, some of them are more annoyances than anything else. Even so, here are some of the more common problems you'll run into on a Tablet PC, along with the solutions.

18

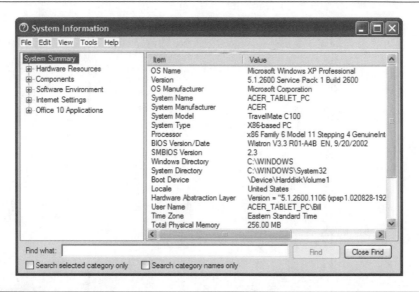

FIGURE 18-8   When troubleshooting problems on your Tablet PC, the configuration information provided by the System Information window can be crucial.

Office XP Pack for Tablet PC Security Warning Appears in Journal

Since Microsoft Office XP applications came out long before the Tablet PC was launched, naturally, they had little integration with Tablet PC features. Microsoft made the Office XP Pack for Tablet PC available as a free download to add some Tablet PC integration to Office XP. And it did. Unfortunately, there was a side effect. Once you install the Office XP Pack for Tablet PC on your computer, the behavior of Windows Journal may change.

If you start Windows Journal after installing the Office Pack, you may see the Security Warning shown in Figure 18-9. If you do see it, you'll also see it the next time you start Windows Journal. And the time after that. And on and on.

While this warning can be quite annoying and looks rather ominous, it isn't a big deal. The reason it appears is that the Microsoft Office Pack for Tablet PC uses an ActiveX control to integrate Office XP and Windows Journal. If you haven't set Internet Explorer to always trust content from Microsoft Corporation, Windows sees the ActiveX control and throws up the message.

The only solution to this problem appears to be this: Set the Always Trust Content From Microsoft Corporation check box the next time you see the Security Warning.

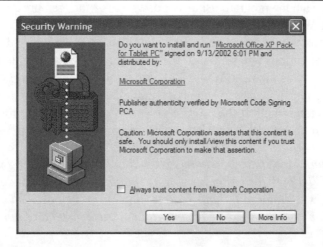

FIGURE 18-9   Unless you know the solution, this Security Warning appears every time you start Journal after installing the Office XP Pack for Tablet PC.

If you'd rather not automatically trust every ActiveX control that Microsoft wants to install on your computer, then you'll have to get used to seeing that Security Warning.

Terminate Hung Programs with Windows Task Manager

Sometimes programs hang. That is, they stop responding to input and just sit there, doing nothing of value. You can use Windows Task Manager to terminate hung programs. You may lose data that was unsaved when the program hung, but normally the program will run just fine the next time you start it.

Before you terminate a program, you should make sure the program is really hung and not simply waiting for you. Sometimes, particularly when you have many windows open on the screen, you can lose track of what's going on with each application.

What appears to be a hung program may be a program that has a dialog box open somewhere on the screen, waiting for you to do something. So, before you use Windows Task Manager to terminate the troublesome program, take a moment to look for a stray dialog box. Minimize the other windows on the screen and, if possible, drag the offending window to a different location so you can "look behind it." Only after you're sure no open dialog box is waiting for you should you terminate the program.

18

To terminate a hung program using Windows Task Manager, press CTRL-ALT-DEL. This opens the Windows Task Manager, which will look similar to Figure 18-10. Tap Applications to view the Applications tab if that tab isn't already visible.

On the Applications tab is a list of the *tasks* (programs and folders) running on your Tablet PC at this moment. If you look under the Status heading, you'll see tasks that are running normally have a status of Running. Any task that's hung will have a status of Not Responding. If the program is hung, you're going to lose any unsaved data in that program, regardless of what you do, so you're no worse off for terminating it.

CAUTION *Sometimes the status of a hung task will be listed as Running when you first open Windows Task Manager. Wait a minute or two and see if the status changes. If it doesn't, that's a good indication the program is waiting for input or crunching away at some difficult task instead of hung.*

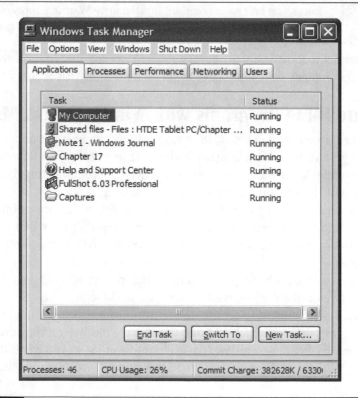

FIGURE 18-10   One of the many uses of the Windows Task Manager is terminating programs that are no longer running.

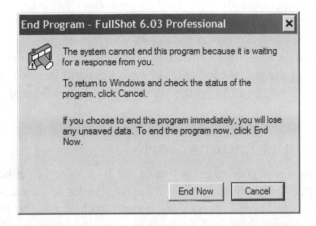

FIGURE 18-11   This dialog box is a sure sign that you'll have problems if you forcibly terminate the program in question.

To terminate a hung program, tap the program in the list, and then tap End Task. After a moment or two, Windows Task Manager should successfully terminate the program.

If you try to terminate a program that needs a response from you (it may need to know if you want it to save a document, for example), Windows Task Manager pops up the dialog box shown in Figure 18-11 to alert you to the problem. Either cancel the program termination and check the status of the program or tap End Now to forcibly terminate the program without providing the response the program is waiting for.

I strongly recommend you only terminate a program that's waiting for a response as a last resort. You'll most likely lose data or cause other problems if you terminate such a program without dealing with the issue first.

Do a Reset to Recover from a Hung Tablet PC

Once in a while, Windows itself will hang up. Nothing will work right. The cursor might move around the screen, but nothing you click or tap responds in any way. The cursor might be frozen in place or even disappear altogether. In a situation like this, you have little choice but to do a reset of your Tablet PC. A reset turns off the computer without regard to what's going on in Windows. Terminating a program that's not responding means you can lose unsaved data in that program. Resetting the computer means you'll lose unsaved data from all the running programs, as well as from Windows. A reset like this can corrupt Windows files, so don't do this unless you've exhausted any other options to recover from the problem.

18

You can do a reset from the keyboard by pressing CTRL-ALT-DEL twice. If pressing CTRL-ALT-DEL twice doesn't reset your computer, you can force it to reset by pressing and holding the Power button on your computer until it shuts down. Wait a little while (at least 10–15 seconds), and then turn the Tablet PC back on again. The chances are pretty good that your problem will be gone and you'll be back in business. If not, you can let the Windows XP Setup Wizard try to repair the problem.

Make the Tablet Buttons Work

For some functions, you need to press two of the Hardware Tablet buttons on your computer. You must press those buttons in the right order or they won't work. For example, on my Acer, I need to press these buttons to change the screen orientation: Fn+Up/Right. If I press them at the same time, nothing happens. If I press the Up/Right button, and then press the Fn button, the active document scrolls up (if I'm working in an application that supports scrolling), and a message appears to tell me that I've activated the Function Tablet button. So make sure you press the buttons in the order in which they appear.

If you don't like the order in which you have to press the buttons, you can change it. See the section, "Configure Tablet Buttons," in Chapter 3 to find out how.

Identify and Deal with Resource Problems

Sometimes your system's performance will drastically deteriorate for no apparent reason. The mouse becomes sluggish and everything seems to take forever. This could be caused by running too many applications and utilities at once. Or, it could be caused by one program suddenly going berserk and grabbing as many of your system's resources as it can. Let's talk about an easy way to decide which situation you have and ways to deal with it.

To decide whether you're running too many programs at once or one program has gone berserk, we'll use Windows Task Manager. To open Windows Task Manager, press CTRL-ALT-DEL on the keyboard or the Security Hardware button on your Tablet PC.

NOTE   *This is one situation where the Tablet PC Input Panel's keyboard doesn't work like a real keyboard. If you tap CTRL-ALT-DEL on this keyboard, you'll get a dialog box directing you to use the physical keyboard or the Security button.*

When the Windows Task Manager appears, tap Performance. This tab, shown in Figure 18-12, gives you a snapshot of the resources in use on your Tablet PC right now. Take a look at the CPU usage. This tells you how intensively your computer's CPU (the microprocessor) is being used.

Dealing with a Resource-Hogging Program

This value fluctuates as Windows does its work and as you use the machine, but unless one of your programs is crunching away at some big job (like recalculating a spreadsheet, running a game, or playing back some big multimedia file), this value should be nowhere near 100 percent. If it is and it stays there for more than a few seconds, your problem is probably a berserk program. To find out for sure, tap Processes to view the Processes tab shown in Figure 18-13.

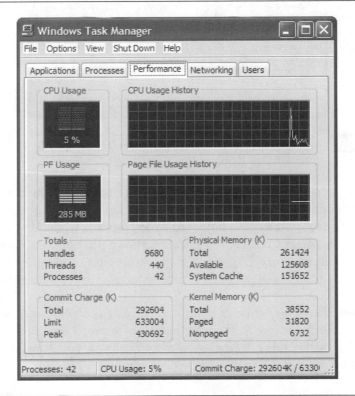

FIGURE 18-12   Get an instantaneous report on how hard your Tablet PC is working by viewing the Windows Task Manager's Performance page.

18

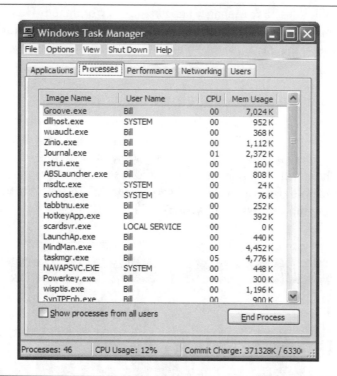

FIGURE 18-13   Use the Processes page of Windows Task Manager to determine which program is hogging all the resources.

This page is dominated by a list of the processes running on your computer. The most important things to look at for now are the CPU and Mem Usage columns. *CPU* shows the percentage of total CPU time used by any process, while *Mem Usage* shows the memory used, measured in KB. Typically, when a program becomes a resource hog, it uses up all the spare CPU time or a huge amount of memory. You can see which processes are using the most CPU time or memory by scanning down the list.

TIP   *If more than one person is using your Tablet PC right now (if you're using Fast User Switching to share the machine), set the Show Processes From All Users check box before proceeding. That way, you'll be able to find the problem even if it's caused by another person's processes.*

These numbers fluctuate a bit but, if all is well, you should find that System Idle Process is using much of the CPU time and none of the processes is using a disproportionately large amount of memory. If some program is hogging the CPU, some process other than the System Idle Process will be using 80 percent, 90 percent, even as much as 99 percent of the CPU time. If you see this, you know which process is causing problems. The trick is determining which program the process belongs to.

Sometimes it's easy to determine which program a process goes with. If you can't tell just by looking at the name of the process, you can apply the process of elimination. Exit one program after another while watching the Processes list. The process should disappear from the list when you exit the program it belongs to.

Usually when you restart the program that caused the problem, everything works fine again. If the problem keeps recurring, you're probably not the only person to experience it and the program's publisher may have a fix. Contact them for help.

Dealing with Too Many Well-Behaved Programs

If you don't see anything amiss on Windows Task Manager's Performance and Processes tabs, you may just be asking your Tablet PC to run too many programs at once. Try closing applications you're not actively using and see if the problem clears up. If so, you may be trying to do too much on your computer at once (not that you do too much at once in your personal life . . .). If you need to run all those programs at once, consider adding memory to your Tablet PC. In general, more RAM translates into the ability to handle more programs at once.

TIP
When all else fails, restarting your computer often clears up resource problems. For various reasons, when you've run a lot of programs or had Windows running for a long time without restarting it, the system can end up with lots of inaccessible resources. If you save your work and close all your programs, and then restart Windows, that frees up the inaccessible resources, greatly improving the performance of the computer.

Repair Windows Problems with the Windows XP Setup Wizard

Sometimes Windows itself gets messed up (corrupted). If you're seeing strange behavior that doesn't seem to be related to a particular program you're running, Windows XP may be corrupted. In cases like this, the Windows XP Setup Wizard may be able to detect and correct the problem. To give this a try, follow these steps:

1. Connect the CD-ROM drive to your Tablet PC and insert the Windows XP Tablet PC edition CD into the drive. After a moment the wizard's Welcome to Windows XP screen appears (see Figure 18-14).

18

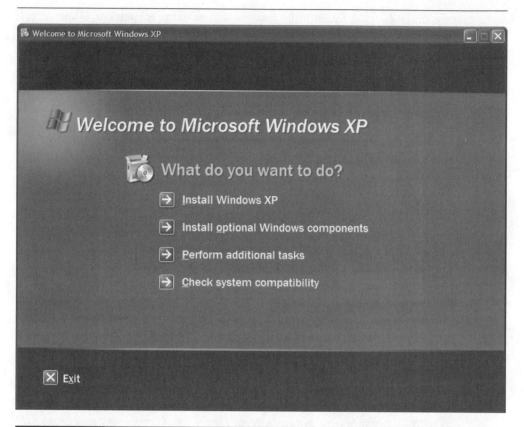

FIGURE 18-14 Although you wouldn't know it from this screen, the Windows XP Setup Wizard can repair the copy of Windows XP Tablet PC edition that's already installed on your computer.

2. Tap Install Windows XP and follow the onscreen instructions.

3. After the wizard reboots your Tablet PC, it should detect that you already have Windows XP Tablet PC edition on your computer. It will then offer you the option to repair the installation.

4. Select the repair option, and then follow the onscreen instructions as the wizard attempts to make repairs.

Get Help with Remote Assistance

For some problems, the best way to get them solved is to allow a technician or other support personnel to use the computer themselves. Having helped people deal with

Did you know?

How Remote Assistance Differs from Remote Desktop?

Remote Assistance and Remote Desktop are similar. Both are Windows XP-specific features. Both allow your computer to be controlled from a distance. Perhaps the best way to understand the difference is to consider Remote Assistance as a special version of Remote Desktop.

The differences between the two reflect the way they're used. Remote Desktop enables you to take control of your computer from another machine, assuming you have an Administrator's account on that machine. The two computers can be connected across the Internet or using a network. When your computer is set for remote access using Remote Desktop, it's locked so that only the person connecting remotely can see what's happening on the screen or control the computer in any way.

Remote Assistance enables you to share control of your computer with another person across the Internet. You can still see your screen and control your Tablet PC when you're getting Remote Assistance.

strange problems myself, I know there are times when letting the helper sit at the computer and use the keyboard and mouse while watching the screen is the fastest, most efficient way to solve the problem.

If you use your Tablet PC in the office, where you have support staff nearby, this isn't usually a problem. All you need to do is get your Tablet PC and the technician into the same room, and then get out of the way. But, if you were on the road or otherwise unable to put your computer and the right person in the same room, you used to be out of luck.

That's all changed since the arrival of Windows XP. All versions of Windows XP, including Windows XP Tablet PC edition, support Remote Assistance. *Remote Assistance* is a tool that allows someone to control your computer across the Internet or a network. Remote Assistance is similar to Remote Desktop, which we discussed in Chapter 7. To understand the differences, see the section, "Did You Know How Remote Assistance Differs from Remote Desktop?"

With Remote Assistance enabled on your computer, you can contact knowledgeable friends across the Internet and let them help you fix your problem, even if they're thousands of miles away. You can also use Remote Assistance to contact Microsoft technicians and request help from them.

During a Remote Assistance session, you always have control of your computer. The helper is always able to view the screen, but needs your permission to control

18

anything on your computer. During the session, a small chat window appears on the screen, so you and your helper can communicate during the assistance session. To use Remote Assistance, you must:

- Prepare your computer to receive remote assistance

- Request remote assistance

- Participate in the remote assistance session

Prepare Your Computer to Receive Remote Assistance

To allow Remote Assistance sessions on your Tablet PC, tap Start | Control Panel | Performance and Maintenance | System | Remote. This opens the Remote page of the System Properties dialog box, as shown in Figure 18-15.

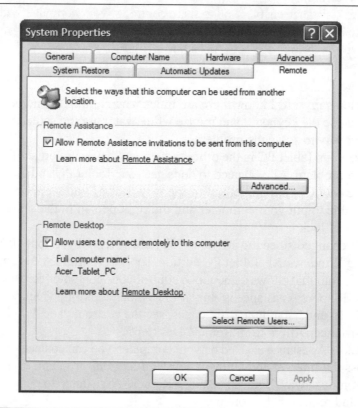

FIGURE 18-15   The first step in receiving Remote Assistance is to configure your computer to send invitations.

In the Remote Assistance section of the page, set the Allow Remote Assistance Invitations To Be Sent From This Computer check box. This enables you to request help, but doesn't control how much control over your computer the other person will have or the amount of time the invitation will remain in effect. If you're concerned about security, the duration of the invitation is an important issue. You don't want to leave an open invitation for someone to connect to your computer, particularly if you've given them the right to control your machine from a distance.

 *If either you or the person you're requesting assistance from is behind a firewall, you may be unable to use Remote Assistance. If this situation applies, contact the appropriate network administrator for assistance.*

To handle these two concerns, tap the Advanced button in the Remote Assistance section of the Remote page. This opens the Remote Assistance Settings dialog box. This dialog box has two sections. One section is for setting the amount of remote control someone has when they respond to your remote assistance invitation. The other section enables you to set the amount of time for which the remote assistance invitation remains open.

If you're comfortable letting the person who's helping you take control of your computer, set the Allow the Computer To Bc Controlled Remotely check box (see Figure 18-16). Remember that with Remote Assistance, you always have

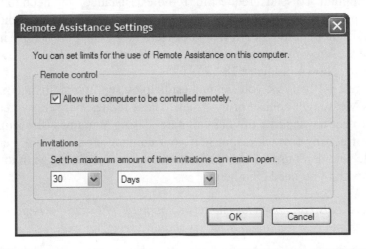

FIGURE 18-16   Control your computer's Remote Assistance Settings using this dialog box.

control of your computer, too. So, it isn't as if the person helping you takes over your computer and leaves you helpless while they do whatever they want.

The general rule for the length of time that you should allow an invitation to remain open is this: the shorter, the better. In the Invitations section of the dialog box, you can set a length from 1 to 99, with units of Minutes, Hours, or Days. Tap OK when you finish configuring these settings the way you want them. You're now ready to request Remote Assistance.

Request Remote Assistance

When the time comes for help, you can send a request across the Internet. You can send this request to any computer expert you know (including a knowledgeable friend) so long as their computer system meets the requirements of Remote Assistance. To render aid with Remote Assistance, your expert's computer must

- Be running Windows XP or another Remote Assistance-compatible operating system

- Be running Windows Messenger or an e-mail program that is MAPI-compliant (Microsoft Outlook and Outlook Express are both MAPI-compliant)

- Have an Internet connection

If those requirements are satisfied, you can send a request for assistance to that person's computer. To send a request for remote assistance, you need to be on the Help and Support Center Remote Assistance home page (tap Start | Help and Support | Remote Assistance). Tap Ask A Friend For Help in the Support pane. This opens a new page in the View pane, where you tap Invite Someone To Help You, which opens the page shown in Figure 18-17.

As Figure 18-17 shows, you can request help by sending an instant message to a Windows Messenger contact or by e-mail. These requests are encrypted while in transit to protect the security of your computer. Using Windows Messenger has the advantage of getting a quick response if your contact is online, while e-mail can reach people who don't use Windows Messenger or who aren't logged in to Windows Messenger when you need their help.

NOTE   *There's also an option to send an invitation as a file, but the regular Windows Messenger or e-mail approaches should serve you well.*

Whichever means you use to send the invitation, the recipient has the opportunity to accept or decline it. You'll receive notification if the person declines the invitation,

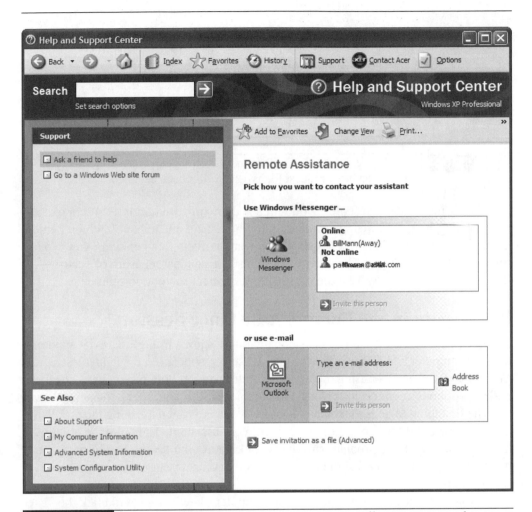

FIGURE 18-17   Use either Windows Messenger or your e-mail program to send a request for assistance.

although it's easy to miss it when you've sent the invitation by Windows Messenger. Look for a Session Is Terminated message in the Remote Assistance Web Page Dialog that appeared when you sent the request. Figure 18-18 shows this message in the dialog box.

CAUTION   *If the person you ask for help uses another MSN Messaging Service application rather than Windows Messenger (Trillian, for example), they may not see your request for assistance. In this case, your best bet is to e-mail the request.*

18

| FIGURE 18-18 | If you see the Session Is Terminated message in this dialog box, you know that your request for assistance has been declined. |

If your invitation is accepted, you will see the words Invitation Is Accepted... in the dialog box, followed by another dialog box. This one tells you which person has accepted your invitation, and asks if you want to allow that person to view your screen and chat with you. Consider this dialog box as a last measure of security—if you're not there to say Yes, the person can't connect to your computer.

Participate in the Remote Assistance Session

If you do say Yes, the Remote Assistance window shown in Figure 18-19 appears on your computer and a copy of your computer screen appears on the helper's screen. You chat with the helper using the Message Entry pane. If both of you have speakers and microphones connected to your computers, you can also speak to each other.

The first thing to do is to send a message to your assistant explaining the problem. Then follow the directions you receive from your assistant. They may be able to help you deal with the problem simply by looking at your screen and giving you directions. Or, they may feel the need to directly control your computer to solve the problem.

If your assistant wants to control your computer directly, they will click the Take Control icon in the Remote Assistance window on their screen. When they do, you see the dialog box in Figure 18-20. Tap Yes to allow the other person to directly control keyboard and mouse input to your computer. Remember, you can still control the keyboard and mouse yourself, and be sure to heed the warning about both of you trying to control the computer at once.

From here on, you should work with your assistant to resolve the problem. If, at any time, you want to terminate the Remote Assistance session, tap Disconnect on the Remote Assistance window, or press the ESCAPE key on your keyboard. The ESCAPE key on the Tablet PC Input Panel also works for this.

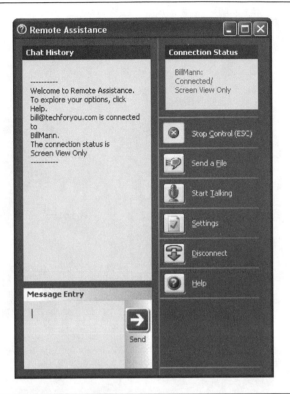

FIGURE 18-19   The Remote Assistance window is your way of interacting with someone assisting you remotely.

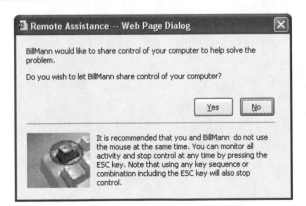

FIGURE 18-20   Tap Yes to let your assistant share control of your keyboard and mouse but, remember, you shouldn't try to control them simultaneously!

18

Index

INTERNATIONAL CONTACT INFORMATION

AUSTRALIA
McGraw-Hill Book Company Australia Pty. Ltd.
TEL +61-2-9900-1800
FAX +61-2-9878-8881
http://www.mcgraw-hill.com.au
books-it_sydney@mcgraw-hill.com

CANADA
McGraw-Hill Ryerson Ltd.
TEL +905-430-5000
FAX +905-430-5020
http://www.mcgraw-hill.ca

GREECE, MIDDLE EAST, & AFRICA
(Excluding South Africa)
McGraw-Hill Hellas
TEL +30-210-6560-990
TEL +30-210-6560-993
TEL +30-210-6560-994
FAX +30-210-6545-525

MEXICO (Also serving Latin America)
McGraw-Hill Interamericana Editores S.A. de C.V.
TEL +525-117-1583
FAX +525-117-1589
http://www.mcgraw-hill.com.mx
fernando_castellanos@mcgraw-hill.com

SINGAPORE (Serving Asia)
McGraw-Hill Book Company
TEL +65-863-1580
FAX +65-862-3354
http://www.mcgraw-hill.com.sg
mghasia@mcgraw-hill.com

SOUTH AFRICA
McGraw-Hill South Africa
TEL +27-11-622-7512
FAX +27-11-622-9045
robyn_swanepoel@mcgraw-hill.com

SPAIN
McGraw-Hill/Interamericana de España, S.A.U.
TEL +34-91-180-3000
FAX +34-91-372-8513
http://www.mcgraw-hill.es
professional@mcgraw-hill.es

UNITED KINGDOM, NORTHERN, EASTERN, & CENTRAL EUROPE
McGraw-Hill Education Europe
TEL +44-1-628-502500
FAX +44-1-628-770224

http://www.mcgraw-hill.co.uk
computing_europe@mcgraw-hill.com

ALL OTHER INQUIRIES Contact:
Osborne/McGraw-Hill
TEL +1-510-549-6600
FAX +1-510-883-7600
http://www.osborne.com
omg_international@mcgraw-hill.com